One Foot Forward

One Foot Forward:
Walks in Upstate New York

Richard B. Frost

Bloated Toe Publishing
Peru, New York 12972

Other books by the author:

Plattsburgh, New York: A City's First Century (2002)
A Day Away: Journeys From Northeastern New York (1999)
(*A Day Away* written under pseudonym of Richard Landon)

Library of Congress Control Number: 2008938285

ISBN: 978-0-9795741-1-5

To inquire about obtaining copies of this title or the titles listed above, write to:
Bloated Toe Enterprises
PO Box 324
Peru, NY 12972

or

Go to Bloated Toe Enterprises website:
URL: http://books.bloatedtoe.com
email: info@bloatedtoe.com

Cover photo: Ripken on the boardwalk at Willie Wildlife Marsh

Printed and bound by
Boyd Printing Company
5 Sand Creek Road
Albany, New York 12205

Manufactured in the United States of America

For
Marty
and
Ripken

Contents

ADIRONDACK – NORTH COUNTRY

Contents

Contents

CENTRAL – LEATHERSTOCKING

Contents

WESTERN – NIAGARA

Contents

Acknowledgments

No human being alive deserves more thanks for this effort than my wife Marty does. When the text indicates "we," it's Marty to whom I refer. She has traveled on most of the outings, giving up precious garden time as she did so. She served as chief editor and most constructive critic. She offered support when I became discouraged at the always prolonged process of completing a book. And she tolerated the moods that somehow seem to accompany such a venture.

No canine alive deserves my thanks more than our Labrador retriever, Ripken. He patiently let me decide our destinations, critiqued every possible water hole or river, and gamely stayed behind when we visited places from which he was prohibited. His older Labrador companion, Camden, also joined us on many of the earlier journeys. Her untimely death kept her from enjoying the completion of the project.

Many other people (and a few dogs) have helped, too. Suzanne Perley has again offered incomparable proofreading skills and general criticism, as she did for my earlier books. My close friend and assistant, Amy Dragoon, helped keep all in order during my "day job," allowing me the freedom necessary for my research and travel. As always, I appreciate the support of the editors at the Press-Republican, Bob Grady and Suzanne Moore. Some of these chapters have appeared in that newspaper, albeit sometimes in altered form.

A partial list of those who made suggestions for destinations, and/ or facilitated visits, include Patti Donoghue of the Greater Rochester Visitors Association; Nancy Vargo, then at Buffalo-Niagara Convention and Visitors Bureau; Diane Johnson-Jaeckel of Wyoming County Tourism; Mary Ann McCarthy of Orange County Tourism; Robin Dropkin of Parks and Trails New York; Bill Lattin of the Cobblestone Society; and Bonnie Hays of Historic Palmyra.

Many people walked with us along the way. Some are mentioned in the text. Among others were Mike and Paige Caldwell; Ben, Nicholas, Kim, and Kayla Dragoon; Sam and Gloria Olivier; and Megan Kavanaugh.

I would be remiss without thanking Larry Gooley and Jill McKee of Bloated Toe Publishing. Larry edited the manuscript meticulously, made many useful suggestions, and set high standards for accuracy in the text. Jill conjured up solutions to layout and map problems when I thought none were available. They both worked very hard to bring the book to publication.

I'm certain I've missed a few people to whom I owe thanks, and for that I apologize. Each person's contribution and companionship has been truly appreciated.

Introduction

In twenty-plus years of travel writing, much of it centered on my home region of northeastern New York State, I've come to view upstate New York as an underappreciated gem. Friends around the country think only of skyscrapers and the Statue of Liberty when they ponder New York. Even many in New York City know surprisingly little about what their state offers to the north and west.

Don't misunderstand me. No place on earth offers the cultural, creative, and culinary possibilities of New York City's metropolitan area. However, I came of age in upstate New York, and after a decade or so elsewhere, I chose to return. Nowhere in the south did I find the glory of an Adirondack autumn. Nowhere in New England did I find the sheer power of Niagara Falls. Nowhere in the west did I find the air of anticipation that greets spring in the Finger Lakes.

To me, upstate New York means mountains, the Catskills and the Adirondacks. Upstate connotes farmland, whether dairying and maple sugaring, or raising grapes for wineries. Upstate includes quintessential small-town life reminiscent of New England. Upstate includes major cities like Buffalo, once one of America's largest, and Rochester, home of Kodak and Xerox.

Upstate reflects history, from Native American presence, through the Revolutionary War and the War of 1812, to the building of the Erie Canal. Upstate embraces celebration, from annual inductions into Baseball's Hall of Fame in Cooperstown, to traditional ceremonies in Waterloo, the birthplace of Memorial Day. Upstate boasts scenery, from the shores of Lake Champlain and Lake George, to the picturesque Catskill views that inspired the Hudson River school artists, to the college campuses high on hills around Ithaca.

Upstate New York invites participation, not just passive appreciation. Therein lies the reason for this book. By walking, one can become immersed in the state's resources, while simultaneously enhancing aerobic capacity, and building up an appetite for knowledge as well as for cuisine.

Some of these walks are leisurely strolls through small villages. Others are visits to outdoor museums. The more serious hiker will find towpaths along once busy canals and challenging trails in the wilderness. Those with creative leanings will find artist colonies and sculpture parks. History buffs will find paths to homes of venerable figures and streets walked by important personages.

Hopefully, readers will find excuses for returning to places familiar from childhood, and also reasons to sample locales they've never seen before. Along the way, the walker should burn a few calories, condition (or recondition) a few muscles, and absorb a bit of information.

A few caveats.

Though walking routes and hiking trails don't change as frequently as do, say, museum exhibits, quite likely some of the places described will be different than when I last visited. All information given, however, was current at the time of publication.

This does not purport to be a comprehensive guide by any means. In fact, I'd be a bit disappointed if both natives and outsiders don't have suggestions for additional excursions in virtually every chapter. I do hope, though, that these essays provide a diverse geographical and thematic approach to seeing what upstate New York has to offer.

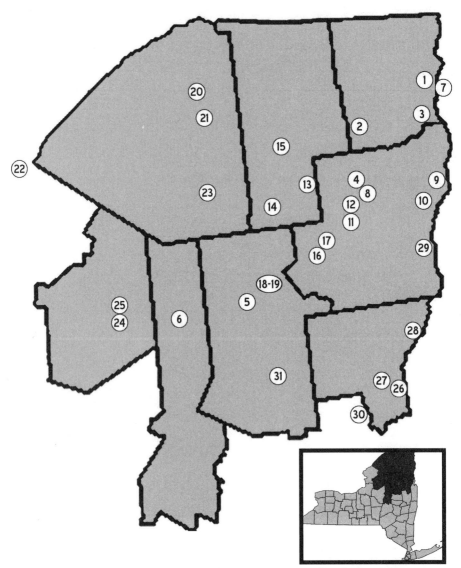

1.	Plattsburgh War of 1812 Trail	12.
2.	Silver Lake Bog	13.
3.	Ausable Chasm	14.
4.	High Falls Gorge	15.
5.	Great Camp Sagamore	16.
6.	Bald Mountain	17.
7.	Valcour Island	18.
8.	Owen and Copperas Ponds	19.
9.	Essex	20.
10.	Coon Mountain	21.
11.	Avalanche Lake	22.

1. Plattsburgh War of 1812 Trail
2. Silver Lake Bog
3. Ausable Chasm
4. High Falls Gorge
5. Great Camp Sagamore
6. Bald Mountain
7. Valcour Island
8. Owen and Copperas Ponds
9. Essex
10. Coon Mountain
11. Avalanche Lake

12. John Brown Farm
13. Saranac Lake and Tuberculosis
14. Fernow Forest
15. Paul Smiths VIC
16. Newcomb VIC
17. Santanoni
18. Adirondack Museum
19. Castle Rock
20. Potsdam
21. Stone Valley Recreation Trail
22. Wellesley Island

23. Cranberry Lake
24. Whetstone Gulf
25. Lowville Demonstration Area
26. Lake George
27. Warrensburg
28. Silver Bay Association
29. Crown Point
30. Hadley Mountain
31. Sacandaga Walkway

ADIRONDACK – NORTH COUNTRY

The Adirondacks connote mountains, to be sure. But the North Country also means waterways, including the St. Lawrence River and Lake Champlain. Then there are all those pristine, remote ponds to be acknowledged.

Much of our nation's early history took place along these corridors. Military leaders became aware of the terrain. So did miners, loggers, traders, and businessmen. In the 1820s, the Champlain Canal linked Lake Champlain with the Hudson River and Erie Canal. Sportsmen began to come for hunting and fishing. Hotels, some grand but others rustic, offered lodging.

The area also claims importance in environmental history. Early concepts of land management and preservation were solidified here. Creation of the Adirondack Park, with its "forever wild" clause, set an important precedent for future wilderness legislation.

Walks in this region range from long hikes and modest climbs, to village strolls and tours of so-called "camps" on a scale almost unimaginable, to spots where battles were fought and abolitionists buried.

Plattsburgh War of 1812 Trail • Silver Lake Bog

A decisive battle during the War of 1812 took place at Plattsburgh. American victory on land and water here in September 1814 went far toward assuring the integrity of a new republic.

Local Boy Scouts developed a walking route that points out important sites during that action. It's a grassroots initiative that heightens appreciation of the area's heritage.

We began downtown on the steps of City Hall. Of course, City Hall was a distant dream when the British invaded Plattsburgh in 1814 as part of their strategy to control Lake Champlain. Inside, the anchor from the British flagship *Confiance* dominates the lobby. Historical murals installed in 1985 include a painting of Commodore Thomas Macdonough, leader of the American fleet.

Across the street stands the Macdonough Monument, an impressive memorial to the American naval effort in the Battle of Plattsburgh. The names of Macdonough's ships are engraved into the base of the obelisk; an eagle stands guard atop the 135-foot structure. For historical purposes, though, it's better to ignore the monument temporarily. Instead look beyond to Plattsburgh Bay, where the decisive fighting took place.

We walked a block to the building that now houses Zachary's pizzeria. Around the time of the War of 1812, Dr. William Beaumont had an office on that site. Beaumont cared for a war casualty, Alexis St. Martin, whose gaping abdominal wounds were expected to be fatal. Amazingly, St. Martin recovered, but the holes in his abdominal wall and stomach never healed. Taking advantage of the situation to observe what happened to foods placed directly into the stomach, Beaumont made major contributions to the knowledge of digestive physiology.

Proceeding down Bridge Street, we passed a marker denoting the first building constructed in what would become Plattsburgh. Another sign commemorates teenage volunteers who held off British troops trying to cross the Saranac River. Across the street sits the home of American officer Benjamin Mooers. A cannonball from the battle still rests in one wall.

We rounded the corner onto Jay Street, coming upon the spot where city founder Zephaniah Platt built his first home in 1799. A turn from Hamilton Street onto a trail along the former Plattsburgh Air Force Base provided some scenery to complement our history lesson.

An informative display brought the particulars of the battle into perspective. One must remember Lake Champlain's crucial strategic importance in those pre-interstate and pre-railroad days. Walking along the shore makes the point more clearly than any textbook can.

A plaque along the trail marks Fort Scott. By cutting over to the current Parade Oval, we approached the location of Fort Moreau. Across South Peru Street on an embankment stands a marker for a third fortification, Fort Brown.

None of the buildings on the former air force base dates to the War of 1812. But it was the importance of the Battle of Plattsburgh that led to a long-term military presence. The oldest structures are stone barracks erected in 1838. The base cemetery marks the final resting place for many Battle of Plattsburgh warriors, including 136 whose identities were never learned. More are buried on Crab Island, visible from several spots along the trail.

You'll now be near the War of 1812 Museum, with its Battle of Plattsburgh Interpretive Center. A visit will provide much more detail on the significance of the event.

Passing two jet planes that pay silent testimony to the long-term air force presence, we continued via McKinley Avenue and Flynn Avenue, and then to South Catherine Street.

Though the actual location probably lies elsewhere, a marker for Pike's Cantonment gave us a chance to ponder Zebulon Pike. The famed general may be better remembered for the Colorado mountain named after him, but he was stationed here during the War of 1812.

After crossing the Saranac River yet once more by bridge, we turned left at Steltzer Road. Soon we reached Riverside Cemetery. Graves of both British and American officers from the Battle of Plattsburgh are located here.

The full trail calls for a spur to Colonel Thomas Miller's home on Quarry Road, another spot at Halsey Court and Boynton Avenue where Captain Leonard and Major Wool resisted a British advance, and Melissa Penfield Park, location of a British campsite. Instead we cut across to the corner of Oak and Court streets. There a British hospital once occupied a building more recently home to the Clinton County Historical Society.

We returned downtown and crossed Trinity Park, stopping to look at monuments honoring soldiers of later wars. Once back at our starting point, we took a "bonus walk" to the Kent-Delord House, British headquarters during the Battle of Plattsburgh. If time allows, the Kent-Delord, now operating as a museum, nicely rounds out an historic afternoon.

A few comments are in order. We spent almost three hours on our tour, walking over four miles. The full Boy Scout route comes close to seven miles. Going on a weekday assures entry into City Hall to see the historic anchor and the impressive murals. There are plenty of places to rest. Restaurants and restrooms, while not omnipresent, are never far away.

******

For an easy walk, consider a visit to the Silver Lake Bog. Due to a lack of signage, finding this very pleasant trail can be a challenge. But it will provide a satisfying afternoon for a modest effort.

To get there, follow Silver Lake Road from Route 3 near Clayburg, and turn right when you hit the T-intersection at the lake itself. Take a left onto Old Hawkeye Road, and keep a lookout for a parking area on the right. Only at the beginning of the trail does a sign appear.

This area, managed by the Nature Conservancy, begins with a boardwalk through a bog area. Take the brochure at the sign-in site; it's keyed to fifteen marked sites.

The well-constructed boardwalk traverses an area dominated by tamarack, black spruce, and Northern white cedar. Hardwoods require better drainage and can't survive in such an environment.

We quickly learned to identify the distinctive clumps of needles that set the tamarack apart from spruce or fir. Tamarack also owns the distinction of being a deciduous evergreen. Its needles turn golden in the fall, then drop off the limbs.

In a bog, one must also pay attention to the ground cover. Grassy

4

swirls and groups of ferns greeted us initially. But the thick carpet of sphagnum moss—fifteen species are represented—dominates the area.

Our guidebook pointed out Labrador tea and mountain holly, additional important components of the understory. At one stop we found an array of pitcher plants, calmly awaiting their next nutritious insect prey.

Higher up are examples of witches' broom. These tangled masses at the ends of black spruce branches result from the effects of parasitic dwarf mistletoe.

None of the amphibians or redbacked salamanders native to the area appeared. We did, however, sit on one bench and listen to the resident birds. Plus, I learned that weasel-like fishers are one of the few animals courageous enough to feed on porcupines. Maybe I should train one to stand sentinel for my dogs, who have a proclivity for finding the quilled creatures.

At the end of the boardwalk, one can retrace steps to the parking area or continue onto the Bluffs Trail. This additional two-mile round trip brought us up a gentle elevation to a splendid view, while our pamphlet assured that we'd continue to learn along the way.

The forest transition is dramatic. Only steps away from the bog, we began to see yellow birch, hemlock, beech, and maples, all denizens of the climax mixed northern hardwood forest. Ground cover changed, and even the smells differed markedly from the bog.

Our booklet alerted us to striped maple, its bark green with white stripes. On hemlock bark, we found small holes made by yellow-bellied sapsuckers. Later we would find much larger openings, courtesy of visiting pileated woodpeckers.

On top of the ridge, red pine predominates. Through the trees we could view Silver Lake below, and Whiteface Mountain in the distance.

Information:
Battle of Plattsburgh Association, 31 Washington Road, Plattsburgh, NY 12903. Phone 518-566-1814.
Adirondack Nature Conservancy, Box 65, Keene Valley, NY 12943. Phone 518-576-2082.

Ausable Chasm • High Falls Gorge

Ausable Chasm, twelve miles south of Plattsburgh, may be one of New York's oldest tourist sites. Seneca Ray Stoddard dubbed it "a Yosemite in miniature" in his first guidebook to the Adirondacks in 1874. Travelers on steamboats and trains made it a routine stop on northern tours.

Signs piece together the geological history. An ancient sea bed, faults in rock ledges, and glaciation all played a role. What they left was a remarkable sinuous channel between cliffs of sandstone that continues to evolve today.

I also gleaned bits and pieces of human history, including early development of waterpower on the river, and purchase of the chasm itself in the 1870s by Philadelphia businessmen. In the silent movie era, a few westerns were filmed here, including one starring Tom Mix.

Tickets are purchased in the gift shop, where a scale model depicts what visitors are about to see. A trip to Ausable Chasm begins with a walk, first on the rim, and then through part of the gorge's interior. Two floods in 1996, ten months apart, combined to erase most previous walkways and staircases. Veteran chasm visitors will notice a new route.

I started with a leisurely stroll past sample rock formations (one with tracks from an animal that's never been identified) and a section of steel bridge torn away during the flooding. I continued toward a view of The Pulpit, a massive rock face set apart by faults on either side. Farther along there's a vista of Elephant's Head, another impressive formation. The "trunk" tapers progressively as it reaches water level.

From there, I retraced my steps, eventually following signs across the Route 9 bridge to the other side of the river. Attendants at a gatehouse checked for my admission bracelet, after which I resumed my hike through very pleasant mixed forest.

Before long, one comes to a classic view of Rainbow Falls framed by the arched steel bridge. Once this was called Birmingham Falls, a name selected when the local iron industry was optimistically compared to that of the famed British city. A desire to impress tourists led to the current name, applied in 1877. Three powerful flows merge in the drop over rock ledges, creating a scene that has been well known for over

150 years.

A few yards farther along, wooden staircases led down to Rocky Point, 150 feet above the river. This proved a good place for gazing upon the layered sandstone ledges across the water.

Now two choices presented themselves, the Rim Trail along the top, and the Inner Sanctum, twisting along closer to the river.

Planning to sample both, I first walked the newly constructed Rim Trail. Signs identified majestic pines, hemlock, and other conifers, whose dark green contrasted nicely with the brown sandstone walls. Later I'd pass oak, ash, and white birch. Though temperatures reached the high eighties that afternoon, shade and steady breezes made for a comfortable walk.

Periodic lookout spots revealed the grandeur of the chasm. At Moonlight Vista, a boardwalk hovered over the canyon. Another viewpoint, called On Top of the World, occupied the edge of a rocky prominence. Peering in both directions, my attention was riveted by the waters churning at the bottom of rock walls.

I returned to the trail branching point and took the Inner Sanctum route. Almost immediately, signs told me I stood atop Elephant's Head. Following a network of wooden stairways and boardwalks, I descended (and descended! and descended!) into the depths of Ausable Chasm.

A spur down metal steps led to Punch Bowl, a large pothole scoured out by hard rocks swirling and grinding down through softer sandstone. From the same viewing ledge, I gazed upon the last remnant of a bridge from the early 1900s. Perched perilously above the rushing waters, it may well have carried me on one of my earlier excursions here.

Other notable landmarks include Jacob's Well, a pothole six feet in diameter and twenty feet deep, and Hyde's Cave. A Philadelphia tourist (should I describe him as foolhardy?) discovered the latter after letting himself down the cliffs with a hundred-foot rope.

Walking carefully on some wet spots along the way, I noted blankets of moss on the walls beside me. I also began paying attention to overhanging cliffs nearby, wondering which might be the next to fall. Soon Column Rock came into view. Signage informed me that this will likely be "one of the first sites ... to be removed by natural frost and wedging forces."

The channel began to narrow. I imagined the sensation of being here at night. Unless a full moon shone directly overhead, all would be darkness—backgrounded by the roar of the waters below.

Soon I reached an overlook above Table Rock, launching point for the water segment of chasm journeys. Visitors can end their experiences with raft rides, opt for inner tubes or kayaks, or simply retrace steps and notice details missed on the first go-round.

******

High Falls Gorge, near Wilmington, opened as a tourist attraction more than a century ago. Since 1961, it hasn't missed a single summer season. As of 1999, the site also began welcoming visitors during the winter.

A steel and wood bridge leads across the West Branch of the Ausable River to the half-mile trail. It's a bit amazing that no entrepreneur ever dammed this spot to take advantage of the waterpower possibilities. The Rogers Company of Ausable Forks lumbered extensively here, and New York State Electric and Gas now owns much of the surrounding land. Yet the river continues on the same course that it's traveled for centuries.

A well-written brochure teaches some geology and points out highlights of the surroundings. Keyed to numbered signs, the leaflet assures that most unique features will be recognized. At two locations, tape recordings add further commentary.

Thus, I learned that the bedrock, anorthosite, qualifies as perhaps the oldest rock on the planet. It's not dissimilar to rocks brought back from the moon. A layer of pink granite overlays the anorthosite. Faults, or cracks, made when the granite hardened have been filled by once-molten basalt.

Once upon an ice age, a glacier dammed a great lake near present-day Lake Placid Village. When the ice melted, an outpouring of water followed the route of least resistance, in this case softer basalt rock. Thus was High Falls Gorge formed.

Surrounding woodland takes on importance, too. This climax mixed forest includes hemlock, spruce, birch, white pine, beech, and maple. The area immediately adjacent to High Falls turns out to be an island of woods never logged, making it one of the few stands of virgin forest in the region.

Stairways descend into the heart of the gorge, bringing one close to torrents of water cascading through the rock channel. Sculpting forces of the river are readily apparent. Three separate waterfalls dominate High Falls Gorge. The Main Falls drops over one hundred feet, while Rainbow and Climax Falls are smaller.

Time should be allowed for studying rock layers and plant types along the walk. Ferns cling to ledges, and I could identify lichens in several spots.

My brochure labels one bridge as "best view." Indeed this vantage point provides a terrific perspective on the entire gorge. Downstream, the water calms into a broad placid stream heading for Lake Champlain.

An observation point overlooks Master Pothole. Formed by the scouring action of sand and small rocks over eons of time, this cavity plunges thirty-five feet deep through a basalt dike.

Forty-five minutes will suffice to see the highlights of High Falls Gorge. But it's a place that invites lingering. A search for the best photo opportunities will certainly lengthen the visit.

Winter provides a wealth of ice and snow formations potentially appealing to artists and photographers. The river continues its flow amidst and around cakes of ice, and frozen forms decorate every ledge and rock face.

Information:
Ausable Chasm, Box 390, 2144 Route 9, Ausable Chasm, NY 12911. Phone 518-834-7454.
High Falls Gorge, P.O. Box 1678, Lake Placid, New York 12946. Phone 518-946-2278.

Great Camp Sagamore • Bald Mountain

Remnants of the nineteenth-century's Gilded Age, during which America's captains of finance would have Park Avenue apartments and sumptuous Newport cottages, Adirondack Great Camps gave the privileged few a sense of "roughing it."

William West Durant, son of a surgeon-turned-railroad magnate, devised the concept. Sensing the possibilities of development in the wilderness, he built rustic complexes to which he invited potential clients for hunting and fishing, and wining and dining—and hopefully seeing the benefits of retreats from hectic and dirty cities. After suitably impressing his visitors, Durant would sell them their own wilderness plots and offer to build more woodland castles. In some ways, this may be no more than the ancestor of today's time-share pitch.

Too few of these Great Camps survive; the number open to public inspection is even smaller. A guided walking tour of Sagamore near Raquette Lake gives an opportunity to experience one.

Durant built Sagamore in the mid-1890s. In 1901 he sold this camp to Alfred Vanderbilt. Vanderbilt died on the Lusitania in 1915, selflessly assisting others to safety as he lost his own life. His widow, Margaret, continued to use the complex until her own death in 1954.

Her will left the camp to Syracuse University. When Syracuse chose not to keep the property, ownership passed to the nonprofit Sagamore Institute, which gives tours and offers a series of workshops and seminars.

Travelers in 1897 faced a thirty-six hour journey from New York City, first by train to North Creek, after which they rode seven hours by stagecoach over corduroy roads. "Fillings were shaken out of their teeth," our guide told us, perhaps as much a commentary on the dentistry of the day as the state of the roads. When the railroad came directly to Raquette Lake in 1901, the journey shrank to a mere twelve hours.

After an introductory slide show in the Visitor Center, we began our two-hour walking tour in the Upper Camp, the work area for Sagamore.

Great Camps sought self-sufficiency. At Sagamore, animals were raised for milk and meat, vegetables were grown, and maple syrup was harvested. And wood was cut. Two or three of the forty year-round employees worked solely to supply the insatiable needs of wood furnaces. The pole barn, still serving as a woodshed, housed up to one hundred cords in the camp's heyday. A series of attractive red board-and-batten buildings housed a carpenter's shop, workers' quarters, and a school for the staff's children.

The carriage barn once protected Vanderbilt's three prized racing carriages. ("Racing carriages?" we asked our guide. "What kind of business was he in?" "He was involved in inheriting," the guide quipped back.) The blacksmith shop included an unusual hand-cranked bellows above the stone forge. Six-foot-thick stone walls protected the nearby root cellar.

Off by itself sits Wigwam, added by Vanderbilt around 1905. This structure has standard frame construction but a wonderful veneer of silver-gray cedar bark siding. Our guide described the process of peeling and preparing the bark. He went on to tell us how Wigwam served as the "men's club" for the property.

Situated between the work area and the more luxurious Upper Camp, the building sits high above a pretty Adirondack stream. We sat in the parlor, with its rich wood paneling and large stone fireplace. Most of Sagamore was fashioned from materials on site, but Wigwam features Southern yellow pine shipped in by rail.

Special pottery and dishware were commissioned. No effort was spared on maintenance. Even the moss on the stone hearth was watered regularly to keep it green.

For those hardy souls desiring a more woodsy experience, there's a lean-to down the hill. A hollowed cedar log served as rain gutter. Servants could be counted upon to line the floor with comfortable balsam boughs.

Now we walked to the Upper Camp, which fills a peninsula jutting out into a private lake.

Two lakeside cottages, named for children Gloria and Alfred, are the newest buildings at Sagamore. They are veneered with brown spruce bark. A picturesque boathouse with steeply pitched roof sits a few feet away.

No one visiting Sagamore will fail to be impressed by the Swiss chalet-style main lodge. Built with spruce logs, the lodge has comple-menting red trim and a broad porch. Doors are modeled on those of medieval castles; keys weighed two and a half pounds.

Inside we found deeply beveled knotty pine paneling, another of Sagamore's twenty-six stone fireplaces, and huge spruce beams (peeled and polished with beeswax) running the length of the building. A dark-room and wine cellar are nestled amidst the lodge's four stories. Acety-lene carbide equipment generated gas for lights.

Durant's Great Camp concept followed the tradition of the Adiron-dack logging camp. Thus, the communal dining room occupies a sepa-rate building. Two Vanderbilt expansions remain true to the original use of log beams, cedar bark veneer, long tables, and iron chandeliers. In 1924 Margaret added a pleasant bay window with a view of Sagamore Lake.

Covered walkways, also typical of Great Camps, took us past an icehouse (five panes of glass in this pre-thermopane era), the laundry (needed largely because women had the habit of wearing different out-fits for each activity of the day), and the caretaker's house.

The Casino, once called the Playhouse, served as an after-dinner gathering place. Billiard and ping-pong tables (a stuffed alligator tradi-tionally held the ping-pong balls) are long gone, but cushioned benches built into the walls still seat visiting groups.

We finished at the open-air bowling alley. Built by Brunswick atop six feet of steel-reinforced concrete, the lanes include newell posts with grooves large enough for cigars. Ball returns work flawlessly even after a century of play.

******

Sagamore offers a variety of trails with which to complement a visit. One encircles Sagamore Lake. Others offer longer treks into nearby wilderness.

Another option would be heading down Route 28 toward Old Forge. John Brown of Providence, Rhode Island—not the famous abo-litionist, but rather one of the family after whom Brown University is named—purchased a huge tract of land here in the late 1700s. His efforts at settlement failed, as did attempts to mine nearby iron deposits.

Tourism was to prove the first successful industry. Hunters and fishermen traveled to the region. In 1871, the first large hotel, The Forge House, opened. Dams along the Moose River created a canoeists' paradise. One can put in at Old Forge and paddle a hundred miles with only a few short carries.

An historic marker notes another important event. Hunting and trapping had depleted the Adirondack Mountains of its beaver population, and naturalists called for repopulating the region with the animal. Seven beavers were kept here in 1904 before being liberated the following spring. Any hiker can testify to the ultimate success of the restocking.

Just ten miles north of Old Forge, turn onto Rondaxe Road. Look for a large parking lot just after the turn. There a hike up Rondaxe (sometimes called Bald) Mountain begins. This is a very popular trail. Don't choose it for solitude. Rather, take it for a splendid view of the central Adirondacks.

The route is a broad, clearly marked path, signified by red markers. There are short walks through conifer forest, but much of the time is spent on a rocky ridge with open views. As one of my guidebooks suggested, it's easy to imagine that the rocks poking up from the forest floor along the long ridge are the vertebrae of a giant prehistoric animal.

After climbing only about a mile, and with only a few steep spots, you'll enjoy splendid views of the first four lakes of the Fulton Chain. Dense forest fills the space between Third and Fourth Lakes; a winding S-shaped channel allows boats through the connection. Fourth Lake is much larger, but islands make it seem like several smaller bodies of water when viewed from high above.

One hopes the fire tower on top will be maintained. A scamper up the steps allows one to see the notched top of Blue Mountain just beyond the end of Fourth Lake, and on a clear day, Mount Marcy in the distance. To the north are Bottle and Slide Mountains, with Big Moose Lake hidden behind.

Above Fourth Lake is Little Moose Lake, part of the extensive holdings of the Adirondack League Club, one of the region's oldest sportsman organizations. You also get a good perspective of the spiny ridge traversed on the way to the top. And despite all the disclaimers, don't be surprised if you find you have the peak to yourself for a while.

Information:
Great Camp Sagamore, P.O. Box 146, Raquette Lake, New York 13436. Phone 315-354-5311.
Adirondack Trails: West Central Region, Adirondack Mountain Club, Lake George, NY.

Elephant Head at Ausable Chasm

Valcour Island • Owen and Copperas Ponds

Valcour Island in Lake Champlain deserves an important place in the nation's history. There had been activity during the French and Indian War in 1759, when British and French vessels fought in the area. The crucial Battle of Valcour during the American Revolution, though, guaranteed the island's place in the pantheon.

Hoping to control the Lake Champlain passage, British leaders began sailing south from Canada in October 1776. Benedict Arnold, commanding the new fifteen-ship American Navy from the flagship *Royal Savage*, could not stand up to this British force's attempt to sweep down to Crown Point and Ticonderoga.

But the colonial forces did manage to inflict damage. Many of the boats were then able to begin a retreat to the south, escaping the British fleet. Though enduring the loss of numerous lives and a few ships, the American effort impeded British strategy sufficiently to prevent a quick movement down the lake. With winter coming on, the British had to return to Canada and plan another initiative for the spring.

That delay gave the American forces time to regroup, an opportunity that helped assure victory in the Battle of Saratoga that next year. Many consider that event to have been the turning point in the Revolutionary War.

The waters around Valcour Island have been more tranquil over the past two hundred years or so. For several decades, farming dominated the island. As leisure patterns changed, the area became a favored spot for boaters. Cottages and camps began to dot the shore.

At one point investors considered large-scale development. This threat mobilized advocates of preservation, led largely by the National Audubon Society. Within ten years the state owned most of the island's 950 acres.

Some state planners envisioned an area that would include two marinas, beaches, a golf course—even giant movie screens for the entertainment of boats anchored offshore. Zoning laws instituted by the Adirondack Park Agency in 1972 assured that the island would remain more primitive. Most cottages and foundations were removed. By 1976, the Department of Environmental Conservation had opened a system of trails.

About nine miles of walking trails now trace the perimeter of the island and cross through its interior. Shore views are outstanding, and the conifer-dominated forest makes for pleasant walking. White cedar, spruce, and pine are most commonly seen. Considerable wetland survives on Valcour, too. Perhaps most notable from a nature point of view, though not easily accessed by trail, is the blue heron rookery on the southern end of the island.

We walked much of the perimeter. Shortly after starting out, we came to the lighthouse. Completed in 1874, the stone structure features a red shingled mansard roof. The thirty-five foot tower housed a light visible for eighteen miles. The lighthouse provided quarters for the lightkeeper's family until 1930, when automated equipment replaced the original light.

Continuing on, we passed rocky outcrops, limestone ledges along the shore (supposedly rich in fossils), and a smattering of raspberry bushes. Though we found plenty of purple loosestrife, we did not find any of the unusual orchids and ladyslippers said to thrive on the island. Whittled trees and an offshore lodge testified to beaver activity.

At the southwest end of the island, we found a stone house with two dormers and a covered porch. Two hefty chimneys, impressive granite lintels under the windows, and a slate roof add to the sense of solidity of this property, formerly the Seaton home.

Henry Seaton bought his 129-acre parcel in 1919, then built a home from rock quarried nearby. Seaton became noted for his knowledge of both the natural and military history of the island. He assisted Kenneth Roberts during the writing of *Rabble in Arms*, and provided both financial and muscular assistance when the ship *Philadelphia* was raised from the lake bottom in the 1930s. Interested in preservation, Seaton was a willing seller to the state in 1973.

There's a square stone structure nearby, perhaps a pump house. Steps descend to the remains of a cement dock.

Continuing on the Indian Point and Nomad Cross Trails, we found more evidence of human occupancy. An empty cistern must have been used by an early homeowner. A lonely chimney stands as silent testimony to another home, one belonging to Plattsburgh native Monsignor

16

Robert Edward Moore.

M. H. Yager, who bought the property in 1953, described a log home built partially from timbers recycled from an old barn on the mainland. From an altar on the balcony over the living room, Father Moore said Mass for Catholic visitors on Sunday. Father Moore, who worked in Catholic Charities in New York City and had a parish near Wall Street before returning north, willed the property to the Grey Nuns, from whom Yager eventually made his purchase.

No remnants remain from one unusual phase of the island's history. The Dawn Valcour Community, formally known as "The Head Center of Advanced Spiritualism and Free Love," set up shop in 1874. Based on Utopian concepts similar to those of the better-known Oneida Community, the group espoused sharing of labor and wealth, but eschewed marriage. Farming, especially of fruit, was to provide the economic basis. Hoping for one hundred members, the number never exceeded twenty during its brief one-year history.

******

For a slightly different experience nearby, drive along Route 86 toward Wilmington Notch and the trailhead for Owen and Copperas Ponds. Though this is a very gentle trail, it provides a satisfying sense of wilderness. We hike here often but always enjoy going back.

We followed a gurgling brook that stayed always just to our right. It's a typical Adirondack trail, too eroded and with lots of exposed roots. The world's largest root-covered, glacially deposited boulder (or "erratic") suddenly came into view, the tree's tentacles a tangled mass fully encompassing the huge stone. My wife exclaimed "I'd learn to paint just to paint this scene."

After seven-tenths of a mile we came to Owen Pond. That day a couple from Michigan, Deb and John, were camped at the lean-to with their three-year-old Labrador retriever, Sadie. They planned to stay for a few days of relaxation and fishing. It has to be as nice a place to spend the night as any in the Adirondacks.

Our own retrievers would have been content to spend the rest of the afternoon romping with Sadie, but we decided to press on. We crossed over a hump of land on the way to Copperas. It wasn't difficult, but it was a definite ascent. Then the trail dropped down again, eventually reaching Copperas Pond via a spur to the left.

This is a wonderfully pristine setting. The lean-to was gone, but there was still a fire ring of stones. We heard the splashes of jumping fish and gazed lazily across at Whiteface. The waters stayed still and clear except for ripples from the fish—and the wake behind our swimming puppy Ripken. Had there been more daylight left we would have trekked another 0.6 mile to a third pond, Winch.

Almost everyone can do the Owen-Copperas walk. Consider one or all of these to introduce your children to the pleasures of the Adirondacks, to give your less active friends and relatives a sampling of the North Country, and to whet your own appetites for more excursions over the summer and fall.

Information:
Adirondack Trails: Eastern Region, Adirondack Mountain Club, Lake George, NY.
Guide to Adirondack Trails: High Peaks Region, Adirondack Mountain Club, Lake George, NY.

Kayla Dragoon by Fort Scott marker on Battle of Plattsburgh Trail

18

Essex • Coon Mountain

The founding of Essex goes back to pre-Revolutionary War days. William Gilliland, that intrepid settler who founded Elizabethtown (named for his wife), Westport (originally Bessboro), and Willsboro (named after guess who), also laid down a few roots in Essex. War against the British undid many of Gilliland's accomplishments, but the small town of Essex proved especially resilient.

Manufacturing and boatbuilding helped anchor Essex in the early nineteenth century. During the War of 1812, two ships led by Commodore Thomas Macdonough in the decisive Battle of Plattsburgh were fashioned in Essex shipyards. Opening of the Champlain Canal in 1823 cemented Lake Champlain's role as a key channel of commerce, further bolstering local merchants.

However, no one could have predicted the arrival of railroads. Suddenly waterways had competition—competition that could run all year, no less. Essex, like many places bypassed by trains, went into economic decline.

There's an upside. Remote until the era of the automobile, and even then off the beaten track, Essex survived as a sparkling remnant of early America. Factories didn't locate here. Urban renewal projects didn't bulldoze venerable properties. Almost like a time capsule, the village retains its character of a century or more ago.

A group called ECHO (Essex Community Heritage Organization), formed in 1969, called attention to the benefits of preservation. ECHO's efforts helped the entire town earn listing on the National Register of Historic Places in 1975.

A colonial shipbuilding and trading port would have supported its share of inns and taverns. One, Wright's Inn (1790), was recycled into the Town Hall during the 1990s. It was there that I picked up an annotated brochure and began my tour.

The first segment along Main Street was then, and is now, the center of commerce for this historic hamlet. Old stone warehouses and brick stores have been transformed into shops, galleries, and small restaurants. Antiques and original artwork are among the goods purveyed. The painted logo for Gold Medal Flour has faded, but still remains clear on the side of a onetime brick store dating to 1840.

The touring public has returned to Essex, and there are hostelries to meet their needs. A columned two-story porch marks the yellow clapboard Essex Inn, built around 1810; it's now returned to its original function of housing guests.

We turned up School Street, and then took a two-block stroll along Elm Street. Here stood some especially fine homes. Hickory Hill shows off Federal architecture at its best. A Palladian window and marble lintels are among decorative details. Down the street stands the elegant Noble Clemons House, an Italianate structure bordered by a wrought-iron fence decorated with fleur-de-lys.

Just around the corner, the brick Cyrus Stafford House features an Ionic-columned entryway. Huge stone slabs above and below the windows must have taxed any pulley system that set them in place.

Among churches is St. John's Episcopal Church, a gleaming white former schoolhouse (1835). In its open belfry hangs a bell once used by a passenger steamboat that plied Lake Champlain. Essex Community Church, built in 1855, is easily recognized by its tall square clock tower. The corners have unusual projecting quoins. Most stone used in Essex construction was quarried locally. However, limestone for this church and for Greystone, a private residence just north of the village, came from the same quarry in Willsboro Point that supplied builders of the Brooklyn Bridge.

Back by the Town Hall, we looked across at the sunburst panel atop the original village fire station. The first time we came to Essex, we approached from the south and were greeted with this splendid sight. Now the building houses galleries.

Heading north, we saw some of the most memorable homes in the area. No place looks as grand as Greystone (1853), built with smooth stone blocks. Cast-iron grilles cover the narrow attic windows. There's a wooden water tower out back. Next door's Harmon Noble House (1835) features an octagonal, enclosed gazebo, with curved red roof, and a porch around the perimeter. Originally, this served as a private one-room schoolhouse for the owner's children.

Dower House, though altered, traces its history all the way back to William Gilliland. Then there's Blockhouse Farm (1836), charming in pale yellow with white Greek Revival columns. An historical marker tells about a fortification built here in 1797 to protect settlers against Indian incursions. From 1799 to 1807, it served as Essex County's courthouse. Now, in a gentler era, the home occupies a knoll with a commanding view of the lake.

There's no reason to adhere strictly to the outlined tour.

On School Street, there's a three-story brick edifice apparently once a school. Unusual stonework atop the windows caught my eye. Nearer the water, small tourist cabins give a nostalgic look at how people vacationed fifty or sixty years ago.

Stone-rimmed Beggs Park, right on the lakeshore, makes a good spot for a picnic. We whiled away time on a bench gazing at the ferry coming in (the first ferry was already in operation by 1790), and across the water to mountain views in Vermont.

******

Coon Mountain rises just outside Wadhams. A leaflet at the trailhead on Halds Road informed us that the property had been donated to the Adirondack Land Trust. For over a decade this entity has been working in tandem with the Adirondack Nature Conservancy to preserve natural areas. Red markers denote the one-mile route.

Initially we walked through shadowy forest dominated by hemlock. Here and there I spotted a prominent burl adhering to a tree trunk. With time, the path opened up, and we began to see American beech, ash, and some red oak.

Wildflowers also greeted us, most notably the deep pink broad petals of primrose.

But it will be rock formations that we most vividly remember. A massive rock face soon began to appear behind the trees to our left. Our trail became steeper, briefly hugging the stone wall as we climbed over a ravine. Though never difficult, this trail provided the satisfaction of working for our goal.

And the goal proved worth the effort. The first lookout point gazed out over a medley of farmland and nearby Adirondack peaks. Once on top, we had a wonderful panorama of pastureland, forest, Lake Cham-

21

plain, the Adirondacks, and the Green Mountains. Beyond the village of Wadhams just below, Hurricane and Giant Mountains loomed most prominently among Adirondack peaks in the distance.

We lingered on top to eat lunch. The trail leaflet mentioned that William Gilliland died on this mountain in 1796. I remembered Gilliland's story as one of the more tragic tales in Alfred Donaldson's classic *A History of the Adirondacks*.

Gilliland bought a large tract of North Country land in the 1760s. Unlike many speculators, he became determined to visit his holdings and develop them himself.

However, Gilliland made one crucial mistake. Though he supported the patriot cause during the Revolution, he somehow alienated Benedict Arnold. In a bitter piece of irony, Arnold had him jailed as a traitor. His lands were ravaged during his absence. Later claims to property were denied by fledgling American courts.

This pioneer settler became reduced to guiding and surveying for hire over huge tracts that he once owned. He died of exposure after becoming lost in winter weather—right here on Coon Mountain. His name, however, lives on.

Information:
Essex Community Heritage Organization, Essex, NY 12916. Phone 518-063-7088.
Adirondack Trails: Eastern Region, Adirondack Mountain Club, Lake George, NY.

Avalanche Lake • John Brown Farm

Tony Goodwin, in *Guide to Adirondack Trails: High Peaks Region,* calls the trail to Avalanche Lake "probably the most spectacular route in the Adirondacks." Adirondack folklore makes the trek that much more interesting.

Fabled guide Bill Nye plays the key role in the story. A Vermonter by birth, Nye traveled widely at a young age. He hired out on whaling ships on the Indian Ocean, worked in the tobacco trade in Charleston, South Carolina, and went to St. Louis with plans to join John C. Fremont on a western expedition before finally settling in New York's North Country.

After homesteading in North Elba, not far from today's Olympic ski jumps, he earned a name for himself as one of the Adirondacks' best guides. Though he worked at various times for such notables as Henry van Hoevenbergh and Verplanck Colvin, he may be best remembered for another set of clients—the Fieldings.

Seneca Ray Stoddard best told the story in his earliest guidebook to the Adirondacks.

One Mr. Fielding (his first name is never given) and his wife Matilda, along with their seventeen-year-old niece Dolly, visited Lake Placid in 1868. They secured Bill's services for a multi-day camping trip through Indian Pass to Tahawus, on to Lake Colden, up Mount Marcy, and ultimately a return to Lake Placid via Avalanche Pass.

The first few days, though undoubtedly arduous, went smoothly. But on the final leg, they reached Avalanche Lake late in the day. Steep cliffs drop directly into the water on both sides. Traditionally guides would construct makeshift rafts to ferry clients along the shores.

Time didn't permit a raft, but Bill knew he could walk a ridge below the water's surface and carry the Fieldings to the next part of the trail.

It must have compromised Matilda Fielding's modesty to be straddling the head and shoulders of her tall, lanky guide. Halfway across, she began to slide down his back into the water. Dolly yelled frantically "Hitch-up Matilda, hitch-up! Why don't you hitch up?" She hitched down rather than up, but Bill managed to complete the carry and deposit her safely on the other side.

Today, planks are bolted into the cliffs on one side of Avalanche Lake. Every Adirondack veteran knows these are called "Hitch-up Matildas."

To visit the legendary spot, we began at the South Meadow trailhead near Adirondack Loj in North Elba. From there, it's a gentle 2.6-mile walk to Marcy Dam. Originally constructed as a fire road in the 1930s by the Civilian Conservation Corps, the route crosses several creeks on plank bridges and traverses stately forest.

Marcy Dam can resemble a minor metropolis on a fall weekend. Thus, the open mountain views beyond the crib dam are always a welcome sight. Phelps and Algonquin are among peaks easily identified.

Trail signs pointed us toward Avalanche Lake. During a pleasant streamside leg along Marcy Brook, we found flat rocks along the water's edge for lunch and solitude. My Labrador retriever rated the brook an "A" for its accessibility to canine frolicking.

Just past the lean-tos of Avalanche Camp, we crossed an especially scenic bridge. Only now did we begin to climb. Strategically placed planks helped us over some wet areas, but we still had to scramble around our share of boulders. A few log stairways made the going easier for us than it would have been for the Fieldings.

A descent brought us to a clearing at the edge of Avalanche Lake. My guidebook informed us we were seeing Mount Colden on our left and Avalanche Mountain on the right. Names didn't seem important. All we really noticed was the steepness of the slopes and how the cliffs indeed did plunge below the water on both shores.

Now we scurried over rocks, climbed a few ladders, and crossed some crevices on planks as we worked our way to the water's edge. My dog had all the challenge she wanted. At the beginning of one ladder I elected to leave her with a companion while I finished my hike.

Soon I came to the first short catwalk cantilevered above the water, and then a longer walk bolted into the rock face. Generations of hikers have been grateful for these "Hitch-up Matildas," which provide a unique vantage point for surveying the area.

Impressive cliffs dominate the view. There are also interesting rock formations along the shore. Carpets of trees clinging to flat projections of the otherwise sheer cliffs add color contrast. A look back gives a good perspective on the catwalks.

Avalanche Lake looks perfect for an inflatable boat, though I'd want to be careful on a windy day. I felt a brief longing for a time when I might reach such a spot and have a guide build a raft for further exploration.

We returned to Marcy Dam, where we lingered a while finishing up our snacks and snapping pictures. Whereas the Fieldings would have still had a substantial hike to Lake Placid ahead of them, we required only another forty-five minutes to reach our car.

The round trip walk to Avalanche Lake measures about ten miles. A thoroughly interesting and engaging hike, it keeps one's attention—and requires it. One must be in good physical condition for the outing, and appropriate hiking boots are a must.

Bill Nye would scoff at the improvements that facilitate today's hiker. He likely felt the traveler should be willing to work harder to reach a goal. But he'd nonetheless be glad so many people appreciate the beauty of the areas he knew so well. Well over a century after the first "Hitch-up Matilda," Avalanche Lake remains a very satisfying destination.

******

New arrivals to the North Country are often surprised to learn that John Brown's body lies "a-mouldering in the grave" just outside Lake Placid.

Born in Torrington, Connecticut, and raised in Ohio, Brown operated a tannery and traded in wool before making his home here in the late 1840s. Abolitionist Gerrit Smith had made land in the area available to freed slaves for farming. Brown came to encourage this new settlement named "Timbuctoo."

His second wife, Mary Ann Day, a native of Granville, New York, and four of Brown's thirteen children lived in the small farmhouse. The family ran the 244-acre farm during Brown's many absences, growing forty acres of potatoes for sale at ten cents a bushel to the nearby starch factory.

Indeed, Brown left frequently, first for antislavery raids in Kansas, and finally to plan the ill-fated attack on an arsenal at Harper's Ferry, Virginia. But Brown called his Adirondack farmstead home. In 1858, he had the headstone carved for his grandfather, a Continental Army soldier with the same name, brought from New York City to this spot in the Adirondack foothills. It would come to mark his own remains only a year later.

The plan at Harper's Ferry had been to storm the arsenal and procure weapons for a slave rebellion. Though his small group of followers successfully captured the building, most were caught within two days by troops led by General Robert E. Lee. Tried for treason, Brown was hanged on December 2, 1859. His body traveled by train back to North Elba for burial six days later.

The historical significance of the farm was recognized early. A group of admirers bought the land as a shrine to John Brown in 1870; New York State assumed ownership in 1895.

I found a weathered, unpainted clapboard home with wood-shingled roof and two chimneys. Furnishings represent a modest Adirondack home of the mid-nineteenth century. The light, airy parlor would have been a pleasant space for relaxing, if such an individual as John Brown ever allowed himself that luxury. The tall desk, bookcase, caned rocker, and a few chairs represent pieces known to have belonged to Brown himself.

His grave lies within a black wrought-iron enclosure across from the house. Three stones attest to the twelve men buried here, a group that includes two of Brown's sons. That headstone originally made for Brown's grandfather, and now marking his own final resting place, stands inside a glass frame.

We walked along the farm trail. A brochure describes the difficulties of living in such a place—black bears breaking into the chicken coop; such severe cold that "our old rooster froze to death last night." Numbers identify trees of the Adirondacks, and the pamphlet details their use.

The scenery—with the exception of the incongruous ski jumps—has probably changed little since Brown's tenure here. In such a peaceful setting, the tyranny of slavery and the gunfire of the Civil War must have seemed very distant indeed.

One considers the single-minded idealism that drove John Brown. The simple provision of food and shelter must have seemed herculean in this remote territory. For Brown's family to have endured such hardship in support of his mission, and for him to have made his way to both Kansas and Virginia in just a few short years, signified a passion of great depth.

Near the parking area, there's a statue of John Brown with his arm around the shoulder of a young boy. This rendition of Brown captures important qualities—an aura of sageness, an intensity of expression, a sense of guidance. It's the image I choose to remember.

Information:
Guide to Adirondack Trails: High Peaks Region, Adirondack Mountain Club, Lake George, NY.
John Brown Farm State Historic Site, 2 John Brown Road, Lake Placid, New York 12946. Phone 518-523-3900.

Greek Revival farmhouse on outskirts of Essex

Saranac Lake and Tuberculosis • Fernow Forest

Few people view Saranac Lake as an industrial town. When the picture of a dominant industry comes to mind, one thinks of a mining community, or a city with lumber and paper mills, or perhaps Hershey, Pennsylvania. But for almost a century, Saranac Lake made much of its livelihood from one industry—health care, specifically the treatment of tuberculosis.

In the mid-nineteenth century almost any small town in the mountains would have been a welcome contrast to crowded and polluted American cities. Some attributed the salutary effect to aromas of balsam fir. Others cited altitude, or dryness provided by sandy, well-drained soil. Hunters, fishermen, and vacationers headed north for recreation and respite.

Including Edward Livingston Trudeau.

At a young age, Trudeau had responsibility for his younger brother, who eventually died of tuberculosis. Likely this experience influenced his decision to study medicine at the College of Physicians and Surgeons in New York City.

In those days, tuberculosis posed a major occupational hazard to physicians, and Trudeau contracted the disease. His course was one of rallies and relapses, but by 1876, he thought that he was dying. An avid hunter, the young doctor returned to one of his favorite places, the Adirondack Mountains, for his final days.

Trudeau arranged to stay at Paul Smith's Hotel on Upper Saranac Lake. The climate clearly agreed with him. His health stabilized, he began to hunt, he resumed reading journals, and he thought about practicing medicine again.

Trudeau had read about the sanitarium movement in Europe for patients with tuberculosis. Wealthy people with the disease were already relocating to houses in Saranac Lake and elsewhere. Trudeau decided to build a sanitarium for those unable to afford more commodious quarters. He also envisioned a research presence, experimenting with new therapies along with prescribing the rest, fresh air, and exercise that constituted standard management.

The Trudeau Institute campus on Algonquin Avenue, built in 1964, continues Trudeau's mission of research into immunology and infectious disease. On a brick patio behind the building, there's a statue of Trudeau created by Gutzon Borglum, carver of Mount Rushmore. Twelve hundred patients joined in commissioning this creation. Dedicated in 1918, the memorial depicts Trudeau reclining in a cure chair and covered with heavy blankets. On the pedestal are engraved the words, "To cure sometimes, to relieve often, to comfort always."

Stroll over to Little Red, an attractive red clapboard cottage that was the first building of Trudeau's sanitarium complex. Two factory girls were its first occupants. With central wood stove, simple white furniture, and hooked rugs, it struck me as somewhere in between hospital and camp decor.

Our next stop was downtown. Buildings on Main Street saw commercial use on the ground level, but housed patients in upper stories. While appreciating sturdy brick and stone construction, and some finely detailed dentil work, we looked primarily for the porches and balconies that symbolized use for "curing."

Initially exercise was seen as the key. As concepts of fresh air grew in importance, sleeping on a porch became part of a doctor's prescription. The reclining cure chair was developed; wide doors were installed so beds could be rolled out to porches. Daily rest periods were so important that radio stations went off the air for two hours each afternoon.

The Church Street Historic District begins just off Main Street. We passed Dr. Trudeau's home, now in its second century of use as a doctor's office. The two shingled Werle cottages preserve a sense of the original cure cottages. Dr. Trudeau was a founding member of the rustic brown Church of St. Luke. Fittingly, one stained glass window depicts a mountain scene with a deer drinking at a lake.

Dr. Trudeau's original Saranac Laboratory on Church Street was America's first facility specifically for tuberculosis research. Construction is unusual, with a first floor of quarried stone, and a second of brick. This site stayed active until the new Trudeau Institute opened in 1964. Plans call for a museum showcasing Saranac Lake's history as a health resort.

Helen Street is laden with cure cottages, as are Park Avenue and

Old Military Road. The sanitarium concept did not provide nursing home care for advanced disease. Mary Prescott set up Reception Cottage for this purpose.

Eventually, a new Reception Hospital was built specifically as a chronic care facility. It's a handsome brick and columned building—with lots of porches—at the end of Franklin Avenue. Renamed Prescott House, the place now functions as a private dormitory for Paul Smith's College.

Now drive to the site of the original Adirondack Cottage Sanitarium. From Little Red in 1884, the campus grew to an eventual fifty buildings. It was easier to raise money for small cottages than for large structures. Once tuberculosis was found to be caused by a microorganism, though, the benefits of having people well separated turned out to be significant.

The American Management Association bought the property after the sanitarium closed in 1954. Twenty-five buildings remain. There's no map to support a self-guided tour, unfortunately, but it's worth looking around.

Six of thirty patient cottages survive, albeit with porches enclosed. Each had a central living room, a bathroom, and four bedrooms. Bedroom doors had transoms to facilitate circulation of fresh air.

Dodd Building, a sprawling stone and brown shingle affair that could pass for a rustic mountain hotel, served as the central dining facility. Another pavilion served as a reception hospital. Doctors with tuberculosis had their own place, James Cottage. Reid Building housed nursing students.

Elsewhere on the grounds are such functional units as the laundry and laboratory. A workshop building provided what we now call occupational therapy.

Patients had use of the Greek Revival-style library, and the chapel, which displays impressive stone masonry. The auditorium and recreation pavilion, built in 1939, represented the last expansion while the campus still functioned as a sanitarium.

Finish your tour with a drive to Stevenson Cottage, where Robert Louis Stevenson spent the winter of 1887–1888. Though Stevenson had respiratory disease, he was never definitely diagnosed with TB. Some rooms are furnished as they were for Stevenson's occupancy. Memorabilia ranges from ice skates he used on Moody Pond, to his signature in Blanche Baker's autograph album.

The village has brochures listing high points for a walking tour. Historic Saranac Lake (518-891-0971) also offers periodic guided tours.

******

In between Tupper Lake and Saranac Lake sits Fernow Forest Nature Trail, as nicely laid out and interpreted a route as you'll find in the Adirondacks. The site pays tribute to Bernhard Fernow, a pioneer in American forest management.

Fernow (1851–1923) immigrated to the United States from Prussia. His interest in forestry led to eventual appointment as chief of the Division of Forestry of the United States. When Cornell University opened the country's first school of forestry, Fernow became its director.

Grants of Adirondack land gave Cornell the opportunity for extensive research. On one sixty-eight-acre parcel, Fernow decided to show how a deteriorating hardwood forest could be successfully transformed into a profitable softwood one.

He logged the site, selling all marketable wood, and burning remaining stumps and brush preparatory to replanting. Norway spruce and white pine seedlings were then placed in alternate rows. To some extent, it's akin to tilling up a vegetable garden to plant an entirely different collection of flowers.

Being a visionary has its costs. From their Upper Saranac estates, rich landowners saw the smoke as an eyesore and demanded a halt to such experiments. Their political pressure led Cornell to close its forestry school. A new state forestry school started in 1911 in Syracuse declined to hire Fernow. His "success" cost him his job.

A century later, Fernow has recognition, along with the likes of Gifford Pinchot, as being an early leader in American forest management. This pleasant, well-marked trail commemorates him.

The self-guiding brochure clearly explains such concepts as forest succession, recycling of nutrients in the woods, and natural selection.

We began in a section dominated by sugar maple, yellow birch, and American beech. The contrast with Fernow's carefully planned softwood plot quickly became clear.

We saw Norway spruce first, but the Eastern white pine is the majestic ruler of the forest. One specimen had a diameter over thirty inches, a reminder of how large that tree can grow over a hundred years.

Pine and spruce have their battles. We saw dramatic examples of the plague brought by white pine blister rust, and by weevils that affect both species. A stop near quaking aspen and white birch taught us that these are among the first trees to repopulate a burned area.

There's a plaque on a large glacial erratic that quotes Fernow—"I have been unusually lucky to see the results of my work. I have been a plowman who hardly expected to see the crop greening, yet fate has been good to me in letting me catch at least a glimpse of the ripening harvest."

Student foresters from Paul Smith's College maintain the half-mile trail. In doing so, they both honor a pioneer in their field and bring public attention to his accomplishments.

Information:
Historic Saranac Lake, Box 1030, 132 River Street, Saranac Lake, NY 12983. Phone 518-891-0971.
Guide to Adirondack Trails: Northern Region, Adirondack Mountain Club, Lake George, NY.

Paul Smiths VIC • Newcomb VIC

When the State of New York decided to build two visitor centers in the Adirondacks, the decision to locate one in the hamlet of Paul Smiths seemed fitting. In the late nineteenth century, plenty of travelers came here to stay at Paul Smith's hotel or in one of his cottages. They got a touch of luxury in the midst of this large wilderness.

A college bearing his name now fills the site on St. Regis Lake where the hotel stood. Students can earn degrees in forestry, recreation, and culinary arts, all subject areas familiar to Paul himself. Just down the road, the Visitor Interpretive Center occupies a spacious log building. Those who haven't come here previously should spend some time perusing the exhibits.

Displays focus on the ecology of the Adirondacks. Geology, water issues, and forest succession receive attention, with emphasis on the impact of humans on the region. Conservation history gets addressed, too.

In 1857, journalist Samuel Hammond wrote, "Had I my way, I would mark out a circle of a hundred miles in diameter, and throw around it the protecting aegis of the Constitution." The "forever wild" clause in the New York constitution, added in 1894, provides some of that protection.

Outside, a series of marked trails offers exposure to a sampling of Adirondack terrain. Even the longest measures only two miles, so most can be done in an afternoon. Interpretive brochures assist in teaching walkers a bit about the environment.

Our warm-up trail was Heron Marsh. Red spruce and balsam fir dominate part of the way, while near the end red and white pines take over. Much of this area burned in 1912, so changes induced by forest fires are explained. Paul Smith built a golf course on some of this sandy soil. Pine forest has taken over that space.

Principles of marsh geology and biological diversity are covered. Steps go up to a lookout over Heron Marsh, a good spot for sighting birds and other wildlife. Two boardwalks go through the marsh. There are also a few log Adirondack lean-tos along the way.

The Forest Ecology Trail continued our immersion into natural

33

history. Factors leading to establishment and maintenance of various forest types are explained. As such, we learned to expect conifers on sand and gravel-laden soil, and hardwood trees on higher-nutrient soil. The latter covers 60 percent of Adirondack land below 2,500 feet in elevation. The impacts of natural disturbances like windstorms are pointed out. So is the effect of disease, such as the fungal process that attacks beech trees.

Especially intriguing are birch trees that appear to stand atop narrow stilts. Our brochure explained that birch often grow atop rotting logs. When, over a period of years, the log fully rots, these tentacled roots are left exposed above the soil.

Another long boardwalk led us over a fen, a bog-like area rich in nutrients brought by a stream. At one stop, we were on a carpet of sphagnum moss atop eighteen feet of water too acidic for most animal life.

The Boreal Life Trail is another nicely laid out route. This 1.1-mile loop has a bit more up-and-down walking than the others. A boreal forest features mainly such evergreens as pine, spruce, fir, tamarack, and hemlock. We learned to look for rows of small holes drilled in hemlocks by yellow-bellied sapsuckers. A large pine shows the results of lightning strikes.

There's a viewpoint by Barnum Pond, named for P. T. Barnum, who frequently stayed at Paul Smith's Hotel. Near the pond's outlet, we found evidence of beaver activity.

Another winding boardwalk, this one 1,600 feet long, crosses a bog area dominated by tamarack and black spruce. Interestingly, tamarack loses its needles each fall, an unusual behavior for conifer trees.

We did two other short walks. The Barnum Brook Trail, a wide, packed-earth lane, can accommodate wheelchairs. Trees are labeled, and signage points out nature observations made by Theodore Roosevelt. It was here in the Northern Adirondacks that Roosevelt got his introduction to the natural world. Early in life he wrote a book on the birds of Franklin County. From a lookout we could see a beaver lodge. St. Regis Mountain with its fire tower loomed in the distance.

The Shingle Mill Falls Trail has as a focus the impact of man. At one time there was a reservoir here. At the outlet of Heron Marsh, a gristmill operated in the 1850s, to be followed later by a shingle mill. Homesites have been reclaimed by the forest. Along the way, we spotted burls high on tree trunks, large boulders called erratics that were carried here by glaciers, and a beaver lodge. This loop ends with a boardwalk over Heron Pond.

Opportunities for further walking and hiking are limitless. Nearby trails go to Black Pond and Long Pond. Those interested in a climb can try Jenkins Mountain (an 8.2-mile round trip) or the shorter but steeper trail to the summit of St. Regis Mountain.

******

The small village of Newcomb offers a remarkable variety of outdoor Adirondack experiences.

For a leisurely outing, consider walking trails that start just outside the Visitor Interpretive Center on Route 28N.

Gentle switchbacks began the walk through a northern hardwood forest of sugar maple, yellow birch, beech, and white ash on the Rich Lake Trail. We came to lookouts above natural sand beaches (ducks and a loon out on the water) and glimpsed a 120-year-old white pine soaring high above.

We veered onto the Peninsula Trail, which took us onto a rocky promontory jutting into Rich Lake. Here we had a rare opportunity to view a primeval forest of Eastern hemlock. Thriving in cool moist areas such as sheltered ravines, these trees can survive up to six hundred years, longer than any others in the Adirondacks.

Unusual sights confronted us from time to time. For example, a huge gneiss boulder, actually a glacial remnant, with polypody ferns growing on its crown, high enough to be out of reach for the deer who relish it; an eroded rock face festooned with lichens and moss, but with trees springing from the top; and a chain around a white cedar at water's edge, survivor from a log boom that held trees before their ninety-mile trip down the Hudson River to Glens Falls.

And we stopped to take pleasure in small details. Fungus growing from tree trunks; delicate white-stemmed mushrooms popping out of the ground; the almost prehensile tails of dragonflies cavorting on a plank bridge.

But this is a forest, and trees take pre-eminence. We lingered by one birch growing atop a boulder, its roots intertwined like tentacled stilts with the roots of two adjacent hemlocks. One tree's cantilevered root system interlaced with roots from neighboring trees looked like an abstract painting. Another gnarled root actually looked like a pelican.

These trails are not long, less than two miles total; adding on the Sucker Brook Trail tacks on just under another mile. They offer an invigorating wilderness experience, accessible to the most sedentary hiker, yet providing a rewarding stroll even to a woodland veteran.

By all means, stop inside the Visitor Interpretive Center. I find the combination log, shingle, and stone structure architecturally pleasing. Plan time for viewing "Living with the Land—The Development of an Adirondack Land Ethic," an exhibit filling one large gallery. The thematic display emphasizes man's relationship with wilderness in general, and the North Country in particular, with clearly written text, maps, and photographs. Let it put into perspective the evolution of these mountains into such a unique ecosystem.

Information:
Paul Smiths Visitor Interpretive Center, Box 3000, Paul Smiths, NY 12970. Phone 518-327-2000.
Newcomb Visitor Interpretive Center, Box 101, Route 28N, Newcomb, New York 12852. Phone 518-582-2000.

Santanoni • Adirondack Museum • Castle Rock

Santanoni dates to 1892, when Albany banker Robert Pruyn commissioned Robert Robertson of New York City to design this Great Camp as the centerpiece of his twelve-thousand-acre wilderness estate. Many of America's most wealthy families bought or built such Adirondack compounds in the late nineteenth century, but few constructed complexes more formidable than Santanoni.

Entry to the Santanoni Preserve, on route 28N just west of Newcomb, is marked by an easily visible sign. We turned, crossed over a bridge, and quickly found ourselves at the gatehouse of this Great Camp. During scheduled summer hours, one can peruse exhibits inside on the history of the area.

The 4.9-mile route to Santanoni and Newcomb Lake, usable for horse-drawn wagons in summer and fall, is comfortably wide and not at all difficult. Except for crowding over to allow three equestrians to pass, we generally had the trail to ourselves.

Towering pines ruled over the Santanoni forest during our early winter hike, though dark hemlock and fir comprise the majority of the trees. The occasional white birch added a dot of light to the scene. In the absence of summer foliage, we had clear views of surrounding slopes, the occasional glacial erratic, and even a few burls high up on trunks.

A gradual uphill took us one mile from the gate to the farm buildings. Typical of the Great Camps, Santanoni boasted a farm and work complex that gave an assurance of self-sufficiency. One large barn burned in 2005, an unfortunate loss, as its weathered wood shakes, red trim, and steeply pitched roofs sheltered a space remarkably intact considering its one-hundred-plus year age.

A stone building with red roof, fronted by a long stone-columned porch, was the Santanoni creamery. Its thick walls helped keep milk and other dairy products cold. Two brown homes nestled in the woods housed a herdsman and a gardener. A few yards farther, we spotted a compact fieldstone cubical structure; this was the smokehouse. Santanoni apparently once produced enough meat, produce, and dairy goods to supply not only its owners' needs, but to sell in nearby Newcomb.

The trail briefly edged downward, before settling into a gentle undulation of ups and downs. We passed some open fields before returning to deep forest. A couple of stone bridges brought us over streams. At 2.2 miles, a spur goes off to Moose Pond. At about 4.5 miles we were teased by a peek of Newcomb Lake to our left. From that point, it was a fifteen-minute descent to the lakeshore. Once across a wide plank bridge, we came upon the camp.

Santanoni's cluster of log buildings faces Newcomb Lake. A nearby boathouse and secluded studio are the only other structures on the shore. Typical of Great Camps, the main lodge and cottages feature broad porches, massive stone fireplaces, and covered walkways between the units. Red window and door trim contrasts nicely with the peeled and darkly stained logs. The diagonally patterned twig doors are unique to Santanoni.

Glimpses into the main lodge revealed impressive decorative features. The split cedar wainscoting remains my choice for camp interiors, and who wouldn't relish one of those huge stone fireplaces? White birch bark covers the upper walls and ceiling.

Walk over to the art studio, an ideal rustic retreat with an arched picture window looking out onto Newcomb Lake. I wouldn't have much difficulty getting inspiration there.

Santanoni has battled back from almost three decades of neglect. The complex's second owners, the Melvin family of Syracuse, left forever after an eight-year-old grandson disappeared in 1971. Ownership subsequently passed to New York State, and the camp fell into the limbo of what to do with man-made structures in a "forever wild area."

Combined efforts of the Town of Newcomb, the Preservation League of New York State, and the organization Adirondack Architectural Heritage have rallied support for Santanoni's preservation. Their success makes the goal of this walk a very satisfying one.

******

Drive to nearby Blue Mountain Lake and tour the Adirondack Museum, one of the state's most impressive regional attractions. Sited on the grounds of the Blue Mountain House, an early Adirondack hotel, the complex offers a broad variety of exhibits in a series of buildings and pavilions.

In fact, a surviving remnant of the Blue Mountain House is one stop. When you're done examining the clerk's area and a guest room, go next door and examine photographs of the many other inns that once hosted guests in this wilderness.

The "Boats and Boating" pavilion proves a favorite. Among the freshwater craft on display are some wooden Adirondack guideboats. Unique to this region, they were traditionally constructed by guides looking to take clients hunting and fishing. Find the ten-pound canoe made especially for George Washington Sears, a writer known as "Nessmuk," who took it on his legendary canoe journey through rivers and lakes in the heart of the Adirondacks.

Before the automobile, there were stagecoaches and buckboards. We learned about these in a long building featuring "The Adirondacks in the Age of Horses." Some of the most popular buckboards were produced in Glens Falls, in the southern Adirondack foothills. The Concord coach on display would have crammed in a dozen or more people en route from a rail station to a hotel. Inspect the luxurious Pullman car that brought wealthier visitors to the region.

I'm especially partial to the exhibits on lumbering in "Work in the Woods." Exceptional dioramas depict the work involved in getting a log out of the woods during winter, and then onto surging spring waterways for travel to mills.

Recreation has long been an industry here, too. Almost anything you might want to learn about fishing and hunting sits inside "Woods and Waters." Look for an Adirondack rifle, manufactured during the nineteenth century in Plattsburgh. A life-size woodcarving portrays hermit Noah John Rondeau working near his cabin. A full-size Adirondack lean-to gives a sense of the camping experience.

Climb the short though steep path up Merwin Hill to Bull Cottage. Inside you'll find examples of another uniquely Adirondack creation, rustic furniture. Birch-bark veneers and intricate twig work decorate many of the chairs, tables, and hutches. One can sleep soundly and securely in a bed crafted from huge Adirondack logs.

When you need respite from strolling the thirty-two-acre museum, take a seat by the moving photo belt and have historic pictures delivered in front of you. They'll make you want to see more exhibits!

******

Include a climb of Castle Rock on any visit to the Blue Mountain Lake area. Beginning alongside Minnowbrook, a Syracuse University education center, the trail traverses mixed hardwood and conifer forest, sometimes along a stream. Finding an appropriate parking space could well be the biggest obstacle on the excursion.

We signed the trail registry, walked on gravel, and passed a few private driveways, until a clearly marked sign directed us into the woods. From there we found an occasional gentle uphill, but the first mile and a half is for the most part level. We crossed a brook, and we cautiously stepped around some sunken corduroy.

At that point, another sign pointed left to a trail with yellow markers. Now we climbed more steadily, finally reaching the base of a rocky outcrop. There was a squeeze between large rocks before the path opened onto a broad open ledge.

The sun at high noon bleached the scene a bit on our last visit, but no weather can mask the beauty of the scenery. Most of what's visible remains in a pristine state. William West Durant had envisioned this as a place for luxury resorts. When he went bankrupt, Harold Hochschild, a copper baron who later founded the Adirondack Museum, purchased much of the acreage. He gave most to a trust set up to protect the land.

The view from Castle Rock offers a splendid panorama. The massive bulk of Blue Mountain, almost 3,800 feet high, dominates the eastern horizon; with binoculars, we could see its restored fire tower. The very top of Snowy Mountain juts up in the Southwest. Beneath us sat Blue Mountain Lake, dotted with numerous oblong islands, some just large enough for a grove of four or five trees.

Lake Durant sits to the south. Eagle Lake, still largely owned by Hochschild's descendants, lies a bit to the west. Utowana Lake, also part of the Hochschild property, hides just out of view. Only campsites maintained for public use betray man's presence there. Beyond we could just barely catch a glimpse of Raquette Lake.

Most of us will never own a lake or a private wilderness. But a climb to the commanding vista from Castle Rock will give a taste of what it could be like.

Information:
Guide to Adirondack Trails: High Peaks Region, Adirondack Mountain Club, Lake George, NY.
Friends of Camp Santanoni, Box 113, Newcomb, NY 12852. Phone 518-582-5472.
Adirondack Museum, Box 99, Route 28N and 30, Blue Mountain Lake, NY 12812. Phone 518-352-7311.

Cottage at Santanoni in winter

Potsdam • Stone Valley Recreation Trail

The city of Potsdam claims an impressive architectural heritage. Two colleges add to the tapestry, as does parkland alongside the Raquette River where it passes through downtown.

Potsdam's settlement dates to 1803, when surveyor Benjamin Raymond, working on behalf of David Clarkson, began laying out a community. Clarkson and his associates had purchased the entire township, one of ten that were part of the fabled Macomb Purchase in Northern New York.

The Raquette River provided waterpower for a sawmill and a gristmill, but the most important enterprise was agriculture. Soon a tannery joined the mix. Within six years, Raymond's fledgling community had risen to over nine hundred people.

Arrival of the railroad in the 1850s helped bring prosperity. Lumber and farming remained important, but entrepreneurs began taking advantage of another natural resource: stone. Distinctive reddish-brown blocks, classified as Potsdam sandstone by State Geologist Ebenezer Emmons, were mined from quarries on both sides of the river.

But as the railroad bringeth, the loss of the railroad taketh away. Automobiles became dominant. Shipping costs for stone became too great. Development of hydroelectric plants on the Raquette led to flooding most of the quarries. Farmers began having difficulty competing with more fertile areas. With the exception of the Raquette River Paper Company, founded in 1891, the local economy plummeted.

However, Potsdam had an ace in the hole, a very important one: education. Potsdam Normal School, successor to the 1816 St. Lawrence Academy, flourished, becoming a four-year college in the state university system in 1948. Meanwhile, Thomas Clarkson Memorial School of Technology had been founded by the three sisters of a leading citizen killed in a quarry accident. Opened in 1896, the school grew into today's Clarkson University. Together, the institutions are the largest employers in the city.

The city has published an excellent self-guided walking tour highlighting the legacy of sandstone, first quarried in 1809. A pamphlet clearly explained changing modes of sandstone construction, while charts summarized basic architectural styles, helping improve our eye for detail.

The central downtown blocks are very impressive. One store on Market Street was the first commercial structure made of the newly available Potsdam sandstone. Built in 1821 essentially as an experiment, it still looks quite solid almost two centuries later. Buildings include such features as cornices, parapets, and arched windows. At 45-47 Market Street, there's an especially interesting rough-hewn marble structure decorated with brown sandstone arches and lintels.

Potsdam's Public Museum, built in 1876 as a Universalist Church, is one of three adjacent Greek Revival style sandstone buildings. The other two, a library and village office built as WPA projects during the New Deal, match their older partner remarkably well. Gleaming white columns front all three.

Residential areas best demonstrate the older sandstone method of slab-and-binder. Stone is cut into narrow rectangles, and then placed in alternate horizontal and vertical rows. The Elks Club owns one such structure, constructed in 1822. Clarkson-Knowles Cottage is another fine example.

Later the ashlar technique became more popular, with its irregular rough-edged stone anchored by corner quoins. Used rarely for private dwellings, this method found favor for public buildings, commercial enterprises, and churches.

Many house styles are represented, including boxy Italianate, Gothic Revival with its fancy gingerbread (made of cast iron rather than wood on one Elm Street house), and Victorian-era Queen Anne. Some of the latter, one with twin turrets and another with onion-style domes, have become fraternity houses.

Churches are quite striking. Though the Methodist has white marble construction, most others favor the distinctive local sandstone. The Presbyterian, with its tall steeple and front spires, can be seen at a distance, as can the formidable tower of St. Mary's Catholic Church.

Just across the Raquette River stands perhaps the most notable one, Trinity Episcopal Church, built in 1835 and expanded several times. A 110-foot sandstone bell tower dominates the design. Inside we admired the Gothic ceiling, finely carved lectern, and seven Tiffany windows.

The Potsdam Public Museum offers a focus on local history, plus several prized collections donated by area residents. I noted a baton used by Julia Crane, a Potsdam native who joined the Normal School faculty in 1884. Within two years, she had established the Crane Normal Institute of Music, the first school in America developed specifically to train public school music teachers. Local drugstore owner Hervey Thatcher contributed advances in milk bottle technology, including that paper cap so ubiquitous before milk began coming only in waxed cartons (which he also patented).

******

There's a very satisfying walk in St. Lawrence County, the Stone Valley Cooperative Recreational Area. This locally notable trail network passes land owned by St. Lawrence County, the Town of Colton, and Niagara Mohawk. The power company maintains the route in collaboration with the Laurentian Chapter of the Adirondack Mountain Club and the St. Lawrence County Youth Conservation Corps. On the west trail we found a plaque dedicated to Lewis Weeks (1920–1999), apparently a leader in bringing the trail to fruition.

One trail begins right at the edge of "downtown" Colton, with paths on each side of the Raquette River. Along the west bank, we passed the dam spillway, eventually crossing a narrow bridge over a flume. Soon we found ourselves walking alongside rapids. Broad rocks began to interrupt the current; then we came to a rock chasm with impressive waterfalls. As the trail descended to river level, our dogs raced ahead to stake out swimming holes.

This place must be a geologist's dream, but with some interpretive markers missing, we couldn't fully appreciate the significance. Near the Narrows, we did find a sign describing the "mylonitization" of the 500-million-year-old sedimentary rock beneath us. The layering we observed apparently comes from a shearing force best compared to sliding a deck of cards.

We also hiked the east side. Water sheeting over broad rocks came into view almost immediately. A sunlight-dappled forest added contrast to the very pretty scene. The trail diverged away from the river, and we had more strenuous walking for a while. When we approached the water again, we found swimmers by broad rocks at a deservedly popular bathing spot.

Staying along the river, we came to a "stairstep" falls, several potholes, and a roaring falls. And more falls. Next came a climb up log-reinforced steps, and a stretch winding along a high ridge. Steep descent brought us to Layer Cake Rock, a small island of metasedimentary rock. A sign told us we were near a fault zone that divides Adirondack Highlands from St. Lawrence Valley lowlands.

Farther on, we saw a group of campers perched atop a rocky outcrop alongside another swimming hole. Cedar, hemlock, and pine appear to dominate the surrounding forest. We found burls, exuberant fungal growth, and plenty of evidence of bird excavation.

The trail on each side is 3.2 miles. A full loop would be 7.5 miles. The river alternates between narrow passages and wider ones. From a churning cascade, the water changes to a broad, steadily charging stream, later to surge with power again, and then returns to a lazy flow. I suspect a hike in the spring, with the water level higher, would be quite a different experience.

Information:
Potsdam Chamber of Commerce, P.O. Box 717, Potsdam, NY 13676. Phone 315-265-5440.
Colton Recreation Commission, Colton Town Hall, Colton, NY 13625. Phone 315-262-2553.

Wingspan chart at Wellesley Island

Wellesley Island • Cranberry Lake

Even by the mid-1800s, the Thousand Islands region of the St. Lawrence River had become a popular vacation spot. President Ulysses S. Grant spent holidays there, as did railroad magnate George Pullman and uncounted thousands of lesser-known people.

Some of the islands are barely large enough to hold a single house. Others have more luxurious accoutrements. None surpasses Boldt Castle, the stone complex built on Heart Island by George Boldt, owner of New York's Waldorf Astoria Hotel. Designed as a present for Boldt's wife, the castle sits unfinished. It lives on as a memorial to her premature death.

Wellesley Island is the largest of these islands. Once the place was a playground for the wealthy. Now New York State maintains stewardship of large parcels of land, guaranteeing public access for all. Our experience at Wellesley Island State Park convinced us of the wisdom of the state's decision. A scenic suspension bridge near Alexandria Bay provides access.

Edison Bradley, owner of Old Grand Dad distillery, once ran a model farm on the site of the current park. From 1911, he spent summers at his "Bungalow," a 240-by-68-foot structure with forty rooms. (The house burned in 1922.) The property changed hands several times before the Thousand Islands State Park Commission purchased over 2,600 acres for public use in 1954.

The state park includes nicely sited campgrounds, a newly built cottage colony, and plenty of river access along its eighteen miles of waterfront. Not surprisingly, this has become a haven for boaters. For those of us who are landlocked, there's still plenty of activity.

The park's centerpiece is the Minna Anthony Common Nature Center, dedicated in 1969. It is named in honor of a woman who contributed nature columns to Watertown newspapers for over twenty-five years. The center offers an interesting museum, plus access to a varied network of hiking trails.

Impressive taxidermy anchors displays on the ecology of the area. The wetland exhibit included a beaver swimming underwater, while a kestrel and red-tailed hawk were highlights in a tall case of bird specimens. Elsewhere, we noted a fifty-one-inch muskellunge caught in 1978, and the fossilized tracks of an unidentified creature that lived nearby 500 million years ago.

A diorama of Wellesley Island pointed out glacial features, preparing us for the conjunction of Picton granite bedrock and Potsdam sandstone plateau we would later see while hiking. In a hands-on room, kids (and we childlike adults!) compared textures of animal pelts and looked at aquarium inhabitants.

Over two days we hiked virtually every foot of the nine-mile trail system. In doing so we traversed gently undulating broad forest paths, climbed over craggy granite outcrops, looked over ponds formed by beaver activity, and found plenty of the gnawed aspen stumps favored by those formidable rodents.

A brochure accompanies the North Field Loop. Commentary highlights concepts of forest and field succession. Along the way, there's a pen formed by tall wire fencing. Inside, where deer have no access, brush and sapling growth flourishes, a marked contrast to the more barren contiguous area. With an estimated 50–100 deer per square mile, Wellesley has three times the density cited as optimal for a healthy population.

The Eel Bay Trail brought us past layered sandstone ledges high above the St. Lawrence River. Descent to Sand Cove gave our dogs a brief opportunity to swim. Soon we came to blueberry bushes (a young girl hollered "snack time!"), and then proceeded on to a series of glacial potholes scoured over the years by sand and gravel to depths as great as fifteen feet.

At the Eel Bay Dock, a 36-foot voyageur canoe sat ready for its next group tour. Signage provided information on shoreline ecology. Fishing here is good for perch, bullhead, pike, and bass. One successful angler confirmed this with his recently landed string of fish.

Our most beautiful views came along the Narrows Trail. Wildlife was most plentiful on the lesser-used South Bay Trail. There were plenty of deer, including one fawn with its mother. We watched a great blue heron float on air currents as he propelled himself against the wind.

Back near the museum, a Geology Wall shows off vertical stripes representing each rock type in the region. Then there's the "How Big

Is Your Wingspan?" diagram. My wife Marty spread her arms for comparison to colored silhouettes of the loon (forty-six inches) and bald eagle (a full seven feet).

No visit should end without a stop at the Butterfly House. Built in 1998, this frame of marine netting encloses a garden full of coreopsis, yarrow, columbine, and other plants. Many inhabitants are orange-and-black monarchs, but there are also painted ladies, red admirals, and black-and-yellow swallowtail butterflies.

An energetic and engaging interpreter called our attention to tiny blue eggs and just-hatched caterpillars. She told us that the butterflies can't be released into the open. Law requires that any wildlife born in captivity remains in captivity. Butterflies aren't exempt.

******

Lumbering and tourism once made Cranberry Lake a prosperous area. The first of a series of dams that formed the lake was completed in 1867. By the turn of the twentieth century, steamboats plied the waters. Sportsmen came, among them such notables as Frederic Remington. Large hotels thrived. The Emporium Lumber Company operated a major mill at Cranberry Lake until the 1920s.

A state campground on the lake draws people throughout the summer. From the campground a network of trails allows a sampling of what Cranberry Lake has to offer. Most popular is a hike up Bear Mountain, with its commanding view of the surrounding area.

We opted for a less strenuous hike along the Boardwalk Nature Trail. The four-mile-plus round trip gave us the exercise we sought. A trail guide available at the campground gave us the chance to learn a little Adirondack ecology along the way.

Markers led us to inspect the understory of the forest, an aspect of the environment that we're always seeing, yet know so little about. We identified goldthread, so named because of the way Native Americans used its stems as a yellow dye. Then there was shining club moss, fuzzy green in appearance. Its dried spores, easily ignited, once found use as flash powder for early photographers.

Something called spotted touch-me-nots served as a native liniment for poison ivy. Indian pipes had no specific use, but these unique white plants are unusual in lacking chlorophyll. Rather than make energy from photosynthesis, they rely on fungi in the soil.

Boulders known as erratics, so named because they don't match the bedrock beneath them, dot all Adirondack landscapes. Close-up views revealed lichens and mosses, the earliest manifestations of soil development.

Maple trees sport the most brilliant fall colors. Our brochure reminded us of the sugar maple's commercial value for sap, as well as for making furniture and hardwood floors. White ash finds use in rake handles, but also for baseball bats. Bobby Thomson's famous 1951 home run was hit with an Adirondack bat.

Beech trees were plentiful. Claw marks alerted us to the species' popularity with bears, who seek beechnuts as food. Striped maple, particularly younger ones, features white lines on the bark. The American hemlock was critical to the tanneries so common a century ago in the North Country.

There were plenty of conifers, most notably balsam fir and red spruce. Moister areas nurtured white cedar, useful in building docks. Tamarack is also common.

Long boardwalks meandered past wetlands, swamps with woody trees and shrubs, and marshes, defined as areas without woody plants. A bog was filled with sphagnum moss. When dried, such moss can be added to gardens for water retention. Native Americans used sphagnum to line diapers.

Some of our route followed lumber roads, a reminder of how man has used the forest. Animals have impacted the landscape, as evidenced by the results of beaver activity. So have natural forces; the area still shows effects from a microburst that swept through much of Northern New York in the mid-1990s.

Information:
Minna Anthony Common Nature Center, Wellesley Island State Park, 44927 Cross Island Road, Fineview, NY 13640. Phone 315-482-2479. Cranberry Lake State Park, 243 Lone Pond Road, Cranberry Lake, NY 12927. Phone 315-848-2315.

Whetstone Gulf • Lowville Demonstration Area

One Adirondack foothills hike has crossed over from "new find" to "favorite" in the past few years—Whetstone Gulf State Park. There's no direct route to this park, located in the Western Adirondacks just south of Lowville in Lewis County. But expect a scenic ride either along Route 3 or Route 28 before cutting over onto Route 26.

By now you'll be on the Tug Hill Plateau, a rolling countryside quite unlike the mountains and lakes that comprise the Adirondacks in the east. The area may be best known for its reliably heavy snowfall, well over two hundred inches during most winters.

Undulating cornfields and a smattering of dairy farms mark the region. This tranquil beauty provides no clue to the dramatic landscape one finds at Whetstone Gulf itself.

Staff member James Chaufty filled me in on the site's history.

This park has seen public use for well over a century. Formerly a farm donated as a town park, Whetstone entered state ownership in the early 1900s when Assemblyman Clarence Fisher obtained a $25,000 appropriation to purchase 1,400 acres. (The park now includes over 2,100 acres.) A few old foundations remain from farming days, as do scattered apple trees, whose drops decorate the green swaths of lawn in fall.

The Civilian Conservation Corps played a major role, Jim told me. They built the ranger's home and planted thousands of trees, including the red pines that soar over all others on the periphery of the park.

After World War II, campsites and picnic areas were built, as was a bridge over the creek. A dam was built in 1961 to control the once raucous water flow through the Gulf; a swimming area was also developed.

Run initially by the state's conservation department before being put under the aegis of the Thousand Islands State Park Commission in 1968, Whetstone Gulf owes much of its pristine state to the vision of manager Mark Frank. Chaufty, a twenty-four year veteran of the park, depicts Frank as a taskmaster who ran the site well. His emphasis on a preserve scrupulously clean and visually appealing filtered down to all employees—and to visitors.

The heritage of the park is further celebrated by a plaque on a large boulder near the entrance. It commemorates William McCarthy, a forest ranger here from 1931 to 1946. He receives credit for development of the campground, and for his devotion to conservation.

A mile-and-a-quarter exercise trail just across Whetstone Creek provides a good spot for limbering up. I suspect many visitors never get any farther.

After putting leashes on our dogs, we set out to hike the gulf. A five-mile route circumnavigates the bluffs atop the chasm, with a cross-over by bridge at the far end of the trail. At one time another trail followed the stream at water level, but footbridges are out, and it's now impassable.

Advised that the north trail was the less steep one, we saved it for our return trip, beginning instead on the south rim. We began climbing almost immediately through a pine forest dotted with many young maple and poplar. The steepness caught us by surprise; the terrain just doesn't look that rugged from the parking area!

After about fifteen minutes, the way leveled off. We took a spur to a lookout platform and gazed over the neighboring plateau toward silos and pastures carved from still forbidding land.

Soon we had our first glimpses of cliffs on the opposite side. Now we could begin to appreciate the uniqueness of the gulf. The melting of glaciers caused a powerful outflow of water across this region at the end of the last ice age. Whetstone is only one of several dramatic east–west channels carved into the land. The depth of the gorge reaches almost four hundred feet, but at some points the edges are barely ten feet apart.

Most of the dramatic rock faces are composed of Martinsburg shale. There's also one layer of sandstone, which early settlers found useful for sharpening stones. It's from this that the creek and gulf get their names.

In general we found an excellent trail through the mixed forest. But there are no guardrails along the top; hikers must pay attention.

A side trail led us down to creek level near a series of pretty cascades. Soon we crossed a stretch of corduroy, and then a bridge that connected us with the north trail. A group of kids fished just above the bridge. They told us they hadn't had much luck that afternoon.

Returning along the north rim, we had excellent views of remarkable notched rock walls on the south, some almost cirque-like in contour. The narrow stream coursed through the chasm far below. Forest growth on top added to the sense of depth; the vertical drop certainly looked greater than four hundred feet at some points.

The trail atop the north rim is not as well defined in some places, but it was never difficult to find our way. There are a few areas disconcertingly close to the edge. I don't think I'd want to ski this trail in winter.

Back at the entrance area, I talked more with Jim Chaufty. He suggested a return for winter skiing, or in April, when the snow has melted, but before bugs stir to life or vegetation blooms. Then, he asserts, Whetstone offers the best views.

I asked about evidence of Native American presence in the area. Jim told me there were trails but no signs of long-term occupancy. He reminded us that the Whetstone Gulf region can be a "terrifically inhospitable area, with swamps, trees, bugs, and three hundred inches of snow."

******

In the western Adirondack foothills, on Route 812 in the hamlet of Dadville, the New York Department of Environmental Conservation maintains the Lowville Demonstration Area. This ninety-two-acre preserve functioned as the Lowville Tree Nursery from 1923 to 1971. Many of the seedlings raised here were planted by Civilian Conservation Corps workers in parks around the state.

A brochure outlined our walk along the Forestry Nature Trail. A one-hour stroll introduced us to forest concepts while bringing us through several woodland plantations, past ponds, and along a wildlife marsh. Trees and plants are well labeled. Panels along the way give clues and encourage visitors to "guess the bird."

Following blue trail markers, we ambled through a sugar maple orchard, learning that Lewis County leads the state in production of maple syrup. Rows of spruce and pine taught us about the important commercial uses of these trees. Pitch pine turns out to be unique in its requirement for fire to open its cones and establish new seedlings. Blocks of hardwoods show off chestnut, white birch, red oak, walnut, and hybrid poplar.

Christmas tree production is explained. Various species of pine, fir, and spruce are harvested after seven to thirteen years to supply the holiday market.

Along the way we absorbed information on ecological succession, concepts of woodland management, and insights into animal habitat. An arboretum highlights three hundred trees and shrubs, both native and introduced, that are hardy enough to thrive in the rigorous North Country climate.

One field has been left alone to demonstrate natural processes of forest succession. Another swath of land shows the impact of 1995's damaging microburst on woodland. Management techniques, including thinning of seedlings to promote hardy growth, are discussed, as well as effects of drainage changes and grade alterations.

Bluebird boxes serve to lure New York's state bird. A pond becomes habitat for varieties of trout. Marshland attracts plentiful bird life along with a host of mammals. Drainage ditches catch spring outflow from the Black River but also support muskrats, turtles, and frogs.

Keep in mind that all sorts of bugs also thrive here. Fortunately, we had brought plenty of insect repellent. Fall hiking, or even snowshoeing in winter, might be more comfortable! There are picnic tables available, and even an old fire tower to climb.

Information:
Whetstone Gulf State Park, R.D. 2, Lowville, NY 13367. Phone 315-376-6630.
New York State DEC, 7327 Route 12, Lowville, NY 13367. Phone 315-376-3521.

Lake George • Warrensburg

From early days of settlement in Quebec and New York, troops, traders, and settlers entered Lake George on travels between Lake Champlain and the Hudson River. The beauty of the lake was recognized early. Father Isaac Jogues, the first white man to see the water, extolled its attributes. Thomas Jefferson visited and proclaimed it a jewel. Thirty-two miles long, with 179 islands, and with no industry along its shores, the water remains crystal clear.

I grew up near Lake George. To me, the battles in this resort town generally meant traffic jams and long lines to get into restaurants and nightclubs. Yet this site also played a significant role in our early history, first as France and England battled for control of North America, and then during the colonial revolution.

In Lake George Village today, signs proclaiming "Big Bob's Burgers and More" or "House of Frankenstein" wax museum crowd out the historical markers. Those coming for the beaches, family activities, and nearby attractions should pick up a "Colonial Wars of Lake George" leaflet and walk the three-mile loop to get a sense of history. The brochure advises two hours for the tour, but we spent much longer.

We began at the handsome brick former courthouse on Canada Street. Built in 1845, its central clock tower still serves as a major landmark in the village. Now the building houses a museum, complete with intact jail cells in the basement.

General Montcalm's troops stayed nearby during the French and Indian War. Indeed, the first few stops on the tour point out places of encampment. Artillery Bay, now surrounded by a large motel, served as a landing place for heavy weaponry as Montcalm planned his attack on Fort William Henry.

Some of the shoreline can be enjoyed via a pleasant boardwalk offering scenic views and plaques describing the local fish populations. Shepard Park, at water's edge, boasts a beach, small bandstand, and stone benches. Markers commemorate the Lake House, a luxury hotel that stood during the 1830s, and the first successful swim of the lake's length, achieved by Diane Strubel in 1958.

(Not on the tour but also worth noting is a mural inside the post office. This pastoral scene of rolling hills and farmland overlooking the lake was painted by Judson Smith in 1942, as part of the Federal Artists' Project during the New Deal.)

Turning onto Beach Road, steamboat piers and the old tile-roofed Lake George railroad station come into view. The Lake George Steamboat Company traces its lineage to 1817; its large boats continue to offer tours.

There's also maritime history on the lake's bottom. One sign tells about the *Land Tortoise*, a seven-gun, twenty-six-oar British warship. Called "North America's oldest intact warship," it can be viewed by qualified scuba divers.

Now the route veers onto Fort George Road and the Lake George Battlefield Park. An impressive statue portrays General William Johnson, commander of British troops during the Battle of Lake George in 1755, in consultation with Chief Hendrick of the Mohawks. The inscription on its base points out that "defeat would have opened the road to Albany to the French."

Nearby a bronze statue pays tribute to Native Americans, who first inhabited the region. Unknown soldiers who perished in the nearby massacre of Bloody Morning Scout in 1755, part of the first Battle of Lake George, are recognized by another marker.

Jeffrey Amherst built a new installation, Fort George, in 1759. Both American and British armies held this fortification at various times during the American Revolution. Stone ruins and earthworks remain visible. Elsewhere a relief bronze plaque maps the route by which General Henry Knox took cannon captured by Ethan Allen's Green Mountain Boys from Ticonderoga to Boston early in the Revolution.

Another statue pays homage to Father Jogues, a Jesuit missionary captured by Mohawks and martyred in 1646. He had called the place he discovered Lac du Saint-Sacrement. (In 1755 General Johnson changed it to Lake George in honor of the British king.) Sloping lawns provide a sweeping panorama of the lake and its surrounding mountains.

Atop the nearby hill, a reconstruction of Fort William Henry dominates the landscape. Over five hundred British troops lived here during its brief period of activity. Built in 1755 under William Johnson, the garrison was burned two years later after British troops surrendered during a siege by General Montcalm's army. The massacre of the vanquished by France's Native American allies as they left the protection of the walls was depicted by James Fenimore Cooper in his novel *The Last of the Mohicans*.

Monuments honor the memory of British troops who manned Fort William Henry. One specifically remembers colonists from the Mohawk Valley who assisted in construction of the fort.

Along with touring the interior of the fort, visitors can find additional walks nearby. The summit of Prospect Mountain can be reached by automobile. Hardier sorts can ascend via a steep trail that begins right at the edge of the village. Most people go for the view. There are also interesting ruins of a resort hotel on the top.

******

Warrensburg is one of those pretty villages that just beckons for exploration. On Route 9, only a few miles north of Lake George, it's notable for some attractive bed-and-breakfast spots and a smattering of antique shops. Every fall the village hosts what it calls the "World's Largest Garage Sale."

It wasn't easy to find a walking-tour brochure. The one I finally obtained, "Olde Warrensburgh Tour," was written in 2001 by fourth graders in a BOCES enrichment class. I like the idea of schoolkids participating in a project to show off their community. The commentary reflects topics that engage students' interest; it's lively and a bit humorous at times.

I started at the Warrensburg Museum, whose exterior wall features a mural I've always liked. Entitled *Warrensburg: A Town in Harmony With its Past*, this 1976 Bicentennial project portrays rural and village scenes, with an emphasis on logging.

Much of the route follows Main Street, past an array of impressive churches, by old commercial buildings, and past a bandstand that has long defined this village for me. Dedicated to native son Floyd Bennett, first aviator to fly over the North Pole, the colonial gazebo dominates a small island at a key intersection.

Sometimes my youthful narrators focus on vanished architecture—a music hall, site of a racetrack ("mainly a play area for adults who wanted to escape from their house and children," read the commentary!), and the venerable Grand Army House that boarded Civil War veterans. Reference is made to the mansion built for tannery owner Colonel Benjamin Burhans, who wanted it to last forever.

However, demolition came in the 1960s—"the Burhans mansion only lasted about one hundred years." I'm also informed that Burhans had a private bank that was robbed three times. On the final occasion, the robber left his tools behind.

Looping across Fourth Street and then down Hudson and Elm, I passed Bennett's childhood home, a simple frame house with porch that blends comfortably into a spacious neighborhood. Several Victorian and Gothic Revival homes caught my eye. The Merrill Magee House, an inn and popular restaurant, was actually built in nearby Thurman before being moved here with horse and buggy. The handsome limestone Richards Library includes a squat turret and a bay window on one corner.

Burhans Tannery and a woolen mill no longer stand, nor does the Emerson Sawmill, torn down in 1983 but survived by a few rusting turbines. However, an 1824 gristmill along the Schroon River survives, now as a restaurant. Empty during my walk was a long, red, three-story clapboard structure, once a factory that manufactured three hundred thousand shirts a year. A walkway connected it to the pale yellow building across the street, where ladies' dresses were produced.

Back on Main Street sits a stone shop dating to 1790. Originally a blacksmith shop, it also once had a ballroom on the second floor.

It's always impressive to see what lies beneath the surface of a village. Neal Herr and his students helped me better appreciate this small Adirondack community. A word of warning, though. The tour is listed as being "four miles long and takes approximately 45 minutes." If your energy doesn't match that of a fourth grader, allow a little more time!

Information:
Lake George Regional Chamber of Commerce, 2176 Route 9, Lake George, NY 12845. Phone 518-668-5755.
Warrensburg Chamber of Commerce, 3847 Main Street, Warrensburg, NY 12885. Phone 518-623-2161.

Silver Bay Association • Crown Point

Sometimes I enjoy the bustle of Lake George Village's tourism economy. But frequently I seek quieter nearby places.

One weekend we drove along the lake's west side to Silver Bay. I'd long known that an organization known as the Silver Bay Association sponsored speakers and conferences. The Association has thrived for over a century, but for us this constituted a new find.

History of the site goes back to a man named Silas Paine, who began building a hotel on the spot in the 1890s. In 1900, one Luther Wishard spent a vacation in the area. An employee of the national YMCA, he pictured the place as a training and education center for his organization. Eventually he convinced Paine to sell the property. By 1902 the Silver Bay Association had begun activities.

Now there are sixty-two buildings on the picturesque seven-hundred-acre campus. Architectural styles as different as Victorian and Adirondack Rustic co-exist comfortably, tied together by small gardens and scenes of pristine lakeshore with mountains in the distance.

The YMCA continues to operate Silver Bay. Conferences, retreats, and workshops attract many of the twenty thousand visitors who come each year. A yearly conference on Human Issues in Management dates back almost nine decades. Creative writing workshops for high school students form another annual event.

Silver Bay puts no restrictions on membership. Four thousand individual members also use the extensive facilities.

Environmental awareness forms part of the organization's mission. So does commitment to the region, as manifested by after-school programs, year-round child care, summer day camp, and respite programs.

We picked up a self-guided walking tour handout at the main office and began strolling around.

The office, officially called the Inn, is quite impressive. When Silas Paine purchased the property in 1898, he transformed a fifty-year-old farmhouse into a small hotel. Subsequent additions and renovations have made the rambling five-story structure a central focus for Silver Bay. Rockers on the broad veranda compete with mission furniture in the lobby as inviting places to sit and relax.

Hepbron Hall looks quintessentially Adirondack with its weathered, brown cross-framing. So does Morse Hall, with its rough stone construction. For almost twenty years (1918–1935), when Silver Bay ran a boys' boarding school, this building served as library and science lab. Now it's a conference building with a museum in the basement.

The auditorium harkens back to the Chautauqua era with its open-truss roof, slanted floor, and wood seats for six hundred people. An outdoor staircase goes to the balcony. Bells ring regularly from the tall shingled tower. Original plans for a stone building fell victim to cost considerations, and a wood structure went up in 1907. Within a few months, the entire place burned down. This exact copy was ready by 1908 and continues to serve the campus a century later.

Looking inside at memorial plaques, we noted one dedicated to a longtime piano tuner. Another honored Reverend Daniel Miner Rogers, the first Silver Bay "martyr." This unfortunate man was killed during a religious mission to Turkey in 1909 "during the Armenian massacres while protecting the girls' school."

Helen Hughes Memorial Chapel is named for the daughter of New York governor and United States Supreme Court Chief Justice Charles Evans Hughes. Granite construction, topped by a slate roof, envelops a medieval-style nave with wooden pews. Stained-glass windows decorate the interior.

The Fisher Gymnasium is another notable spot. There are two full-size basketball floors, a weight room, and living space upstairs. A huge fireplace looming over a ping-pong table feeds to the large central stone chimney. We appreciated the fragrant aroma of wood, probably a nice balance to that of sweat worked up during a tough game.

Clusters of cottages dot the landscape. These can be rented by conference attendees and Silver Bay members. Dormitory-style quarters accommodate summer staff, many of them college students from all over the world. Other buildings house classroom space, practice studios for musicians, and a library.

An informative guidebook taught us some forestry as we walked the one-mile Horn Memorial Sanctuary Nature Trail. Then we veered onto the Lakeshore Trail back to the main campus. Along the way we saw foundations of a sawmill operated by the boys' school in the 1920s.

Two plaques denote the Council Ring, an outdoor amphitheater at which the Boy Scouts of America conducted their premier leadership training session in 1915.

From benches along the water's edge we enjoyed the vista across Lake George to the mountain backdrop. A classic Adirondack boathouse, dating to 1905, framed the scene at one end. Behind us, the Silver Bay campus spread up the hill. These are wonderful views with which to end a day.

******

Drive north from Silver Bay. Pass Fort Ticonderoga, the reconstructed bastion where Ethan Allen made his surprise attack, and go on to Crown Point. Though Fort Ti, with its museum, refurbished quarters, and uniformed guides, certainly merits a visit, Crown Point was once the more important military post.

The French built Fort St. Frederic in 1731 to guard this narrow part of Lake Champlain. In keeping with engineering concepts of the time, a tall citadel stood within the compound, essentially a fort within a fort. British forces under Jeffrey Amherst captured the installation during the French and Indian War in 1759. Rather than leave the fort for enemy occupancy, French soldiers destroyed the structures before leaving.

Amherst designed a larger star-shaped complex, farther uphill from Lake Champlain. Bastions and barracks surrounded a four-acre parade ground. Outside the walls, a waterless moat filled with limestone provided additional protection. Only a small company of soldiers was left, however, after the end of hostilities in 1763. This regiment was no match for American troops led by Seth Warner, who captured Crown Point in 1775. British forces retook the fort later. There was no further significant fighting in the area.

Local residents salvaged plenty of rock from Crown Point before New York State took ownership in 1910. Now trails bring visitors by the remnants of Fort St. Frederic near the lakeshore. Remains of brick-lined beehive ovens survive alongside the stone foundations; when in use each could turn out 900 six-pound loaves of bread twice a day.

Walking up to the site of Crown Point, one finds more substantial structures. Two-story stone barracks, built symmetrically in Georgian design, are impressive even two centuries later. Each small room would have held twelve to fourteen soldiers. Interpretive signage told us each group would have been allotted a half cord of wood weekly for heating and cooking, plus a pound of candles for light.

A stroll around the perimeter of the British fort offers commanding views across Lake Champlain into Vermont. Additional trails penetrate nearby woods, allowing a bit more vigorous exercise. Many visitors conclude a stay by walking on to the handsome columned lighthouse near the Crown Point Bridge. Originally built in 1855 and operational into the early twentieth century, the site was converted into a Samuel de Champlain memorial in 1909.

Information:
Silver Bay Association, 87 Silver Bay Road, Silver Bay, New York 12874. Phone 518-543-8833.
Crown Point State Historic Site, R.D. #1, Box 219, Crown Point, NY 12928. Phone 518-597-3666.

Abandoned stone barracks at Crown Point

Hadley Mountain • Sacandaga Walkway

Most Adirondack climbing takes place in the High Peaks and Central Region. For an interesting change in scenery, Hadley Mountain, in the southeastern part of the park, can be a good choice. A restored and staffed (usually) fire tower promises views of Sacandaga Lake and its environs. The 1.8-mile trail, with an ascent of 1,525 feet to the peak elevation of 2,675 feet, is of modest difficulty. Thus, this hike should be suitable for all ages.

The *Guide to Adirondack Trails: Eastern Region*, published by the Adirondack Mountain Club, directed us off Exit 21 of the Northway to Luzerne, and then past Rockwell Falls, a pretty cataract between Hadley and Luzerne. Hadley Hill Road featured forest alternating with occasional rocky pasture; the mountain's tower loomed far ahead on a long ridge.

Turning onto Tower Road, a well-maintained gravel route, we cut through beautiful mixed hardwood-conifer forest. Logging roads diverged, and we noticed a weathered sugar shack to our right. Trailhead parking accommodates quite a few cars, a good thing since this trail can be crowded on peak weekends.

Informative brochures are offered at the site, an addition that we applaud. We stopped at every numbered spot to consult the guide. Red markers denote the trail, which began to ascend almost immediately.

Initially, the forest featured delicately needled hemlocks, whose bark fed the nearby tanneries in the nineteenth century. White birch added lightness to the green canopy. We noted the unfortunate presence of graffiti carved into the smooth bark of several beeches. We would encounter maple and oak as we climbed higher.

As on most Adirondack trails, we found large boulders left by glacial activity, but here bedrock proved the dominant feature. Soil erosion has exposed immense quantities of this rock. In fact, our Adirondack guidebook points out that some stretches simulate paving, or "slanted city sidewalk."

More prominent birch groves appeared farther along. Our brochure taught us that these are pioneer trees, those that establish themselves first after a forest fire. Over twelve thousand acres burned in this area during a series of devastating fires in the early part of the twentieth century.

After alternating steep and gentle sections of the trail, a well-marked left turn brought us up to rock ledges. Here we enjoyed our first views of Sacandaga Lake. The tail of the lake twists behind a low ridge, and curlicues out to the main body of water. The long rock ledges enhance this impressive perspective on the largest man-made lake in the region.

The last part of the two-mile trail turned out to be quite gentle. A detour leads to the brown plank cabin once occupied by rangers, while the straight route goes to a cairn atop the rocky summit. And to the tower!

The summit boasts a 270-degree view, but a climb up the tower increases the panorama to 360. We have a propensity for forgetting binoculars and picking hazy days. Still, we could easily locate the High Peaks, the mountains around Lake George, and the two arms of Sacandaga twisting toward the main body of the lake.

Great Sacandaga Lake didn't exist before 1930, when the Conklingville Dam came to completion. Built as a flood control measure, the dam raised the water level over sixty feet. Older residents of the area still tell stories about the villages—and amusement park—that were flooded by the project.

Our trail brochure offered a map for orienting ourselves, thus allowing more accurate identification of the bodies of water, mountains, and clearings in the distance. Forested land dominates the area. Although paper companies have extensive holdings, much of what we saw falls into the "forever wild" category of the Adirondack Forest Preserve.

The text suggested we might be able to see the foothills of the Catskills, but that sight eluded us. We tried to convince ourselves, however, that we could make out Lake Champlain and the Green Mountains of Vermont on the eastern horizon.

The tower itself dates to 1917. Over one hundred such structures once formed the first line of fire detection in the state. Aircraft surveillance began to supplement the role of the tower ranger as early as 1932. However, public reporting of fires grew so significantly by the 1980s that both tower observation and air patrols found themselves superseded by 1990.

Broad-based local efforts led to preservation of this tower. It is manned most days between the Fourth of July and Labor Day, and sporadically thereafter.

One frequent visitor expressed mixed feelings about the tower. He's pleased to see the educational contribution and the increased interest in the environment. But the tower draws crowds and takes away the sense of wilderness that first brought him here decades ago. It's a dilemma that accompanies any improvement in the backcountry.

We picnicked before leaving, and then started the trek down. Take your time when you descend. It's steeper than it seemed on the way up. Plus, those bedrock passages, so comfortable when climbing, can be slippery when wet or covered with leaves.

******

The Sacandaga Walkway in the town of Speculator offers a pleasant stroll through forest and wetland, with views of the Sacandaga River thrown in for good measure. Well-maintained trails and interesting interpretation offer an introduction to the natural and human forces at work in the area.

A rustic archway separates the trail from adjacent Sacandaga River Community Park, where a gazebo and open pavilion offer good spots for picnicking. Just after beginning, we read a display crediting the community effort that created this enclave.

Varied forest, with birch, maple, beech, and a variety of conifers, marks the initial stretch. Soon, though, we entered wetlands, with a mix of swamp, marsh, and peat bog. Colorful posters pointed out trees, undergrowth, and animal life that we'd see along the way.

Poor soil limits woodland growth in such an area, and lack of root support allows frequent blowdowns. Over years of decay, these fallen trees begin to create hummocks with abundant fern growth and other understory.

Well-built boardwalks float above some of these hummocks, bringing us close to thick sphagnum mats and the occasional pitcher plant. Such conditions attract plenty of bird life. We managed to spot some geese and ducks, plus a lone blue heron.

Wild flowers are abundant in season. Signs alerted us to be on the lookout for pink lady's slipper, purple trillium, and other specimens.

Several outdoor alcoves offer further interpretive information. One is devoted to the heritage of the Adirondack guide, explaining his/her tasks and the necessary skills required. Photos show French Louie Seymour, and Ann Telfer, a woman known for her prowess in the Lewey Lake region.

Another exhibit, by the end of the first boardwalk, paid tribute to lumbering. Logging was quite an arduous process a hundred years ago or more. A picture of the boom controlling logs at nearby Lake Pleasant contrasts vividly with the peaceful scene today. These logs, marked with each lumber company's logo, would then float down the Sacandaga, and eventually to the Hudson River. Vintage photographs show the work—and the danger—of the log drives.

Other displays highlight native presence and early settlement.

A few markers are missing, and we diverted from the main route several times. Rather than detracting from the experience, however, this led us to make more observations on our own. Indeed, the sight of a couple of white-tailed deer heading for the river made our day that much more memorable. Our final views came at an overlook above the river, where a labeled panoramic photo identified nearby land features.

The hour or so spent walking this approximately mile-long trail proved restorative and educational, just what we'd want from an interlude in the southern Adirondacks.

Information:
Guide to Adirondack Trails: Southern Region, Adirondack Mountain Club, Lake George, NY.
Sacandaga River Community Park, Route 8, Box 358, Speculator, NY 12164.

1. Saratoga National Historic Park
2. Salem
3. Saratoga Springs
4. Granville
5. Feeder Canal
6. Glens Falls
7. Troy
8. Mount Lebanon
9. Clermont
10. Pocts' Walk
11. Pratt Rock
12. Mine Kill State Park
13. Storm King Art Center
14. Kaaterskill Falls
15. Museum Village
16. Fort Montgomery
17. Delhi Outdoor Education Center
18. Stone Bridge
19. Stephen Crane
20. Overlook Mountain
21. Byrdcliffe

22. High Falls
23. Wallkill Valley Rail Trail
24. Minnewaska State Park
25. Olana
26. Vanderbilt Mansion
27. Hyde Park
28. Mohonk Preserve
29. Mohonk Mountain House
30. Albany
31. Thacher Park

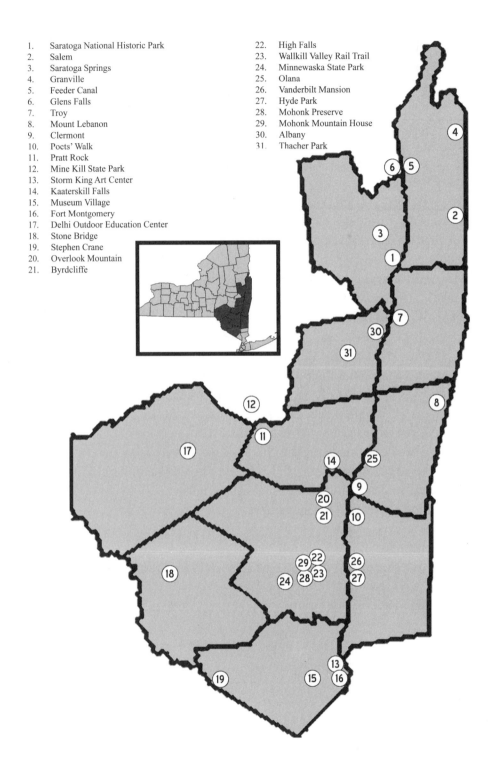

HUDSON – CATSKILL

From the time Henry Hudson sailed up the river that bears his name, this has been the route by which commerce and culture have entered New York. Dutch and then English settlement developed along this valley. Not surprisingly, the area was deemed strategic during the Revolutionary War and the War of 1812.

Completion of the Erie Canal solidified the importance of the Hudson River in commerce. Industry developed in places like Troy. The Delaware and Hudson Canal opened Pennsylvania coal fields to the markets of major cities. New York experienced the growth that would earn it the nickname "Empire State."

Meanwhile, writers and painters began to visit. Washington Irving immortalized the region in his early works. Thomas Cole gazed across the river to the Catskill Mountains and recognized a beauty that demanded to be put onto canvas. Soon the river found its name attached to the first indigenous school of American artwork.

Steamboats offered cruises up the river. Railroads crisscrossed both hill and valley. Resorts began to appear. Recreational opportunities in the Catskills began to lure fishermen, much as the scenery had attracted artists and tourists.

Walking in this region offers the chance to learn about famous individuals and the not-so-famous. Remnants of military activity add historical perspective. Monumental hotels surviving from a golden era still welcome visitors; all that remains from others is the view. Artists still work and exhibit here, sometimes outdoors in wide-open spaces.

Saratoga National Historic Park • Salem

Just a few miles east of Saratoga Springs, colonial troops defeated the British in a 1777 battle that was perhaps the turning point of the American Revolution. Upon learning about the American victory here, the French lent their support to the patriot effort. The now bucolic battlefield has long been preserved as Saratoga National Historical Park.

A visit should begin with the introductory video, followed by a perusal of exhibits in the Visitor Center. One thereby learns how British forces planned a tripartite campaign to secure the Hudson River. General John Burgoyne was to march troops south from Canada along Lake Champlain, while Colonel Barry St. Leger crossed east along the Mohawk River and General William Howe moved north from New York City.

Nothing went as planned. Howe moved his forces to an attack on Philadelphia. St. Leger met resistance at Fort Stanwix and Oriskany, and subsequently retreated north. Burgoyne, meanwhile, captured Fort Ticonderoga, marched past Fort Edward, and headed south along the Hudson. What he didn't expect was such concentrated resistance at Saratoga. But Colonel Thaddeus Kosciusko had designed very effective fortifications for the colonial troops at Bemis Heights above the Hudson River.

There were actually two battles at Saratoga. On September 19, 1777, three lines of British troops converged and fought vigorously at Freeman Farm. American soldiers had to retreat, but Burgoyne's army suffered significant losses.

After waiting fruitlessly for reinforcements from New York City, Burgoyne chose to fight again rather than to withdraw. On October 7, American forces routed the British at Barber Farm, and then successfully attacked strongholds at Balcarres Redoubt and Breymann Redoubt. Burgoyne's troops retreated to the Great Redoubt before heading north. The inspired Americans surrounded the fleeing British, forcing Burgoyne to surrender on October 17.

Artifacts on display range from flintlock pistols and tomahawks, to a metal camp stove and a 1774 silver coin from Germany. There's a cannon used by Burgoyne, plus examples of muskets employed by both sides. One diorama depicts General Daniel Morgan's sharpshooters in a nearby forest. Another shows the American attack on Breymann Redoubt.

Full-size mannequins show off uniforms of the day. Interestingly, British artillery soldiers didn't wear the storied red coats, but instead sported dark blue, so as to better hide the black powder associated with cannon firing. A reproduction of a Boston newspaper of April 30, 1778, features Burgoyne's own rendition of the events at Saratoga.

The 4.2-mile Wilkinson Trail traverses much of the contested terrain. A collaboration between the Boy Scouts of America, Friends of Saratoga Battlefield, Lever Brothers Inc., and the National Park Service, it takes its name from British Lieutenant William Wilkinson, who mapped the battleground in 1777. Gray posts mark the route. Plank benches provide plenty of places to rest.

Wide, grassy lanes took us across fields where hundreds of soldiers died in 1777. Quite likely, some of their remains still lay untouched beneath our feet. Much of the area was actively farmed at the time, some by Loyalists, some by Patriots. The British plundered unharvested crops when their own supplies ran low.

Parts of the trail took us through forest. In 1777, the woods provided timber for fortifications and for fuel. Climbing to a height of land offered broad vistas over the battleground.

At times we walked on the same trails British soldiers or their German mercenaries took during the hostilities. Other interpretive stops revealed the locations of farms owned by Samuel McBride and John Freeman, both British Loyalists who lost their land after the Revolution.

On a couple of occasions, our hiking trail intersected with the nine-mile driving route through the park.

Diagrams at Stop 6 interpreted the Balcarres Redoubt on Freeman Farm, with its log and earthen-work construction. It's important to understand that these albeit modest defenses had to be built quickly by British soldiers under duress. A walk along the long paved loop here helped give us a better sense of troop movements.

Near Stop 7, we crossed over to an interpretive exhibit on the Breymann Redoubt, a crude log defense line captured by the Americans on October 7, 1777. A large monument turned out to be a boot commemorating Benedict Arnold. Arnold was still a hero in those days. His rallying of forces helped General Morgan's troops capture the Breymann

Redoubt that day.

It's worth completing a visit with a drive along the park road. Several stops helped us understand why Americans built where they did. Stop 3 underscored the genius of Kosciusko, a Polish engineer who made optimal use of the natural terrain in his planning. Stop 9, The Great Redoubt, gives a panoramic view from high bluffs above the river. The rolling hills and fields of Washington County create a beautiful vista, but soldiers would have been more concerned about cannon range to the floodplain below.

Additional walking tours can be enjoyed in the nearby village of Schuylerville, and along the Champlain Canal. Brochures are available in the Visitor Center.

******

Every rural village has history and architecture to explore. Salem, in Washington County, makes such exploration easier with its Landmarks Tour.

This settlement on White Creek dates to 1764. As such, its heritage includes much about the American Revolution. A number of eighteenth-century structures still stand. At the edges of the village, there are scenic farmland views that likely haven't changed for decades, perhaps centuries.

Two perpendicular routes are described on the tour's brochure. The north–south tour along Main Street includes an 1866 fire house still in use. An 1899 "shirt shop," with two brick stories atop a stone foundation and bottom level, must once have been a pride of the village. Sadly, it now sits empty.

The classic nineteenth-century downtown core, though small, shows off its share of ornate detail. One store is fronted by tin textured to simulate stone. Another boasts a cast-iron facade shipped by rail from St. Louis. Fine dentil work adorns a 1795 building restored to house a bank.

Walking east–west along Broadway showed us a rich sampling of residential architecture. Greek Revival, Federal, and Victorian features are abundantly present. Many of the houses feature deep lots that back up to White Creek.

An especially fine example is the Georgian-style Blanchard-Mc-Clellan House, one of two built by Revolutionary War General John Williams for his daughters. Revolutionary hero Richard Montgomery's body lay in state here in 1818 while en route from Canada to New York City. That event eerily foreshadowed the mansion's current use as a funeral home.

Celebrated artist John J. Audubon's grandchildren grew up in the brick Federal-style Audubon-McClellan House built in 1810. It would have been interesting to see its interior, which includes an oval dining room and bedroom.

Historic markers denote sites of Revolutionary War blockhouses and stockades. The white clapboard First United Presbyterian Church dates to 1797; a glimpse inside revealed enclosed pews and a large pipe organ. Another ecclesiastical structure, distinguished by a clock tower, has been recycled into a community theater.

A handsome three-story brick complex built as Washington Academy in 1819 now serves as Academy Apartments. Present-day Salem Central School, erected in 1938, offers a pleasing colonial style with decorative crests as part of its design.

We gathered a few snippets of local pride. It's appealing to learn one fine house was inherited by a family's gardener and chauffeur. Another was occupied by an animal trainer known for bringing his talented pigs to the St. Louis World's Fair of 1904.

Our tour ended with a lingering visit to the peaceful, well-maintained village cemetery where flags mark the graves of over a hundred Revolutionary War soldiers. Family vaults stand atop a few small knolls. Sandstone, granite, and marble markers incorporate a variety of funereal art symbols. A few stones are especially poignant, like one for three infants "who died in 2 days sickness."

Information:
Saratoga National Historical Park, 648 Route 32, Stillwater, NY 12170. Phone 518-664-9821.
Salem Chamber of Commerce, Box 717, Salem, NY 12865. Phone 518-854-9296.

Saratoga Springs • Granville

A perfect village stroll should be somewhere with nice parks, some impressive commercial and residential architecture, and plenty of shops and eating spots for breaks.

Saratoga Springs certainly qualifies.

It's best to begin in the renovated 1915 trolley station that serves as Saratoga's Visitors Center. After browsing the exhibits, we picked up a variety of self-guiding walking tour pamphlets. One can roam between the springs that brought Saratoga its initial recognition, wander a choice of impressive neighborhoods, or go past one of America's oldest horse-racing tracks.

We started our walk across the street at Congress Park. Ponds and varied terrain make this central place interesting. Following our brochure, we found pavilions over Congress, Columbian (its iron-laden waters were known for "strengthening the stomach"), and Deer Park Springs (this last one an unusual green and white iron creation).

Perhaps the park's most famous feature is the *Spirit of Life* memorial, a bronze sculpture commissioned in honor of financier and local benefactor Spencer Trask. Trask's wife Katrina arranged to have the project created by Daniel Chester French, whose other credits include the Lincoln Memorial in Washington, D.C.

Canfield Casino is an impressive brick building built by boxing champion John Morrissey in 1870. It served as one of many watering spots during the heyday of gambling in Saratoga. Monuments commemorate the Civil War and World War I. At the north end of the park, a carousel offers rides.

Taking another leaflet in hand, we made our way up Broadway, laid out by Saratoga founder Gideon Putnam in the early 1800s. Still one of New York State's most thriving downtown streets, it takes a mere glance to sense the wealth that must have accumulated here in the late nineteenth century.

Only one of Saratoga's grand hotels remains—the Adelphi. Narrow columns connect three stories of porches. It's worth a stop inside the lobby to admire the scene. But we're happy just to walk leisurely past one striking building after another.

The white marble, Greek Revival-style Adirondack Trust building is one. Apparently the bronze doors were created by Louis Tiffany. Italianate design marks the brick structure of City Hall, which once had a theater on the third floor. At 510 Broadway, the Algonquin Building reflects Richardson Romanesque style.

Once past the Prime Hotel and Conference Center (and I should note that even newer structures like this and Borders Books blend smoothly with the town ambience), we were on North Broadway. Here begins one of the region's truly sumptuous architectural collections. Our guidebook for this area was comprehensive, allowing us to more fully appreciate details of design.

Homes are set back behind large lawns, some of which retain hitching posts out front. Most date from the mid- to late-nineteenth century. More than a few saw use only as summer cottages for businesspeople from Troy and New York City. Others gained reputations as boardinghouses in a time when that term connoted an atmosphere of social elegance.

The oldest home on the street, at 581 North Broadway, dates to 1834. It's built in Greek Revival style, with columns and pilasters. Queen Anne style is common, as typified by the structure at number 605 with a board-and-batten gable that almost looks Tudor. The Gambrel roofs common to Dutch architecture in the Hudson Valley are in evidence. So is the gingerbread trim characteristic of Gothic Revival.

Several truly remarkable places stand out. Hathorn House (number 740) seeks to recapture the French chateau. Red Stone Villa (number 795) matches roughly hewn sandstone with attractive terra-cotta tile. The broad portico with Corinthian columns (number 760) would look appropriate on a southern plantation.

A few more modern creations merit mention. The Victorian at 737 North Broadway was actually built as recently as 1966. Number 766 turns out to be modular, a sample of early prefab work.

Parallel streets feature carriage houses once part of North Broadway estates. Most have been remodeled into homes, some of them quite sumptuous in their own right.

Skidmore College's new campus fills the area beyond North Broadway. Lucy Skidmore Scribner founded the institution in 1903. Before becoming an accredited liberal arts college in 1922, it bore the less than grand name Young Women's Industrial Club of Saratoga.

I remember when the school still occupied its multitude of Victorian buildings in the middle of Saratoga. A certain nostalgic feel has been lost by the need for relocation after the 1960s. On the other hand, this allowed a unity of architecture, most of it modern and post-modern, that many universities never attain.

Had our approximately three-mile route not been sufficient, we'd have found plenty more to explore. The West Side neighborhood shows the impact of immigrant settlement over the years. We could have walked through Saratoga's East Side neighborhood, and up past Union Avenue's Victorian homes, before proceeding to the National Racing Museum and the Saratoga Race Track.

******

When glaciers melted eons ago from a narrow belt straddling New York and Vermont, they left exposed rich outcrops of slate. Around 1839 entrepreneurs began taking advantage of this natural resource. By the late nineteenth century, over 250 quarries were in operation. Though Depression and war took its toll on this industry, production never ceased.

The Slate Valley Museum, established in 1995 at Granville, celebrates this history, which continues through the present day. Thirty-eight companies, with five hundred workers, still produce over $50 million worth of roofing slate annually.

Go inside. Study the display on the geology of slate. Look at the replica quarry stick, typical of poles often a hundred feet high and laden with guy wires and pulley systems. These anchored the operation of pulling huge chunks of slate out of the ground, and then dropping them at nearby shanties.

Stop at the fully equipped shanty, representative of those in which skilled workmen processed huge blocks of rock into thin slate shingles for roofing.

Gaze upon a true treasure, the mural *Men Working in Slate Quarry*, painted by Martha Levy in 1939 as a WPA project for Granville High

School, and restored as a Bicentennial Project in 1976. This detailed mural pays tribute to the slate industry with vivid and colorful renditions of all aspects of the trade.

Once you've enjoyed the museum, pick up the brochure for a walking tour past an array of slate creations in Granville. Pay attention to not just roofs, but sidewalks, and occasionally even house siding.

You'll begin by crossing a covered pedestrian bridge over the Mettowee River—note that it, too, has a slate roof. On the other side, there's an impressive carriage house once part of a slate magnate's estate. Next pass Pember Library and Museum, a stolid stone building with a red slate roof. After completing your walk, it's worth returning to see the wonderful natural history exhibits on the second floor.

Over twenty additional examples of slate use are denoted. There are striped mansard roofs, varying geometric patterns, and colorful scalloping. Note the building on 1 East Main Street. Entrepreneur Hugh Williams had his sales offices here. The roof boasts inch-thick slate in all colors available from local quarries.

Other places show slate cladding (or siding) and sculping (another means of covering a structure). And don't overlook the purple slate grave markers by Peniel Presbyterian Church, placed in 1858 and quite well preserved.

The walk, including one relatively steep segment, should take about an hour. For those so inclined, there's a leaflet for another self-guided walking tour in nearby Poultney, Vermont.

Information:
Saratoga Springs Urban Heritage Area Visitor Center, 297 Broadway, Saratoga Springs, New York 12866. Phone 518-587-3241.
Slate Valley Museum, 17 Water Street, Granville, NY 12832. Phone 518-642-1417.

Feeder Canal • Glens Falls

Completion of the Champlain Canal in 1823 changed trade patterns significantly. Previously, most commerce flowed to the north. This new water link from Lake Champlain to the Hudson River opened the way between the North Country and New York City.

Unpredictable water levels drove the need for another canal, a smaller one in Warren and Washington Counties. Only seven miles long, the Feeder Canal diverted water from the Hudson River near Glens Falls to the Champlain Canal. Opened in 1832, this canal became a commercial force in its own right.

Thirteen locks helped boats through the Feeder Canal. Cargoes included lumber, paper, limestone, black marble, and agricultural products. Goods still traveled the canal as late as 1928.

By the 1960s, towpaths were overgrown with trees and brush. In the few places where the canal was visible from roadsides, the water looked none too appealing.

Enter a group called the Feeder Canal Alliance, formed in 1987. Envisioning the abandoned canal as both recreational and economic resource, organizers published an ambitious master plan in 1990. The Feeder Canal now attracts canoeists and fishermen. A reclaimed ten-foot-wide towpath beckons to hikers and bicyclists. Interpretive signage conveys the historical significance of the route, "the last remaining original canal in New York State."

After taking Exit 18 off the Adirondack Northway, we turned onto Richardson Street in West Glens Falls. We parked in a small lot, tightened the laces on our walking shoes, and set out by the dam diverting water from the Hudson River into the Feeder Canal.

Lumber mills once stood on both sides of the river here. Just upstream was the "big boom," capturing point for logs floated downstream from a myriad of places in the mountains. River drives continued into the 1950s.

After crossing a small bridge, we noticed stone remnants of one early sawmill. Then we proceeded along the towpath, following the same trail from which mules once towed canal boats. Pretty forest and continuous river views marked the way to Haviland's Cove, a city beach for Glens Falls.

Soon we left the river's edge. Remnants of old abutments appeared on the left. Signs of industry began to spring up on our right. Massive log piles reminded us of the importance of lumber and paper products throughout the region's history. On Pruyn's Island, new companies continue the area's manufacturing presence.

There's the serendipitous apple tree, later a blue heron sitting atop a rock, and suddenly a first glimpse of downtown Glens Falls. A stone headquarters building anchors the Finch Pruyn Company's presence on one side of the river. Across, on the other bank, stands Encore Paper, once New York State's largest paper recycler.

We saw a dam spillway just above the falls that gives Glens Falls its name. A sign told how the city was founded near this site, with Abraham Wing establishing sawmills, a tavern, inn, and store by 1765. Gristmills and kilns soon followed. Black marble quarried from the riverbed became nationally known, finding use in the Washington Monument and the White House.

Native Americans called the falls Chepontuc—"difficult place to get around." The bridge between Glens Falls and South Glens Falls provides a good view. Water drops fifty-six feet when flow is high, but dry conditions during our visit made this hard to appreciate.

Just under the bridge is Cooper's Cave, immortalized by James Fenimore Cooper in *The Last of the Mohicans*. Decades ago a spiral staircase off the bridge gave access to the cave. Now a terrace on the South Glens Falls side of the river offers a good view of the site.

Canoeists can continue on the waterway through the Finch Pruyn paper-making complex. Walkers and cyclists must leave the towpath and walk up Warren Street. Access resumes on Shermantown Road, near remains of some of the eighty kilns that once produced limestone here. Jointa Lime, just behind us, traces its company's history back well over a century.

We watched the water's gentle current. Grass waved along the canal bottom much as cilia beat in the respiratory tract. A few ducks floated along. Minutes later, we approached tall silos on both sides of us, and the whirring of machinery filled the air. This marked Glens Falls Cement Company, another longtime industrial presence.

After resting on a strategically placed bench, we proceeded past an open area where Imperial Color and Wallpaper once made the green for dollar bills. Then we crossed the highway, one of two spots along the canal where we confronted significant automobile traffic.

Quiet returned quickly. Cattails caught our eye, as did such wildflowers as turtlehead, purple loosestrife, and wild iris.

At Route 4 in Hudson Falls, the Feeder Canal Alliance has developed a small picnic park. An adjacent ice cream stand provides sustenance for hikers and bikers.

Continuing east, we came to residential areas; some yards backed right up to the towpath. At Martindale Avenue, a former turnaround basin, where canal boats transferred cargo to horse-drawn wagons, has become an attractive park.

Farther ahead loomed five tall cement silos. These were built to store coal brought by barge from Pennsylvania. A nearby industrial site with low-slung buildings and a brick smokestack would appear to be ripe for future interpretation.

We approached Lock 13, its huge stone blockwork very much intact, and Lock 14, with secure iron bolts and screw mechanisms. Another tiny park with benches and antique street lamps came into view just before we crossed Burgoyne Avenue. Now we enjoyed a wonderful view of rolling Washington County farmland ringed with low mountains on the horizon.

Soon we reached a succession of locks known as the Five Combines.

In canal days, boats took fifteen minutes to traverse each lock. Oldtimers in the area tell tales of being allowed onto boats here. They'd have the excitement of an hour and a quarter going through the locks, traveling a distance taking but a minute on land!

A sign directed us to an underground stone aqueduct. This four-hundred-foot channel once served as a sluice, diverting water around the locks when the gates were closed.

The last half mile of our walk brought us by five more locks, each still showing the integrity of its construction. At a T-intersection, we could have turned right along the former Champlain Canal to Fort Edward, or left, to a creek feeding into the current canal. Straight ahead, we saw iron rails, evidence of the railroads that eventually superseded the canals for commerce.

******

A printed walking tour of Glens Falls starts and ends at notable museums.

We began at the Chapman Museum on Glen Street. Along with its period furnished rooms, this site presents a sampling of Seneca Ray Stoddard, once the pre-eminent photographer of the Adirondacks.

Notable architecture along Glen Street includes venerable bank buildings, the city's original YMCA building with its unusual third-floor porch, and the impressive brown and green terra-cotta decoration on the Saunders Building.

City Park includes the brick colonial Crandall Library, named after lumber magnate Henry Crandall, whose carriage house survives nearby. At his height of success he gave every child in Glens Falls a bank account with one dollar, so as to stimulate a life of thrift.

When the route turns briefly onto Ridge Street, look high up for impressive architectural features. My favorite, the Star Building, somehow didn't make the cut for the tour guide.

We moved on to Warren Street. A corner business with especially nice cornice and brackets has local significance. Abraham Wing, city founder, built his tavern on this site in 1775. St. Mary's Academy was designed by the man who also served as architect for much of Princeton University. St. Mary's Church, built in 1869, boasts a Gothic interior with beautiful stained glass.

At 79 Warren Street stands the Joubert and White Building; the name Empire is now engraved at the top. This company gained a national reputation for its buckboards, which were essentially the Cadillacs of horse-drawn vehicles. If you didn't notice the one on display at the Chapman Museum, see it on your way back.

A few steps off Warren, on Center Street, is the home in which Charles Evans Hughes was born in 1862. Glens Falls' most important native son, he served as governor, then later secretary of state and chief justice of the United States Supreme Court. Hughes ran against Woodrow Wilson for president in 1916, and came within only a handful of electoral votes of winning.

Unique is a row of two-story columned homes tucked between factory buildings on Fredella Street.

The walk ends at the Hyde Collection, an Italian Renaissance mansion-turned-art museum, complete with skylit interior courtyard. Art treasures inside include works by Rembrandt, Renoir, Rubens, Picasso, and Remington. Most visitors come away admiring the house itself almost as much as the artwork.

Information:
Feeder Canal Alliance, P.O. Box 2414, Glens Falls, NY 12801. Phone 518-792-5363.
Chapman Historical Museum, 348 Glen Street, Glens Falls, NY 12801. Phone 518-793-2826.
Hyde Collection, 161 Warren Street, Glens Falls, NY 12801. Phone 518-792-1761.

Five Combines along the Feeder Canal

Troy • Mount Lebanon

The history of Troy proves the value of location, location, location. Already provided water access by the Hudson River, and close-by westward passage via the Mohawk River, the city benefited even more as the junction between the Erie and Champlain Canals at their completion in the 1820s. Railroads grew along the same routes, cementing Troy's command of trade routes until obviation by the automobile era.

Add waterpower to the mix, with its impetus for early iron and steel manufacturing, especially of stoves, and then textiles. The idea of detachable collars on shirts may be an antiquated one. Once, though, being the Collar City served as a key to amassing fortunes.

A walking-tour brochure is available at the city's RiverSpark Visitor Center on River Street. This one- to two-hour stroll gives an introduction to Troy's history, while revealing a sampling of what this wealth helped build. First we browsed the center's exhibits on history and industry, and then we set out on our way.

Monument Square pays tribute to Civil War dead. It also acknowledges Troy's industrial output and how this influenced the conflict. Steel from the city built the rails that carried supplies for the Northern effort. Its iron covered the Monitor, first metal-clad boat used in conflict.

River Street followed the curve of the Hudson, making clear the relationship of the commercial district with the waterway. Venerable buildings over a century old still form the backbone of the area. City Hall, unfortunately, is a modern replacement, but nearby, structures dating back to the 1830s remain.

Second Street, described in our brochure as "one of the great nineteenth century streets in America," lives up to that reputation. Greek Revival and Federal architecture incorporate elaborate moldings, formidable doors and entryways, as well as plenty of locally manufactured ornamental ironwork. Hart-Cluett Mansion, home to the Rensselaer County Historical Society, stands out amidst the elegance. Stone in construction and Federal in style, it features a balustrade and dormer windows on its third level.

The William Howard Hart Memorial Library, privately built but for public use, boasts a remarkable ornate interior. Interior marble columns define the space, giving a classicism to go along with computerization. Behind the main desk, an ornate Tiffany window portrays the publication of Dante's *Divine Comedy*. Looking outside, we saw an adjacent courtyard.

Next we found ourselves on the Russell Sage College campus. Originally the Troy Female Seminary, and later the Emma Willard School until its relocation, these brick buildings would blend well into Washington D.C.'s Georgetown neighborhood. We were impressed also by Gurley Memorial Hall, with its contrasting colors of stone.

Our next phase brought us by Troy Savings Bank; we've enjoyed concerts in its second-floor music hall. St. Paul's Episcopal Church, built in 1828, boasts more Tiffany work. Its massive brass bell was made in a Troy foundry. Elaborate terra-cotta work distinguishes Proctor's Theater.

Do not overlook the Troy post office at Fourth and Broadway. Typical of 1930's-era Federal architecture, its jewels are the WPA murals inside. Themes pay homage to Washington Irving and his fictionalized Sleepy Hollow in their depictions of a headless horseman and Rip Van Winkle and friends with long white beards.

Fires impact every city's history and topography, it seems, and Troy is no exception. A blaze in 1862 leveled seventy-five acres of residences and businesses. It's no coincidence that fireproof iron features soon became commonplace on Troy's new construction.

Brownstones along Fifth Avenue typify some of what sprang up after the tragedy. Here also are Troy's earliest "skyscrapers," a full five stories tall. Up on a nearby hill can be seen the city's other notable cradle of higher education, Rensselaer Polytechnic Institute, better known as RPI.

Back along River Street, at the corner of Third Street, stands a statue of one of Troy's luminaries, Samuel Wilson. Wilson supplied meat to the army during the War of 1812. When packages arrived stamped "US," soldiers lightheartedly suggested that the initials stood for Uncle Sam. Years later, spurred by the images drawn by cartoonist Thomas Nast, this otherwise unknown merchant became entwined in our national character.

There now is parkland along the river where miles of warehouses and mills once stood dominant. One unmarked building survives to mark the era of collar and shirtmaking. Cluett, Peabody and Company operated here, producing its nationally known line of Arrow shirts. Next time you happen to think of preshrunk ready-made clothes, remember the process was developed here.

******

Mother Ann Lee brought a small group of religious believers from a poor area of Manchester, England, to America in 1774. They settled in Watervliet, near Albany. Additional communities later became established as far north as Maine, south to Florida, and west into Ohio and Kentucky.

Her mission was the quest for perfection. Life was to be communal, based on concepts of "hands to work, hearts to God." Formally, the group was called the United Society of Believers in Christ's Second Appearing. Their fervent dancing to shake off sin during religious services led them to become known as the Shaking Quakers, or Shakers.

Shakers were never rooted to their past. Interaction with non-Shaker neighbors was commonplace. New technologies were rapidly assimilated. Shakers gave us such innovations as the flat broom and the seed packet, as well as their distinctive functional furniture.

It wasn't lack of business sense that led to their decline. Belief in celibacy played a role. So did changing economic conditions in the world around them.

The Shakers relied on a constant stream of new adherents. In an unsettled world, joining a Shaker community offered the promise of stability. Not surprisingly, widows and orphans always comprised a significant percentage of Shaker families. Indoctrination had its limits, however. Youths were given a choice at age eighteen of whether to stay, or seek opportunity in the outside world. Industrialization and the development of a middle class promised other options.

The last Shaker community in America lives on at Sabbath Day Lake, Maine.

Mount Lebanon, southeast of Albany and near the Massachusetts border, was established in 1787. Eventually the largest Shaker community, it served as spiritual headquarters. Once over six hundred residents lived in eight communal families here amidst six thousand acres. Not until 1947 did the last stragglers relocate. Much of the land and buildings was sold to the Darrow School. Followers of the Sufi faith purchased some property. Other holdings entered private hands.

We parked near a small visitor center. Just beyond stands the massive shell of the Great Stone Barn, a full 196 by 50 feet in dimension. Fire ravaged this remarkable structure in 1972. Restoration is in the works, after which a well-established Shaker Museum in nearby Old Chatham will be moved to this site.

Exhibits upstairs in the red clapboard Granary gave information on the Shakers. Items made at Mount Lebanon were on display, including cloaks and classic Shaker chairs. There's a small gift shop. Scheduled tours leave from here.

We walked down Shaker Road, and then Darrow Road, to the eponymous school. Buildings dating to the Shaker era are striking. There's the original 1785 Meeting House, a three-story white clapboard structure. The attractive brick Elders' Ministry House incorporates a few Victorian features. Marble steps rise to the barrel-roofed Second Meeting House, now used by Darrow School as a library. One well-vented structure formerly served as a Wash House.

Even more impressive is the Main Dwelling House, a five-story brick building completed in 1875. Admission and administrative offices fill the space now. Also notable are the stately five-story brick Brethren's Workshop (1826) and the Trustees' Office (1827), of yellow clapboard and brick atop a foundation of massive cut stones.

A cluster of dark red buildings sits by a pond. One, known as The Tannery, has become the site for regionally notable summer chamber music concerts.

Extension of our walk beyond the Darrow School brought us past privately owned homes, and eventually to Abode of the Message, owned by a Sufi group.

Information:
Troy RiverSpark Visitor Center, Hudson Mohawk Urban Cultural Park, 251 River Street, Troy, NY 12180. Phone 518-270-8667.

Shaker Museum and Library, 88 Shaker Museum Road, Old Chatham, NY 12136. Phone 518-794-9100.

Spring pavilion in Saratoga

85

Clermont • Poets' Walk

Establishment of large landholdings on the Hudson River was underway well before the American Revolution. The oldest one open to the public makes a worthy destination.

Robert Livingston (1688–1775) arrived in America in the 1720s and prospered almost immediately. Successive generations accumulated even more wealth; once the family owned thirteen thousand acres. The family estate, Clermont, remained in Livingston hands late into the twentieth century.

British troops burned the home early in the Revolutionary War. The task of rebuilding fell to Margaret Beekman Livingston (daughter-in-law of Robert). Her project met completion in time for George Washington's visit in 1782.

Though several notable individuals lived here, perhaps another Livingston (1746–1813)—again Robert—became best known. A signer of the Declaration of Independence, he wrote the New York State Constitution, administered the oath of office to George Washington, and helped negotiate the Louisiana Purchase. Interested in transportation as well as agriculture and politics, he financed Robert Fulton's efforts to develop the steamboat. Fulton's first successful ship carried the name of Livingston's estate, *Clermont*.

Alice Clarkson Livingston, seventh generation to own Clermont, left the estate to New York State in 1962. A network of trails winds through the five hundred acres preserved as a state historic site. Two detailed maps serve as useful guides.

Perhaps the Farm Road Trail best gives a feel for the property. Former farm roads brought us past entry posts to a grazing field for cattle, a weathered plank "cow barn" (actually used for horses) dating to 1875, and cottages over two centuries old. A deer herd still makes Clermont its home.

The Ice Pond provided water for animals, gardens, and greenhouse, and hosted skating parties when temperatures turned cold. Its outlet stream once scoured out a small ravine. Down below, a Model T truck chassis stands as proof that even the wealthy tossed old machinery into gullies!

86

Though the family's burial spot has been sealed and their remains moved elsewhere, a lane of tall white pines, framing views of the river and distant Catskill Mountains, stands as a worthy memorial.

Near the mansion, the short Formal Garden Trail offers both views and a sense of the intensive landscaping efforts made by Alice Clarkson Livingston during the early decades of the twentieth century. The "long view" looking south indeed gives a commanding panorama across the Hudson. With effort, remains of a dock can be sighted. Fulton landed his boat, the *Clermont*, here in 1807.

Mock oranges, lilacs, and the state's largest black walnut tree grace the walk. A lawn once served as the croquet court. A footbridge crosses a gentle wandering stream. Rusting metal framework and the foundation remains of a greenhouse are visible, and there's a shed that once served as a children's playhouse. A rustic arbor adds further interest.

A formal Walled Garden proves a highlight. Built around 1930, the Italian-style design includes stone walls and iron entry gates that enclose a variety of shrubs and flowers. Famed English gardener Gertrude Jekyll served as inspiration for a Wilderness Garden, replete with flowering trees and perennials encircling a pond.

Though the Riverside Trail and Chancellor's Trail focus on natural features of the landscape, I found these most fascinating for man-made artifacts. Just beyond an avenue of locust trees, there are the eerie brick and stone ruins of Arryl House. Chancellor Livingston began building the H-shaped mansion in 1793; apparently it dwarfed the current home in size and luxury. Arryl House burned down in 1909, perhaps victim of a blaze started from a railroad ember.

Train tracks come into view. The Livingstons could plant trees to obscure large structures on the rail line, but even today I'm surprised that so influential a family would let the tracks be built between the estate and the river. Farther along the way, there's the Saugerties Lighthouse, a reminder of the days when river traffic dominated transportation.

A fifth trail, the Rose Alba Trail, branches off the Riverside and Chancellor's Trails. The trail guide points out oak and hemlock forests, fungi, and evidence of a lightning strike. Once a private horse-racing track was maintained here.

By all means, tour the mansion before leaving. Unlike many historic sites, this one always remained in the hands of one family. Generally furnished as it looked when remodeled in Colonial Revival style during the 1920s, the random accumulation of items over time adds character. Unlike your home or mine (or at least mine), the miscellany includes Chippendale pieces fashioned by Thomas Chippendale himself and portraiture by Gilbert Stuart.

For a further glance into the life of the Livingstons, one can visit Montgomery Place, a few miles south. Historic Hudson operates this site, which offers a guided tour of the mansion and walks on the grounds.

******

A one-mile stroll at Poets' Walk, near Red Hook, gives an idea of how landscape architects designed so-called "picturesque" landscapes in the nineteenth century. The path gradually descends two hundred feet to river level. At stopping points along the way, placards provide some history and commentary on natural features of the setting.

This land once held the country home of John Jacob Astor's son William. Descendants continued to use the property until 1967. An organization called Scenic Hudson acquired the 120-acre site in 1993, opening the grounds to public access.

Landscape architect Hans Jacob Ehlers was commissioned to design this parcel in 1849. The country was in the midst of the "romantic" movement at the time, a time of new appreciation for man's relationship with nature. Many urban parks and state preserves were being developed. Some chose formal, structured designs. Ehlers opted for the "picturesque," which "emphasized the natural."

Thus, trails at Poets' Walk follow land contours, leading to viewpoints and rustic shelters. There's a mix of field and forest. Hickory, black walnut, and maple distinguish the forest. Open areas are dotted with purple loosestrife and Queen Anne's lace.

At the steep-roofed wooden "pavilion," an open exposure shows off silhouettes of the Catskills in the distance. The best view, however, comes at the "flagpole lot." Here we had a commanding vista. To the left, we saw the 1857 bridge crossing the Hudson River at Kingston

Flats. Boat traffic moved through the water. The forested far shore was dotted with mansions. Bold mountain profiles filled the background.

Then we dropped down into woodland paths, walking north and crossing a footbridge over a small stream. The next point of interest was the summer house, a rustic structure of peeled logs and shake roof that blends into the landscape as smoothly as an Adirondack lean-to might. A forested trail led back to the "pavilion," from where we retraced our steps back to the parking area.

Washington Irving and Fitz-Greene Halleck allegedly roamed these grounds, leading to the decision to name this "Poets' Walk." One need not be an artist or writer to take away inspiration from a visit.

Information:
Clermont State Historic Site, One Clermont Avenue, Germantown, NY 12526. Phone 518-537-4240.
Poets' Walk, Scenic Hudson, 914-473-4440. Trailhead is reached by heading west from Route 9 along Route 199. Turn right on River Road; continue one-half mile. Look for Poets' Walk on left.

Carving at Pratt Rock

Pratt Rock • Mine Kill State Park

Learning the history of the Catskills requires an understanding of the importance of tanneries. One name that popped up in my reading was Zadock Pratt (1790–1871). Seeking more information, we drove to Prattsville, the village that bears his name. Approaching the area, we noticed carving on rocks high up to our right. These are integrally tied to the Pratt story.

We parked at the Pratt Museum, a handsome white Federal building on Main Street. A historic marker lists tanner, banker, congressman, and village planner among Pratt's occupations. Inside we learned more.

A video made by local students revealed that Pratt arrived here in 1824 looking to build a tannery. He began with a modest factory. Eventually the operation grew to be the largest in the world.

Hemlock bark was long the key to tanning. Bark was first peeled, and then ground in the plant's mill. Leaching with water extracted the tannins needed to cure raw hides. These hides, largely from South America, came by boat to New York City. Horse-drawn wagons (later trains) completed the transport to Prattsville.

Tasks involved in tanning sound less than romantic. Hair and flesh must be removed. Then hides are soaked in large vats of tannin liquors for a designated time. Drying (a ten-day process), oiling, and rolling complete the process. Pratt boasted special techniques that made his product more pliable.

Pratt's strategies worked. He marketed his cured hides in New York City quite successfully. He employed thousands of men. When it came to living conditions for workers, Pratt wouldn't settle for simple shacks. Rather he constructed over a hundred solid homes of hemlock planks. A century and a half later, over ninety percent of the dwellings are still standing.

The tannery thrived for twenty years. Profits proved sufficient for Pratt to open a bank, build a company town, and enjoy a long, public-spirited life. The town flourished, too, enough so that Prattsville received at least passing consideration as the capital of New York State.

By now we wanted to do some walking. About a mile east of the

90

museum is Pratt Rock. Our guide told us a bit about its genesis.

Itinerant worker Andrew Pearse came to Prattsville asking for a place to stay. Generous, but believing in the need to work, Zadock Pratt offered accommodations in return for a memorial on a nearby rock. Unfortunately (or perhaps not, as things turned out), the rock sat on property owned by a man not especially enamored of Pratt. So the future congressman sent the carver to a plot of land he owned outside town.

One carving led to another. When done, Pearse had created a cluster of carvings on a high ledge that gave a capsule summary of Pratt's career and family. (At one point Pratt asked to have his burial place cut into a ledge, but the rock proved too hard.)

A kiosk at the base provides more detail on Pratt and Pearse. Lower reaches of the twenty-eight-acre park are nicely terraced, with stairs between levels and plenty of picnic tables. A steep but easily followed trail leads up the hill. My guidebook states the total distance as a mile, but I'd judge it to be a bit less.

We wound our way up serpentine switchbacks, catching glimpses of Pearse's work along the way. There are sweeping views across the river to rolling farmland and the Catskill Mountains. A chair carved into the rock at one point marked a good place to rest.

Up on the gray sandstone ledge containing most of the carvings, we took our time sorting out the pictures. Pratt liked to say "Let the rocks tell my story."

One relief carving depicts Pratt himself. Another shows his son George, who died during the Battle of Manassas in 1862. Elsewhere we found a plaque honoring daughter Julia, and the Pratt family coat-of-arms, including his motto: "Do Well and Doubt Not."

A hand with a circle around it symbolizes "This hand for my country." An arm-and-hammer pays respect to working men. The hemlock tree refers to the forests so important to his tannery's success. A lone horse reflects ownership of over a thousand mares and stallions during his lifetime.

Two congressional terms are symbolized by a hand holding a scroll labeled "Bureau of Statistics 1844," a reference to one bill Pratt introduced. (His favorite bill, the Postage Act of 1838, called for lowering rates from twenty-five cents to a nickel. Another Pratt initiative, in

1845, authorized repairs to the White House. When other legislators balked, Pratt threatened to simply pay the cost himself and tell the world about Congress' cheapskate ways!)

Even the inevitable graffiti on the rocks turned out to be ornate. Calligraphic carving reminded me of inscriptions found at El Morro National Monument in New Mexico.

A memorial at the base of the park commemorates local World War I veterans. Nearby, amidst a small grove of hemlocks, stands the grave of three horses and three dogs belonging to Pratt. The marker simply states "the following were favorites."

One writer described Pratt as "an unassuming citizen, who, by force of his native genius, has risen from obscurity to distinction, from poverty to wealth ... and ... has ever maintained the character of a straightforward, honest man." Any person would be proud to be remembered with such words. Engravings in rock further reinforce that memory.

******

Mine Kill State Park marked its opening in 1973, when the New York Power Authority inaugurated its nearby Blenheim-Gilboa Pumped Storage facility. Reservoirs for the latter add scenic appeal to the area, but the natural features of Mine Kill are more inviting.

An approach west on Route 23 put us in the mood for our exploration. Waterfalls, country hotels, antique shops, and flocks of sheep and herds of cows gave a rural feeling that we needed after fighting heavy traffic on the New York Thruway.

The park itself sits off Route 30 in the Schoharie Valley. From the southern entrance, it was a short drive to the picnic area where we parked. A quick walk brought us to an overlook with a nice view of the major waterfalls. The upper falls is partially obscured by a highway bridge. Then the lower cascade, narrower but taller, goes into a graceful curve near stream level.

One may be tempted to just stop there for the day, but don't succumb. The falls looks ordinary, even modest, from here. You must walk down to see what a special cataract this really is.

Take the trail to the bottom, where the water drops into a deep green pool. You get an impressive perspective of the stream cutting its twisting course through an imposing rock cliff. One clearly sees two segments join to form the upper falls, before the water continues in a gentle turn, finally spreading out into the broad, lower bridal-veil falls.

Look right, where trees bend over from the top of a hundred-foot cliff wall. Water gently cascades down the rock face, looking a bit like icicles in motion, and supporting a bed of dark green moss along the rock. When the rivulets join to form a broad curtain, there's a sense of the flowstone one finds in limestone caves.

Perhaps thirty feet away from the pool, we found a pleasant shaded grove perfect for our picnic lunch.

Another one-mile trail continues on to the New York Power Authority's Visitor Center. There we learned concepts of pumped storage, based on water being recycled between two reservoirs. During the day, downward flow activates turbines and generates power. At night, when there's less overall electric usage, the water is pumped back up to the top reservoir.

Adjacent is Lansing Manor, a restored 1819 homestead owned by the Power Authority. Tours of the interior interpret early nineteenth-century life.

On the way home from Mine Kill, it's worth detouring to Blenheim Bridge, at 232 feet the longest covered single-span bridge in the world. Built in 1855, this National Historic Civil Engineering Landmark carried traffic until 1931.

Information:
Zadock Pratt Museum, Box 333, Main Street, Prattsville, New York 12468. Phone 518-299-3395.
Mine Kill State Park, North Blenheim, NY 12131. Phone 518-827-6111.
Lansing Manor and Blenheim-Gilboa Visitors Center, North Blenheim, NY 12131. Phone 1-800-724-0309.

Storm King Art Center • Kaaterskill Falls

My family grew up only a few miles from Lake George. Time on the beach or at the arcades became a significant part of my childhood. Occasionally my parents would try to interest us in activities more cultural.

Several times my father suggested a ride to nearby Bolton Landing, where we could see oversized sculptures in fields surrounding the home of David Smith. It wasn't easy to tell me anything when I was an adolescent, especially if it concerned art. I never took that ride.

Others had more appreciation and more vision.

Businessmen Ralph Ogden and Peter Stern purchased land in the Hudson Valley, including a 1935 mansion constructed from granite salvaged from a century-old Greek Revival home. They planned to make the place into an art gallery featuring painters from the region.

In the 1960s, Ogden happened upon those same fields of David Smith's that I had avoided. Stunned by the work on display, he completely changed his proposed concept. Rather than a typical gallery, Storm King Art Center would become a monumental setting for large outdoor sculpture, primarily abstract pieces created after 1935.

Our journey took us south of Newburgh, New York, then west of the Hudson River and towering Storm King Mountain, from which the center derives its name. From the entry road, it's simply more of the rolling, well-kept farmland so prevalent in the area.

The Arch by Alexander Calder, a black steel sculpture fifty feet high, stood just beyond the admission booth. Continuing our ascent up the access road, we began to see the campus spread out before us.

There are many ways to enjoy Storm King. None of them require advanced knowledge in sculpture. Certainly the expert will find much to appreciate, but so can the rank amateur (I'm one). Bring a sense of curiosity, a sense of wonder, and good walking shoes.

We began with a guided walking tour on the hilltop surrounding the museum.

Five tall Ionic columns immediately attract attention. These architectural remnants lay unnoticed in a forest until found and moved here. They provide unique framing through which to view monumental sculptures by Mark di Suvero on sloping fields opposite.

Some sculptures move. In *Sea Change* by George Cutts, two long steel tubes are continually turned by motors. George Rickey's *Five Open Squares Gyratory Gyratory* depends on the wind to keep its components constantly in motion. On the other hand, with *Spheres*, Grace Knowlton has fashioned simulated boulders of concrete over a mesh structure; they look as if they've been here since the glacier retreated.

Thirteen pieces of work by David Smith were among Storm King's first purchases. Eight are clustered on a lawn east of the museum. Smith, once a banker, learned welding during his days in an automotive plant near South Bend, Indiana. He adapted that skill to production of oversized metal works crafted from such found objects as blacksmithing tools and car fenders.

At first I wasn't certain what to think of his accomplishments. A few minutes studying *Portrait of a Lady Painter* helped convert me. Using a type case and a stool, Smith created an evocative piece. I walked around his brushed-steel sculptures several times. Patterns of light are seemingly embedded within the metal, creating impressive visual effects.

A thirty-minute tram ride through the five hundred acres let us rest while gaining appreciation for the center's evolving design. Landscape architecture has been important to Storm King since its beginnings. Natural though the surroundings may appear, a considerable amount of earth has been moved in the process of optimally setting the artistic creations.

This devotion to interplay between location and artistry has led to commissioning works by major sculptors specifically for Storm King. To my untrained eye, some ideas worked better than others. I didn't quite understand the concepts behind Richard Serra's ten-acre creation *Schunnemunk Fork*. However, Andy Goldsworthy's *Storm King Wall* fits the southwest corner perfectly. Almost 2,300 feet long, this stone border curves around trees and crosses a pond. It took Scottish artisans two years to complete the project.

Once off the tram, we resumed walking.

After viewing *Mozart's Birthday* and other dramatic sculptures by Mark di Suvero from afar, it's an entirely different experience strolling down and standing next to them. A distant view doesn't convey the enormity of the works. *Mother Peace*, comprised of steel I-beams painted red and carefully welded into place, stands as tall as a four-story building.

Works by di Suvero, an American born in Shanghai of Italian parents, were among my favorites. Soaring lines, vibrant color, and a sense of playfulness, especially as juxtaposed upon the landscape, captivated me. I wanted to see them from every possible angle. *Joie de Vivre* looks exactly that with its orange beams reaching toward the sky. Only in an outdoor setting could it realize its potential.

In contrast, smaller sculptures amidst a grove of trees give a more intimate feel.

Varying conditions dramatically impact perception of the sculptures. Our visit was long enough to let us appreciate how pieces looked different in late afternoon as opposed to the harsh light of noon. Changing seasons and weather conditions must have their effect.

Storm King has worked to preserve the perimeter views. Ironically, the New York Thruway is easily visible on one side. Somehow its proximity made me appreciate this sanctuary for reflection all the more.

******

Thomas Cole, founder of the Hudson River school of painters, first brought Catskill Mountain scenery to international attention.

Born in 1801 in England, seventh of eight children (and only son) of a textile manufacturer, his dreams of seeing America began early in childhood. The family moved across the Atlantic in 1818.

Seven years later, Cole took his first steamboat ride up the Hudson River. He returned with several sketches of scenic vistas, and then did a trio of oil paintings based on them. The canvases sold rapidly, springboarding the young man into his career as an artist.

He married Maria Bartow in the parlor of her uncle's house in Catskill. Called Cedar Grove, this became Cole's home for the rest of his short life. He died of pneumonia in 1848.

Following extensive restoration efforts, the estate opened for public tours in 2000.

The Federal style house, pale yellow brick with green shutters, is built into a small hillside. From the broad piazza, we looked west to the mountain views that Cole found so inspiring. Many of the paintings that established his reputation depicted scenes within fifteen miles of this spot. Reproductions of some of his most famous scenes, including Kaaterskill Falls and the Catskill Mountain House, highlight the house tour.

Imbued with Cole's spirit, we visited some of his favorite spots. Driving along Route 23A, one comes to parking for the Kaaterskill Falls trailhead. Walking along the often busy road to our starting point may have been the most treacherous part of our journey.

The trail begins just to the north of Bastion Falls, a broad sweeping cascade easily visible from the road. Recent rain made the going slippery, so we tread carefully on the rocky, eroded, 1.1-mile route. It's a steady climb through mixed forest, often over rocks and occasionally across a narrow stream. When the roaring sound of water began drowning out conversation, we knew we were nearing our goal.

Kaaterskill Falls, highest in the state, falls 260 feet in two tiers. The top cascade comes seemingly from nowhere, dropping high from a ledge and spraying its force beyond the perpendicular cliff. The second drop, much wider, cascades to the streambed below, where turbulent waters begin their ferocious run over rapids downstream.

We tried to guess Cole's thoughts upon first seeing this landmark. In an era when people feared wilderness and saw it as a phenomenon that had to be tamed, considerable emotion must have been evoked. Let me tell you, our dogs were certainly awed.

Walking to the site of Catskill Mountain House was much easier. Built in 1824, the fabled hotel had thirteen white Corinthian columns marking its entry. Capacity exceeded four hundred guests. Patrons came by steamboat, railroad, and/or stagecoach to arguably the country's top destination.

From the parking lot of North Lake Beach, it's barely a quarter mile along broad trail to the open ledge. Two lonely stone posts stand silent sentry at the final ascent to what was once America's most famous view.

For the final few yards, it's as if you walk to this broad ledge, and then the world falls off in front of you. If given full discretion on where to site a grand hotel, one would hesitate to imagine a vista as grand as this one. Gone since 1963, the Mountain House isn't even survived by traces of its foundation. As a historical marker states, "only the commanding view of this historic resort now remains."

Information:
Storm King Art Center, P.O. Box 280, Old Pleasant Hill Road, Mountainville, NY 10953. Phone 845-534-3115.
Guide to Catskill Trails: Catskill Region, Adirondack Mountain Club, Lake George, NY.

Meadow of Mark di Suvero sculptures at Storm King

Museum Village ● Fort Montgomery

Although an increasing number of New York City commuters are choosing to live in Orange County in New York's lower Hudson River valley, this is in no way what one would consider a suburban setting. Agriculture brought settlers to the area, and the rural atmosphere still prevails.

We found beautiful villages like Warwick, crossed the "black dirt" region that still leads the country in production of onions, and enjoyed picture-postcard vistas of rolling countryside almost everywhere we turned.

Historic venues are plentiful. A bevy of excellent restaurants made it mandatory that a visitor seek some exercise. Converted rail beds like the Orange Heritage Trail, which extends from Monroe to Goshen, help fill that need. For a full afternoon's stroll that included some heritage, we spent a few hours at Museum Village, near Monroe.

People who give back to their community deserve admiration. Here's an example of a man giving an entire new community to his community. Roscoe Smith (1877–1976) grew up on an Orange County farm. As a boy he shoveled coal for boilers, a harbinger of a lifetime commitment to energy development. In 1905, Smith founded the first electrical utility in the area. Despite his role in technological advance, he retained a nostalgia for traditional skills being lost in a changing world.

So he created Museum Village on forty acres that were once part of his great grandmother's farm. Smith built replicas of representative buildings and homes typical of Orange County two centuries ago. A stone schoolhouse duplicates a 180-year-old one in which his grandmother taught. The pharmacy includes the entire interior of a drugstore from the nearby hamlet of Florida. The general store reflects an actual operation in Marlboro.

The complex opened to the public in 1950. Of course, it's people that bring such a place to life, and Museum Village boasts an impressive staff of interpreters.

A veteran weaver explained a series of looms in the James Alexander Weaving Shop, named for Orange County's first such artisan. It

99

takes twenty hours to set up the four-harness loom before it's ready for an expert to use a beater and comb to create a complex pattern. I began to understand the need for a seven-year apprenticeship.

At a chandlery modeled after one in Newburgh, kids got to dip their own candles. An associated exhibit on lighting revealed the little-known reluctance with which some housewives greeted electricity—it made the dust more visible!

Farmers generally had forges to make small items and do simple repairs. For larger jobs, they came to a blacksmith like the one in this re-created stone building. A crank operated the bellows for the charcoal forge.

A hearth filled most of one end of the stone schoolhouse. The schoolmaster told us how students brought logs each day for the fire. Teachers had to be unmarried; their average age was a mere sixteen. Lipstick was prohibited.

I lingered in the print shop. The printer stressed the role of news-papers and posters as he demonstrated the flatbed press, and then the faster Gordon press, with its capacity of three hundred pages an hour. We learned the derivation of "minding your p's and q's," an admonition to return type to the proper compartments after printing.

The broom shop proved similarly fascinating. We learned about preparation of broomcorn, and then saw the intricacies of the treadle-operated wrapping machine which bound the broom with leather or wire. Craftspeople produce actual brooms for sale.

Elsewhere on the grounds, we found a pottery shop (kids exclaimed, "Wow! All of this is made out of clay?"), a bootery, and a wagon shop. There are also a few buildings set up specifically for exhibits, including one of farm tools, and another detailing the evolution of cast iron and soapstone stoves. The village's Natural History Museum boasts a mast-odon skeleton discovered just two miles away.

Our final stop came at the two-century-old log cabin, an exception in Museum Village for being the sole authentic old building. Inside we found whitewashed walls and a stone hearth. Today's plank floor would have represented an improvement over the original dirt surface. Trundle beds reminded how as many as five or six would have slept in a single room.

The interpreter here made a previous era come alive, especially during her clear and engaging descriptions of open-hearth cooking. The necessary collection of legged skillets (spiders), Dutch ovens, and variously sized hooks allowed one to control heat exposure. Even the youngest visitors could see how much harder it was to make dinner in a time before carefully modulated stoves, much less microwave ovens. Such work had its perils, too—only childbirth exceeded fire as a cause of death for young women.

******

Not far from West Point sits one of New York's newest historic sites, Fort Montgomery.

In 1777 the British planned a three-pronged attack to crush the American Revolution. General Burgoyne would come down from Montreal, while General St. Leger secured the Mohawk Valley and General Clinton headed north from New York City. This spot on the Hudson River became an important point of resistance for the colonials.

Redoubts and barracks were built. Wooden rafts floated a chain across the Hudson River to halt British ships. Cannons with a range of three miles were set in place. Immediately south, Fort Clinton, reached by a pontoon bridge, would provide further protection.

But Loyalists tipped off the English. The naval force reaching Fort Montgomery in October 1777 was only a diversionary one. American soldiers were surprised by redcoats coming by land from the west. The British destroyed the fort before heading north to burn the state capital of Kingston.

Destruction of Kingston galvanized the Americans, much as the murder of Jane McCrea near Fort Edward did. The army regrouped at West Point. Enough delay had ensued that British reinforcements did not reach Saratoga in time. American success at Saratoga led to French entry into the war, a key to ultimate victory.

Bordered by deep ravines, this rocky promontory has seen little change over two centuries. Iron mining took place briefly. In the 1960s, Jack Mead led some archaeological efforts. When an initiative developed to bring the area back to public attention, the Palisades Interstate

Park Commission had a remarkably untouched terrain with which to work. In Regional Historic Preservation Supervisor Rich Goring's words, this offered "a chance for doing the right thing the first time around."

The newly organized Fort Montgomery Battle Site Association chose to emphasize both military significance and the contributions of archaeology. Remains would be preserved, but no reconstruction would take place.

Trails lead to remnants of earthworks, foundations of barracks, a guardhouse, redoubts, and a powder magazine with eight-foot-thick walls. A Native American shelter lay amidst large glacial erratics. At one point we came near shafts from old iron mines.

Platforms above each site give access and views, while protecting the actual ruins. Artists' renditions and Acoustiguide narration give further insights into military issues and everyday life.

When you're finished exploring the fort, a steep path leads down to the Hudson River. A new suspension bridge, on the site of the 1777 pontoon bridge, takes walkers to adjacent Bear Mountain State Park. The views downriver are sufficient reward for the modest effort.

Information:
Museum Village, 1010 Route 17M, Monroe, NY 10950. Phone 845-782-8247.
Fort Montgomery State Historic Site, c/o Bear Mountain State Park, Bear Mountain, NY 10911. Phone 845-446-2134.

Stone Bridge Park in Sullivan County

102

Delhi Outdoor Education Center • Stone Bridge • Stephen Crane

On our first prolonged journey to Delaware County, we were awed by the continuous flow of beautiful scenery. Foothills of the western Catskill Mountains, rolling meadows, and bottomland pasture combine with meticulously kept farms for a landscape that rivals any rural county.

Perhaps the major walking route in the county is the Catskill Scenic Trail. Traversing old rail right-of-way for the Ulster and Delaware Railroad, the route between Bloomville and Grand Gorge offers nineteen miles of continuing views. In fairness, we only walked a few short segments, but that whetted our appetite for more.

On a more manageable scale for a day's outing is the Delhi College Outdoor Education Center. Just south of Delhi on Route 28, it offers fifty acres with a variety of trails and natural settings. A poster near the parking lot gives an overview of the property. The Catskill Outdoor Education Corps, an AmeriCorps project, oversees the land and offers regular programs for both adults and children.

Set amidst rolling fields with a beautiful mountain backdrop, grassy paths wind up and down the hills. We took our time walking along a ridge before descending toward bottomland. Sitting in two Adirondack chairs near the crest, we enjoyed a commanding view of all before us.

Along the way we gazed at weathered farmhouses in the distance, and pink mallow flowers up close. Reddening sumac added color on this autumn day, while milkweed pods blew past on their way to new rooting spots. Man-made accompaniments included a grotto-like stone bridge crossing a small stream, picnic tables, and a variety of benches made of stone and wood. Bluebird boxes offer respite to avian visitors.

Settings along the lower levels are varied. There's a pioneer garden with three separate plots bordered by logs. The largest section is devoted to the classic native "three sisters"—corn, beans, and squash. A rusting hay rake stands sentry.

Elsewhere we found a fire circle, a sundial on a stone slab base, and large green spaces used as outdoor classrooms. Nearby is a butterfly garden with four butterfly houses.

A labyrinth begins at a small arbor. Signs told us the labyrinth's history as a "sacred tool" and a "metaphor for life's journey." There are no tricks or dead ends, as in a maze. We walked the route, our two retrievers ("Labs in the Labyrinth" I entitled the requisite photo) running back and forth alongside. At the center we found a circular rock wall covered with spearmint.

The trail followed along a quiet creek. We saw no activity during our visit, but I suspect during fishing season anglers frequent the spot. Before heading back up to our point of origin, we found another set of Adirondack chairs. We sat and enjoyed the vista back up the hill. "Just so peaceful," my wife aptly described the scene.

We climbed back up along a pretty wooded path that I suspect was an old farm road. White pine, red cedar, American beech, sycamore, and apple were among the tree species we identified.

A brochure indicated the breadth of programs offered here. Apparently we missed the reptiles and amphibians that inhabit this ecosystem, and my wife wasn't upset that we saw no bats. Especially intriguing are the winter offerings. It's certainly a nice place for snowshoeing. But it also turns out to be the spot to learn igloo building!

$$******$$

In the days when wilderness was still something to be feared rather than appreciated, travelers looked for what they termed "the picturesque." Man-made attractions included ruins, castles, bridges, and the like. The Stone Arch Bridge in Sullivan County, south of Jeffersonville, captures much of that appeal.

Two Swiss German immigrants, Henry and Philip Hembot, built the three-arch span sometime around 1880. At the time, a main route between the old Newburgh & Cohecton Turnpike and Callicoon Valley crossed the bridge. Apparently a locally infamous crime, called the "hex" murder, was committed on the bridge in 1882. Now the Sullivan County Parks and Recreation Commission maintains it as the centerpiece of a peaceful twenty-acre park.

We parked at a small picnic area just beyond the Stone Arch Restaurant. A broad, easy trail brought us up a series of steps, and then across the bridge.

On the other side we found easy walking on the Worthington Trail. Signage labels it "steep and rough"—it's not. Names of the crew that cleared the trail in 1990 are memorialized. Similarly, by our point of origin, credit is given to those completing the Bridge Trail in 1991.

At a fork, the right branch sports No Trespassing signs. We turned left down toward the stream and continued on our way. Passing a stone foundation, the path continued by stone walls that must have fenced pastures once upon a time. After briefly paralleling another wall on our left, the way veered right, then petered out. The one-way journey is probably less than half a mile.

Retracing our route along the broad, gently flowing stream, we noted sycamores, the largest trees along the banks, along with maple and beech. Right by the bridge, water cascades over a shallow ledge. Huge rocks in the flow allowed access to nice streamside vantage points for photos.

A close-up look at the arches shows them to be built for the ages. I couldn't find information on the Hembots and their building techniques, but this is construction that should still be intact a century from now. The children's playground and pretty picnic area alongside invite lingering a while.

At a small plaza on the far side of the bridge, there's a flagpole, an old millstone, and an engraved marker commemorating Christopher McCann, county commissioner of public works from 1980 to 1982, and apparently a leader in creating this park. The area is described as "a sanctuary for those of all ages traveling the road of life." We're glad we found it.

******

Stephen Crane's *The Red Badge of Courage* stands as a classic of the Civil War. I can remember my amazement upon learning that Crane (1871–1900) never saw battle himself. It turns out much of his inspiration came from tales told by veterans gathering for a reunion in Port Jervis, the Delaware River village that he called home. A one-mile walking tour passes spots relating to his residency there.

We picked up a map at the handsome Port Jervis Free Library on

Pike Street. The sturdy 1903 pale yellow brick building features fine dentil work and pediment. It was built with a donation from Andrew Carnegie, who helped establish some 1,600 such libraries across the country.

Across the street we found Orange Square. The city's oldest park, it's distinguished by a very handsome Civil War memorial. Over ten thousand people attended its dedication in July 1886. Crane sat and talked to soldiers of the 124th New York Regiment, nicknamed the "Orange Blossoms." Their detailed stories gave him both the inspiration and the material to begin writing *The Red Badge of Courage*, based partly around their involvement in the Battle of Chancellorsville.

Along our route we passed the Drew United Methodist Church where Crane's father Jonathan, a minister, preached from 1878 until his death two years later. Among other impressive churches nearby was the First Presbyterian, where Crane's brother William, a local attorney, sang in concert. Deerpark Reformed Church was designed by the same architect who did the state capitol in Albany.

William Crane's home on East Main Street had Queen Anne and Colonial Revival features. William practiced law in Port Jervis from 1883 to 1901. Among other houses pointed out was one on East Main reputed to have been the setting for another Crane work entitled *The Monster*.

The dark red brick Erie Depot opened in 1892 when Port Jervis was a major railroad center. Crane used the station multiple times. Passenger service ended in 1974.

Port Jervis also offers the self-guided Delaware River Heritage Tour. We passed markers denoting events from both the French and Indian War and the American Revolution. The impact of the Delaware and Hudson Canal (the village was named for John Jervis, engineer on the project), built to bring coal from Pennsylvania to the New York market, and the Erie Railroad is highlighted.

One notable spot is Tri-States Boundary Monument, where New York, New Jersey, and Pennsylvania all come together. Although an interstate bridge incongruously carries traffic high above, the confluence of the Neversink and Delaware rivers makes for a peaceful river scene.

This trail runs five miles in its entirety. In some stretches the orange rectangular markers were few and far between, making the route difficult to follow. Exhibit boards along the way helped introduce us to selected aspects of local history.

Information:

Delhi Outdoor Education Center, Delhi College, Delhi, NY 13753. Phone 607-746-4051.

Sullivan County Visitors Association, 100 Sullivan Ave., Box 248, Ferndale, NY 12734. Phone 800-882-2287.

Port Jervis Free Library, 138 Pike Street, Port Jervis, NY 12771. Phone 845-856-7313.

Minisink Valley Historical Society, 125-133 West Main Street, Port Jervis, NY 12771. Phone 845-856-2375.

Civil War Memorial in Port Jervis' Orange Park, where Stephen Crane gathered stories that inspired *The Red Badge of Courage*

Overlook Mountain • Byrdcliffe

One spring I had seen pictures of an abandoned hotel atop Overlook Mountain in the Catskills, and I wanted to see the place for myself. We picked up our friend Megan, ready for a break from her graduate school interviewing schedule, near Albany. Our trailhead lay about an hour farther south, just outside Woodstock.

The Adirondack Mountain Club's *Guide to Catskill Trails* gave excellent directions to Meads Mountain Road. Our trailhead lay five miles up from the turn off Route 33.

My guidebook told me that the building across the road from our trailhead once did business as Mead's Mountain House. Somehow I expected an abandoned ramshackle affair. However, it has apparently been spruced up and reincarnated as a Tibetan Buddhist monastery.

Our two-and-a-half-mile trail was easily followed. Originally created as a carriage road, the path is much wider than most mountain routes. We passed through mixed forest, crossed a few small streams, and encountered a fair number of moss-covered rocky outcrops and impressive boulders.

With two dogs in tow, rest stops weren't easy to enforce. We found ourselves pulled consistently upwards. In about an hour, we came to the site of the Overlook Mountain House. (An incongruous, tall antenna just before the hotel site must have a purpose, but we chose to ignore its presence.)

Research revealed that the ruins facing us marked the third time around for a hotel on this site. The first, built in 1871, burned only a few years later. A second inn opened by 1878, but met the same fiery fate in 1924. *Resorts of the Catskills*, a compendium of essays and photographs published by St. Martin's Press in 1979, confirmed that both merited categorization as grand hotels.

Owners in the 1920s wanted no risk of a repetition. Consequently, construction plans called for stone and concrete, rather than wood. However, a different kind of catastrophe hit, this one economic.

The Great Depression led to financial reverses, and the final attempt at establishing a rebuilt Overlook Mountain House had to be abandoned. What we found, then, was not so much a set of ruins as an incomplete project.

Our first glance showed a formidable three-story structure. Tiered stairs to the entryway looked inviting, dentil work remained in place, and arches over first-story windows added a nice touch. In back, a two-story building with casement windows that once housed staff and a few guests had its skeleton intact. I had thoughts of putting a roof on, bringing in a drywall team, and making plans to finish the job.

Not surprisingly, a closer look dashed my hopes. Indeed, the walls remain remarkably intact, and brick-lined fireplaces are hauntingly present. But flooring has rotted away. The stone-edged grand staircase leads up to emptiness. A few trees have managed to take root inside.

Informative posters plastered onto the interior walls give some historical perspective. One offered fading pictures of the Overlook Mountain House in 1871, with its ornate lobby and elegant dining rooms. Another regaled us with a tale of "The Ghost of Overlook Mountain."

There's also a reprint of a 1993 letter to the *New York Times* decrying the state's burning of the Catskill Mountain House, perhaps the most famous of all early hotels in the region. I wondered if such sentiment has been responsible for the decision to leave these remains in place on Overlook Mountain.

On one placard, we were challenged to "imagine how it was here and how it will be fifty or a hundred years from now." I'm firmly committed to preserving some remnants of mountain resort history. Leaving Overlook Mountain as it stands allows us to ponder early development in the Catskills and consider the changing use of leisure time in America.

We continued to the top of the mountain. Unusual layered rock formations made the way interesting. Peering at the ridges close-up, we saw thick lichen growth and rock patterns reminiscent of the brain's sulci.

A ranger cabin with dark brown plank siding stands sentinel near an opening onto a rocky ledge with a fire tower. Nearby picnic tables invited lingering. My wife tended our dogs, while Megan and I succumbed to our temptation to climb the tower.

Our efforts were rewarded with fine views of the surrounding mountains. To the east we saw a narrow ribbon of the Hudson River.

Prominent on the southern horizon was a vista onto the Ashokan Reservoir, important for New York City's water needs. My guidebook boasts that seven states can be seen from this vantage point. It's one of the more panoramic views in the Catskills.

A few comments on this hike are in order. We found it quite satisfying both in terms of effort and scenery, but this is not an undiscovered or sparsely traveled route. Though the guidebook depicts the trail as a gradual ascent, it's actually a fairly persistent climb. I don't envy the horses that had to pull stagecoaches and wagons up to the hotel a century ago. Should you bring children, they need to be watched carefully within the interior of the foundations.

******

Woodstock, in Ulster County, offers the opportunity to wander Byrdcliffe, the arts colony that first gave that village its cultural reputation.

The Industrial Revolution allowed broad-based consumption of less expensive goods, while also spawning a working class that could afford them. Some people complained, though, about the accompanying urbanization, and the shoddy nature of some products. Others bemoaned the depersonalization of factory processes that supplanted the work of artisans and craftsmen.

Such influential personalities as William Morris, a printer in England, and Elbert Hubbard, who set up a craft community in East Aurora, New York, countered with the so-called "Arts and Crafts" movement. Ralph Radcliffe Whitehead, also British, and his Philadelphia-born wife, Jane Byrd McCall, put such tenets into practice with the establishment of a 1,500-acre complex on a hillside outside Woodstock.

Named Byrdcliffe, an amalgamation of the couple's middle names, the place opened for occupancy in 1903. Artists, sculptors, furniture makers, and other artisans took up residence. Both by fashioning their wares and training new devotees, they hoped to build somewhat of a utopian craft society.

Practicalities often derail utopian ideas. Such is what happened at Byrdcliffe. Although the communal concept dwindled, the tradition of

110

an Arts and Crafts campus persisted. Painters, musicians, writers and others spent summers in the cabins and dormitories. A host of noted visitors dropped in along the way. When Whitehead's son died in 1976, Byrdcliffe was willed to the Woodstock Guild of Craftsmen, which continues the legacy.

We parked outside the barn-like Byrdcliffe Theater, originally an art school and now used as a concert and performing arts venue. Maps available here detail a mile-long walking tour that passes some thirty sites of interest.

What we found was a rustic colony nestled into a forested hillside. Weathered pine siding and green roofs fit well into the landscape. Some of the smaller cottages, like Wake Robin and Morning Star, are camouflaged so well that we didn't notice them even when twenty feet away. The occasional stone foundation denotes the site of a former studio or home.

Arts and Crafts supporters eschewed the complexities of Victorian design. Thus, we found generally straightforward architecture, enhanced here and there with dormer windows and other simple features. Porches are ubiquitous, encouraging the camaraderie that the Whiteheads desired.

One large building, Eastover, has housed the likes of Chevy Chase and The Band during its lifespan. A more compact one, Chipmunk, served as Helen Hayes' summer home in 1924.

Small studio structures make idyllic summer and fall retreats for artists, writers, and composers.

White Pines is perhaps the most imposing structure. This served as the home of Ralph and Jane Whitehead. In this fifteen-room house, they entertained such notables as Thomas Mann, Wallace Stevens, and Isadora Duncan. A covered bridge connects to an adjacent weaving studio. The screened second-story porch must offer fine views.

Restoration was in progress when we visited. When completed, this will be a handsome historic site. On Sundays during the summer, there's an exhibit on the colony here. Only stone walls remain from the gardens that once flourished. One hopes re-creation of these might be in the game plan, too.

In its heyday, Byrdcliffe had a large working farm that supplied vegetables, milk, and eggs. The barns still look solid and ready for use. A short walk led to Yggdrasill (Norse for "tree of life"), an especially appealing cottage/studio by a babbling brook. Jane Whitehead lived here after her husband's death in 1929, until her own passing in 1955.

Information:
Guide to Catskill Trails: Catskill Region, Adirondack Mountain Club, Lake George, NY.
Byrdcliffe, The Woodstock Guild, 34 Tinker Street, Woodstock, NY 12498. Phone 845-679-2079.

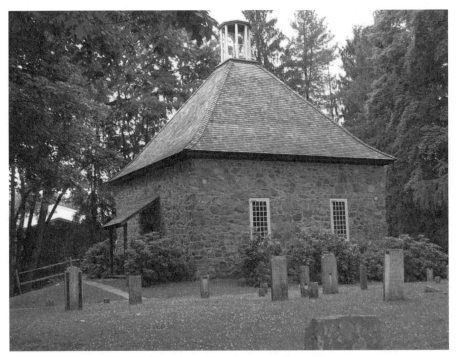

Huguenot church in New Paltz

High Falls • Wallkill Valley Rail Trail

This story begins with the Wurts brothers, dry goods merchants in Philadelphia during the War of 1812. When the government pays them for their wares partially with land, they find themselves owners of anthracite mines in Pennsylvania.

This might sound good, except that Americans are accustomed to softer bituminous coal. Furthermore, the potentially profitable New York City market lies too far away across undeveloped terrain.

The Wurts brothers are solid businessmen, though. They point to the recent war as evidence that the United States shouldn't rely on foreign sources for fuel (sound familiar?). In a New York tavern, they demonstrate the effectiveness of heating with anthracite coal. And they begin to raise money for a canal that will take the coal from the hills of Pennsylvania to the Hudson River.

So begins the story of the Delaware and Hudson Canal Company.

That coal demonstration in a tavern turns out to be a marketing coup. Soon the Wurts brothers have capitalized America's first million-dollar business. Hiring engineers and workmen trained through experience on the Erie Canal, they manage to complete a 108-mile water channel, with 108 locks, in under three years.

Coincidentally, natural limestone cement is discovered only a few miles from Kingston, New York, near the end of the canal route. Add this to the coal coming from Pennsylvania, and the company records profits right from its opening in 1825. Twice the canal gets widened. Trade flourishes all the way into the 1890s, when trains, which don't have to worry about winter freezes, supplant the waterway.

Cut to High Falls, New York, in the foothills of the Catskill Mountains. It took six locks in under a mile to overcome the elevation change here. When the canal closed, High Falls began to fade. Cement production continued, but with the development of Portland cement, this, too, dwindled. The population fell until this community of well-preserved, nineteenth-century buildings became rediscovered by tourists.

Your first stop should be the engaging Delaware and Hudson Canal Museum. Two highly detailed replicas of canal boats are creations crafted by former canal men. One impressive diorama shows a scene between Locks 17 and 18 in High Falls. Another portrays the tending of mules that pulled the boats.

Be sure to see the depiction of a suspension bridge that carried the canal over Rondout Creek. John Roebling's claim to fame may be the Brooklyn Bridge, but he perfected his engineering techniques and invention of wire cable while building four aqueducts for the D&H. What audacity to think one could suspend a wooden trough across a broad stream and render it sturdy enough to support four feet of water and continual boat traffic!

On a carefully constructed working model of Lock 16, all the gates, hinges, gears, and cables work just as designed for the actual canal. We watched as water filled the lock, then appreciated how the boat entered and left at a new level.

After a visit inside the museum, amble along the one-mile Five Locks Walk, a complex built during the canal's expansion in the 1840s.

The trail begins just behind the DePuy Canal House, built by tavern-keeper Simon DePuy in 1797, and now an inn boasting a reputation as one of the outstanding restaurants in upstate New York. Burns from towropes pulled by mules over a century ago dent one corner of the building.

The canal has seen encroachment from adjacent forest. Still, the locks, made of Shandaken conglomerate, maintain a sturdy appearance. At Lock 16, we looked at stone blocks placed so carefully that mortar wasn't needed.

Farther along, it was impressive to look at Lock 18's structural integrity a century after its last use. Snubbing posts may have resembled tombstones, but they still looked strong enough to hold boats tied to them. Spikes for attaching cables were likewise intact. Locks measured 14 feet 6 inches in width; boats were just four inches narrower. Talk about a tight fit!

Behind Lock 16, stone walls denote a canal slip, or loading dock. Weirs, designed to drain excess water, can be seen by Locks 16 and 19. A couple of lock-tender's houses survive, including an attractive white cottage across from Lock 20. Some stone foundations denote sites of long-gone stores and warehouses.

We then walked across Route 213 to explore along Rondout Creek.

An off-road path took us to the upper and lower falls. Placards explained how mills lined the stream soon after the village was founded in 1676. Boom times came after the canal opened, and again after gristmills changed their focus to grinding newly discovered natural cement in the mid-1800s. Now there's a hydroelectric plant in place.

Another short trail begins across from DePuy Canal House, passing Lock 15 on the way to ruins of a Roebling aqueduct. Huge pillars are still standing, as are the abutments of an earlier stone aqueduct. Nearby, kids dove off rocky ledges into deep pools. Imagine swimming there a hundred years ago and watching a boat cross above you!

Strolling the streets of this tiny village, with its onetime feed stores and canal warehouses now offering antiques and crafts, can complete an afternoon of walking.

******

I guess I developed a sentimental attraction to the Wallkill Valley Rail Trail since this was the first such recycled corridor that I'd walked. It turns out to be the seventeenth reincarnated route in New York.

The Wallkill Valley Railroad started operation in the late 1800s and carried produce to market. For farmers in Ulster County and, later, workers traveling to New York City, the train fulfilled an important function.

By the 1930s, however, other forms of transportation, i.e. cars and trucks, had largely superseded the rail line. Passenger traffic ceased by 1940. In 1977 freight traffic likewise stopped. Within a few years of the closing, community activists began envisioning a multi-use trail in its place. Their success led to the Rail Trail's opening in 1993.

The route travels just over twelve miles between Gardiner and the Rosendale town line. Be prepared to search a bit if starting at the latter. Pay attention to that trestle high above as you enter Rosendale on Route 213. Cross the bridge to St. Peter's Church, take a right on Keator Avenue, and another right on Mountain. There's a small parking area just after that last turn.

We traversed everything from farmland to young second-growth forest to mountain views to residential development. My wife found wildflowers galore, naming off such specimens as bee balm, wild phlox, Queen Anne's lace, and black-eyed Susans. There's plenty of wetland on either side, making you appreciate how well the rail line had to be surveyed and graded.

In Rosendale we had access to that former railroad trestle high above the town. Walking halfway across a newly planked surface, we had views up and down the Wallkill River, and across to impressive rocky ledges. There's a nice glimpse of stately St. Peter's Church below, and also of Century House with its nearby cement mine and kiln.

Just under four miles away sits the college town of New Paltz, a good intermediate destination. We walked a few blocks along Huguenot Street, one of the oldest neighborhoods in the United States.

French Huguenots faced religious persecution under Catholic European monarchies that had little tolerance for Protestants. Some fled to Holland, England, and Germany. Eventually a few decided on emigration to the United States. Twelve families arrived in Kingston, New York, around 1670.

In time they purchased over forty thousand acres of land from the Esopus natives and prepared to farm. Their new settlement was named New Paltz, after Die Pfalz, a region in Germany that had given them refuge. Along with New Rochelle, New York and Charleston, South Carolina, this became one of the main Huguenot communities in the country.

Early Huguenots in New Paltz constructed wooden houses. The second generation built with stone, a material that became a local tradition for homes. Some of these dwellings are in private hands. Others are operated as a museum by the Huguenot Historical Society, and are open for guided tours.

Information:
D&H Historical Society Museum, P.O. Box 23, Mohonk Road, High Falls, NY 12440. Phone 845-687-9311.
Wallkill Valley Rail Trail Association, Box 1048, New Paltz, NY 12561.
Huguenot Historical Society, 18 Broadhead Avenue, New Paltz, NY 12561. Phone 845-255-1889.

Minnewaska State Park • Olana

In 1876, Alfred Smiley, who had begun Mohonk Mountain House with his brother Albert a few years earlier, bought this large nearby property. In 1879, he opened the Lake Minnewaska House (later to be called Cliff House), followed by a second hotel, Wildmere, eight years later.

As vacation and transportation patterns changed, visitors no longer spent entire summers in one place. Such projects as winterization of Wildmere, and construction of a golf course and ski slope, were attempted in order to keep the business afloat.

By the 1970s, however, both inns had been destroyed by fire. A trusted employee owned the land and wanted to see it preserved. New York State purchased 6,700 acres, and eventually added another 2,600. Reaction to a plan by Marriott Corporation to build a resort led the state to acquire 1,200 more acres—which included Lake Minnewaska—in 1986.

Today the park offers over fifty miles of walking trails, half of them originally developed as carriage roads. They access two large lakes, Minnewaska and Awosting, plus smaller Mud Pond, and lead to extraordinary views of the Shawangunk Ridge and beyond.

A kiosk at the main parking lot tells much of the story. From there, it's a short walk to cliffs overlooking Lake Minnewaska. The glacially carved lakes and the impressive conglomerate rock dikes are nicely framed by hemlock forest. This certainly would have made a spectacular setting for a nineteenth-century hotel.

These so-called "sky lakes" depend solely on rainwater. There are no natural springs and no buffering capacity. Though clear and clean, with solid conglomerate bases, the lakes are acidic and support no fish.

We set out for the Castle Point Trail. There would be junctions for the Scenic Sunset Carriageway and the Upper Awosting Carriageway before we followed red markers through a forest of pine, birch, maple, and hemlock. Eventually we took a right onto a blue-blazed trail.

Mountain laurel had begun to bloom in time for our June hike. Lower bushes with pink blossoms, we learned, were sheep laurel. The taller mountain laurel burst forth large white flowers.

Staff members (there are five full-time, all-year staff, with addi-

117

tional seasonal staff and volunteers) told us that this was originally a chestnut-oak forest. Lumber from the American chestnut (and some still survive here), plus blueberries and huckleberries from the many bushes still in evidence, provided income for local residents.

Fires were often set to enhance berry proliferation, and this had an impact on the forest. Fire-resistant trees like pitch pine and chestnut tended to thrive. Now in the absence of fire, there's more red maple and striped maple.

We passed a tee from the old golf course, where there was a view down the fairway to Ashokan, and across the Rondout Valley. Just ahead, a small, rocky outcrop gave an incredible panorama of Pomogot Ravine.

Across from us stood a boulder, actually a glacial erratic, known as Patterson's Pellet. The Hudson Highlands presented to the south and east, with Storm King Mountain and a narrow ribbon of the Hudson River visible. In front were the Hudson and Wallkill Valleys; behind us lay the Rondout Valley. Focusing on the rock ledges themselves, we saw old anchoring points for gazebos and railings. Peregrine falcons are common here, though we didn't have the good fortune to see one.

Soon we came to another rocky outcrop, giving another unbelievable vantage point. Wonderful views are so commonplace here that this stopping point didn't even have a name. (Looking closely at maps later, I realized this may have been Kempton Ledge.) Consequently, we expected quite a show at Castle Point.

And we weren't disappointed. Vistas on both sides of the ridge are unlimited. The Hudson Highlands are clearly seen; so are the Catskill Mountains. We had our first glimpse of Lake Awosting far beneath us. Just to add a bit more drama, we had the opportunity to watch a thunderstorm moving in the distance.

Descending, we passed the Hamilton Point Carriageway (yellow markers). A left here would have led back to the Lake Minnewaska Carriageway, and eventually the parking lot, a round trip of about seven miles. We instead lengthened our walk with a lower trail toward Lake Awosting. When we came to our first good open vantage point on Lake Awosting, one fellow walker commented, "Isn't it amazing that when these lakes were created, they all had such good viewing points?" And they certainly do.

Walking down to the lakeshore, we saw the original concrete dam built to sustain water levels, and then saw some examples of recent erosion along rock walls. Completing our loop back to the parking area, there was just no end to the mountain laurel blooms—"like Christmas in the summer," another hiker proclaimed.

The Mohonk Preserve and the grounds of the Mohonk Mountain House are close by. Each of the three reserves has its own character. Walks complement, rather than substitute for, one another. All three deserve some time.

******

Artists of the Hudson River school introduced new concepts of nature and wilderness to American audiences. Thomas Cole stands recognized as the founder of the movement. Frederic Church (1826–1900), however, became one of its most celebrated practitioners.

Though comfortable with his growing fame, Church sought seclusion in his private life. He and his wife Isabel purchased 126 acres of farmland on the Hudson River in 1860 and built a cottage. Within a few years, Church decided to build a grander home atop the hill.

Exposure to Moorish culture during a trip to Europe and the Middle East led him to choose a Persian design. Multicolored brick and brown stone quarried on the property were used in construction. Two Moorish towers, arched doorways and windows, and columned upper-story porches characterize the mansion, which he named Olana.

The home remained in the Church family until 1964, when a nonprofit group purchased the property so as to assure preservation. Since 1966, New York State has operated Olana State Historic Site.

A guided tour of the interior reveals both beauty and fine craftsmanship. Views across the Hudson River to the Catskills, carefully chosen by Church, are impressive.

For Church, creation of the landscape around him was also an artistic endeavor. Using forest, hills, and stream as his media, he carefully planned his largest and most enduring work of art. Natural though the terrain may appear, siting of roads, planting of trees, and dredging of a pond all sought to capture the artist's vision. People traveling Olana's seven miles of carriage road were to enjoy a series of carefully selected scenes.

We walked these grounds for several hours. Taking gently undulating switchbacks through an airy forest, we wandered down to Cosy Cottage, the first home built on the property. Richard Morris Hunt, more accustomed to designing mansions in New York City, served as architect. Simple in contrast to Olana, the lapboard siding construction, gables, and hooded windows produce the sense of a quiet, pleasant retreat.

Our path took us through onetime orchards and past two red barns. Farming continued here until the 1940s. Olana once included a granary, icehouse, sawmill, pump house, and corn crib. There were also garden sites. Church wrote that "Mrs. Church has a digging fit, she flits about with a trowel in one hand and juvenile plants in the other all day."

A peaceful picnic grove just beyond the barns offered a nice place for lunch. We took time to reflect on Church's accomplishments, both as an artist and as the creative force behind Olana.

Thousands zoom past this spot on the New York Thruway every day, not even knowing it's here. Yet, barely a century and a half ago, this constituted wilderness. Preservation of Olana highlights the life of a notable painter and commemorates a crucial phase in the history of American art.

The home at Olana may ultimately be Church's most comprehensive achievement. His architectural vision, complemented by his "romantic landscape," leaves an important legacy, one matching any that he captured on canvas.

Information:
Minnewaska State Park Preserve, Box 893, New Paltz, NY 12561. Phone 845-255-0752.
Olana State Historic Site, RD 2, Hudson, NY 12534. Phone 518-828-0135.

Vanderbilt Mansion • Hyde Park

Before the advent of income tax, a millionaire was really a million-aire. The Vanderbilt clan, with its steamboat and railroad enterprises, belonged to that exclusive realm. Though this family, like others with similar fortunes, gave generously to worthwhile causes, they also spent lavishly on material comforts.

By the late nineteenth century, the lower Hudson River Valley had become a "place to be." With scenery made famous by painters like Thomas Cole, and nearby resorts in the Catskill Mountains, the region became a favored playground. Railroads and steamboats provided convenient transportation, making places like Hyde Park quite accessible

Frederick Vanderbilt, grandson of Cornelius, originator of the family fortune, chose to have a home there. Frederick was shy and unpretentious, and the only one of Cornelius' grandchildren who didn't squander the millions bequeathed him.

In 1895, he and his wife found a scenic spot with six hundred acres overlooking the Hudson. With the forty-room Greek Revival mansion there already unsound, they leveled it, and then hired the best architects available, Charles McKim and Stanford White, to design a new place. Construction took twenty-six months.

Since 1940, Vanderbilt Mansion has been open to the public as a National Historic Site. Rolling lawns, a brook crossed by one of the country's first steel and concrete bridges, and commanding views of the Hudson River introduce a visitor to the environs.

The house is stately from the outside with its limestone construction. Inside, the work of Italian craftsmen and skilled Swiss carvers, complemented by European antiques and artifacts collected by White, creates as sumptuous an abode as one can imagine.

A tour can prove entertaining and informative. Looking at columns, dentils, porticos, and remarkably thick doors, descriptors coming to mind aren't "modest" or "cozy." There's a small intimate study, darkly paneled, with walls of books. It's the exception. Marble columns, tile floor, and central balcony can make the place seem more like a bank than a home.

None of us will own such an estate, so it's nice to have the chance to roam as though we were Vanderbilt guests. I began a loop walk out-side the Visitor Center. Taking a left on the park road, passing the park-ing lot and expansive lawns, I headed toward The Overlook.

Rumbling of trains far below became apparent, but the view from The Overlook blocked out all other sensations. The spectacular vista included river, islands, and steep hills on the far shore. Without binocu-lars, I couldn't identify castle-like structures on the other side, though I suspect the Vanderbilt Mansion is a clear landmark from there.

The route continued toward Bard Rock, first on paved road, before switching to a dirt path between tall pines. Steep lawns fanned out to my left. Soon I found myself back on a paved road, descending along-side stone fencing shaded by maples. At the bottom of the hill, a sign indicated I'd gone 0.8 mile.

Finding the pedestrian bridge to Bard Rock, a popular picnic site and viewpoint, closed, I turned left onto a dirt and gravel trail. My next mile was a woods walk through maple-dominated forest broken up by occasional rocky outcrops. Periodically I had glimpses of the river. I also saw iron fencing buttressed by concrete posts, with railroad tracks just beyond.

Just after crossing a small rivulet, I spotted chimneys of the Van-derbilt Mansion. The columned back portico came into view, and then the forest opened for a good look at the entire length of the house.

At an unmarked fork, I bore right, staying along the river. Soon the route curved, bringing me closer to the iron fence. I walked through a break in the fencing for a commanding view of the Hudson. Almost as if on cue, a train sped by beneath me.

I came to a chain barrier. To the right was the estate's lower gate-house. A sign reported I was a quarter mile from Riverfront Park. Had I desired to extend my hike, I could have gone 2.7 miles and reached the Franklin D. Roosevelt Home.

To complete the Vanderbilt Loop, I turned left and began a gradual uphill climb on a park road. Another spur to the left brought me back along the forest, steadily climbing to the crest of a ridge. Soon I came alongside the Vanderbilt gardens, a nice place to end my 2.6-mile out-ing.

Frederick Vanderbilt had a degree in horticulture from Yale. For him the gardens were more than just another nicety.

Three acres in all, and maintained by an army of volunteers, the gardens are divided into several levels. Brick walls, stone retaining walls, and a wooden pergola help define the space. Vanderbilt's five greenhouses are no longer here. Otherwise, the gardens largely duplicate his original concept.

Paths lead past brightly colored annuals, including blue salvia, zinnias, and crescent-shaped beds of petunias. Over four thousand plants are set each year. Perennial beds fill the next level. Walkways pass rows of lupine, columbine, yarrow, and pink sedum, ultimately leading to a reflecting pool. Dyed black with a botanical dye, and studded with water lilies, this pool is an impressive sight.

From here, the Vanderbilts would have led guests to the lowest levels, where the rose gardens lie. The fourteen hundred bushes, when in full bloom, must be beautiful. Tea served in the central loggia often concluded the visit in halcyon days.

******

There are myriad other walking possibilities around Hyde Park.

A trail connects the Vanderbilt Mansion with Franklin Delano Roosevelt's home three miles south. Another route heads east to Val-Kill, Eleanor Roosevelt's retreat during her husband's presidency, and later her permanent residence until she died in 1962. The home and grounds certainly deserve a visit. A one-mile woodland trail on the grounds allows a pleasant workout. Gentle, wide paths go through a forest with hickory, beech, maple, oak, and a variety of conifers.

We chose to do the Pinewoods Nature Trail, just outside the village in a park of the same name. Signs told us this was once part of the property owned by eighteenth-century settler Jacobus Stoutenburgh. In fact, the surrounding settlement carried the name Stoutenburgh until it was changed to Hyde Park in 1812.

In 1945, the parcel was left by a later owner to three local churches. They in turn leased it to Hyde Park for a town park, charging a mere one dollar for the hundred-year rental. Once farmland, the land now features a playground, baseball field, tennis courts, and a very pleasant

0.7-mile woodland trail.

We began by the tennis courts. Immediately we saw some of the folded rock ridges of "dirty sandstone" characteristic of the area. An old stone fence to our left testified to former use of the land for farming. Oak, hemlock, locust, and maple trees could all be easily spotted. The park's namesake, the pine tree, turned out to be much more scarce.

Crossing a dirt road, we began to hear the sound of rushing water. Just after passing a massive rock ledge tilted at a 45-degree angle, we caught a glimpse of a small waterfall.

Walking down toward Crum Elbow Creek, a tributary of the Hudson, we got a better look at the falls. Stone foundations beyond looked as though they may have been part of an old mill. Lumber, plaster, flax, and nails once emanated from enterprises fueled by power from these falls.

Upstream the creek becomes a broad, quiet stream with a few gentle rapids. We turned back into the woods, gradually winding our way back to the trailhead. Plans call for a bridge across the creek at some point, giving a connection to trails in adjacent Hackett Hill Park.

Information:
Vanderbilt Mansion National Historic Site, Albany Post Road, Hyde Park, New York 12538. Phone 845-229-9115.
Hyde Park Recreation Department, 4383 Albany Post Road, Hyde Park, N.Y. 12538. Phone 845-229-8086.

Mohonk Preserve • Mohonk Mountain House

The heyday of the Smiley hotels on Mohonk Lake and Lake Minnewaska had long receded, although the Mohonk Mountain House continued to thrive, when in 1963 the brothers' families placed a large parcel of land—over six thousand acres—into a nonprofit entity, the Mohonk Preserve. Maintained by annual memberships and day-use fees, this vast wilderness resource offers a broad spectrum of outdoor opportunity.

Rock climbers look to this as an important haven. Hikers and walkers can choose among twenty-five miles of carriage road and forty miles of footpath, starting from three major trailheads.

Be sure to spend some time in the impressive stone and wood Mohonk Preserve Trapps Gateway Visitor Center. Materials were all cut or quarried locally. Note the huge oak columns crafted from trees on the property. Displays give insight into the environmentally conscious design. Especially engaging exhibits on the lower level explain the cutting-edge geothermal heating system.

A scale model of the Shawangunks highlights notable landmarks and hiking destinations. There are nature displays. Historical information ranges from the Native American presence, through early settlement, to the rock climbers who first conquered the slopes in 1935.

After our stop at the Visitor Center, we took the East Trapps Connector Trail to a major hiking area. This turned out to be quite a trek. Passing the rustic gazebo behind the center, we walked through parking lots before climbing steadily uphill past some modest rock monoliths, and into another parking area.

Now the work began. We climbed up a short, wooden staircase before beginning our way up literally hundreds of stone steps. A volunteer at the Visitor Center told us we'd take over 250 steps in all. There's no reason to disbelieve her.

Eventually, however, we reached Undercliff Road, one of the carriage roads constructed over a century ago (at the cost of a dollar a foot!). Our difficult access issues behind us, we had miles of easy walking along the wide, graded path.

Walking just beneath the high rock ledges of the Shawangunk

Ridge, there are stunning views of the valley below—some a bit vertiginous—at almost every turn. You know you're high when a few hawks soar by at eye level.

I noticed occasional yellow paint blazes to the left. Many of these led to stone steps up to the ledge. Frequent emergence of sweating but exhilarated men and women helped me realize these were rock-climbing access points. The ledge itself is largely hidden by trees, but with patience, we eventually reached some impressive open vistas.

Interesting rock formations, one quite cave-like, added to sights along the road. So did the sudden appearance of two beautiful fawns not ten feet away from me, their mother just out of sight uphill. Plenty of walkers shared the route with me, along with a few bicyclists.

I chose to turn around at Rhododendron Bridge and retrace. One can make a five-mile loop by turning onto Overcliff Road. That route offers more views of the Rondout Valley and also of the Catskills.

It's easy to design longer loop excursions. There are also a few very nice, short, self-guided walks. The Laverne Thompson Nature Trail near the Visitor Center gives an introduction to the terrain and vegetation. Sixteen numbered stops are keyed to a brochure, giving information on forest composition, the conglomerate rock characteristic of the Shawangunk area, and geologic forces of the ice age.

Another, the Trapps Mountain Hamlet Path, goes through an abandoned town site. We very much enjoyed this mile-and-a-half round trip that gave insight into the hard existence of settlers a century or more ago.

Old roads, a few cellar holes, and stone fences stand in memory of the fifty or sixty families who carved out a subsistence living here. It's actually a bit hard to believe the oak and hemlock forest we traversed grew up during the eight decades or so after people left; this would have been pasture back then.

One stop showed unfinished millstones. Settlers shaped the hard conglomerate into such stones, earning money by selling them to gristmills. Blueberries, maple syrup, and handmade barrel hoops were other key sources of income. The trail led to a small abandoned graveyard. A handsome four-sided marker memorialized the four young children of George and Rachel Coddington. It's a beautiful place to hike, but a lonely place to rest.

A cabin built about 1890 has been preserved. Candles and kerosene lamps provided light; water came from a spring down the hill. Our brochure drew attention to a large boulder by the home; a shelf was cut out for use in cooking and washing.

******

The Mohonk Mountain House on Mohonk Lake, high on a ridge above New Paltz, just minutes from New York Thruway Exit 18, seems a world apart. The oldest part of the seven-story hotel dates to 1878; several stone sections and a brown shingled segment were added between then and 1910. Described in brochures as Victorian and Edwardian in architecture, complete with turrets, towers, and broad covered porches, the effect comes across as part castle, part grand hotel, and part bungalow run amuck!

Every employee seemed to know the history of the complex. One Alfred Smiley, a Quaker teacher in Providence, Rhode Island, came upon the spot during an outing in 1869. He fell in love with the site immediately, and, with his twin brother Albert, purchased the property. Stokes Tavern occupied the lakefront niche then, and the Smileys remade it into a forty-room inn.

Growth continued, with acquisition of enough land to total 7,500 acres, along with enlargement of the Mountain House. After a third brother, Daniel, joined the venture in 1881, the group developed gardens, and over sixty miles of carriage paths and hiking trails. They added such components of self-sufficiency as greenhouses, an electric power facility, and an icehouse. The fourth generation of Smileys now reigns over Mohonk.

There are 273 guest rooms, but Mohonk also welcomes day visitors. For a fee, individuals can park near a gatehouse and walk (or, in summer, take a jitney) to the main grounds.

On a perfect early spring day, we began with the three-and-a-quarter-mile hike to Sky Top. Though listed in the Mohonk brochure as strenuous, the wide shale path should be accessible to anyone in reasonable physical condition.

Our destination, Paltz Point, marked the edge of a prominent ridge. Along the way we could overlook the Mohonk gardens. Odell Outlook provided an awesome view of the surrounding valley. A cliff dropped straight below us, and we spotted a blue-shirted climber working his way to the top. Gnarled pines fought for survival at the rock's edge.

Sky Top Tower, built in 1923 as a tribute to Albert Smiley, offered an even more panoramic vista from the top of its winding staircase. Made of stone, Sky Top replaced three prior wooden structures built as fire observation points. Two of those towers burned. This stone replacement served as an official fire-watch point until the 1970s.

Another route, The Eagle Cliff Trail, brought us through hemlock groves to remarkable views of the Trapps, prominent cliff ridges in the area. At the Huntington Gazebo, we had a great look at the Trapps and the Clove Valley. Going a bit farther, we found a gazebo (have I told you that there are 127 rustic gazebos on the Mohonk property?) perilously perched atop Artists' Rock from which we saw—and I quote the trail guide—a "breathtaking view of Sky Top (Paltz Point) with its sheer 300-foot cliff."

I'd strongly recommend that day trippers make reservations for a meal. Breakfasts and lunches are above-average, hearty buffets, and dinner truly sparkles. More importantly, this allows access inside. An alcove near the entrance presents the history of the hotel in text and vintage photos. Spacious public rooms with high ceilings combine grandeur and informality. Lake Lounge, with its fireplaces, proves an inviting spot for afternoon tea and cookies. The library off the Winter Lounge lays claim to being the first in an American hotel. And there's no end of hallways to explore.

Information:
Mohonk Preserve, Box 715, New Paltz, NY 12561. Phone 845-255-0919.
Mohonk Mountain House, Lake Mohonk, New Paltz, NY 12561. Phone 800-772-6646.

Albany • Thacher Park

Albany's history goes back to Henry Hudson and the discovery of the river that bears his name. Dutch arrivals settled first, later to be supplanted by British colonization of New York. Fur trading spurred the early economy of the area. Arrival of the Erie Canal brought new heights of prosperity, as did the railroad.

Iron casting became a major industry during the nineteenth century. In 1875, fifteen companies were turning out wood stoves. Agricultural equipment came from Albany factories. The modern billiard ball, fashioned from celluloid when ivory became a rare commodity, emanated from Albany. So did lots of beer. The Dutch established breweries early, and the tradition lasted into the 1970s.

Most of all, though, Albany centered around politics. Having beaten out Hudson for designation as the state capital in 1797, this city has been synonymous with government ever since. Five presidents (and four candidates who lost elections), a vice president, and two chief justices of the Supreme Court sprang from power bases in Albany.

The Albany Heritage Area Visitor Center provides a nice refresher course on area history.

We learned that early Albany was a stockaded city, guarded by Fort Orange, a garrison built along the Hudson River. Construction on roadways along the water unearthed evidence of this early occupation. Archaeology now seems to be a major interest of local residents.

Scale models depict the walled Albany settlement of 1695. A couple of handsome black stoves represent the varied output of that industry, and there's a bottle of Beverwyck beer. Other items range from early native wampum beads, to animal furs, to the largest (and still structurally integral) artifact, a brick smokestack for boilers that drove pumps when this building operated as a waterworks.

One alcove detailed Albany's involvement in the Underground Railroad. Other panels related economic, political, and transportation history. Superb color photographs provided a preview of nearby architecture.

We picked up walking-tour brochures and began exploring.

Right next door there's a lone remnant of the early Dutch occupancy. Quackenbush House, the oldest building in the city, dates to 1736. Constructed with brick from Pieter Quackenbush's brickyard, and enlarged in 1790, this served as home for seven generations of the Quackenbush family before being sold in 1868.

Crossing a small park dedicated to Raoul Wallenberg, whose efforts saved thousands of Jews from Nazi extermination during World War II, we reached the First Church of Albany. Built in 1798, this is the city's oldest religious establishment. Other churches on our route included St. Mary's Roman Catholic (paintings on the ceiling and alongside the altar make the interior beautiful), and St. Peter's Episcopal.

Houses rented by President Martin Van Buren and fledgling author Herman Melville no longer stand, but there's a nice sampling of venerable residential areas along Columbia and Elk streets. The Kenmore Hotel, hangout for gangsters like Legs Diamond in its heyday, has become an office building. Its lobby has been restored to elegance with columns, a fountain, and skylit atrium.

The New York State Court of Appeals proved a highlight. The columned white marble exterior looks more modern than would be expected for 1842 construction. Inside, an atrium stretches to a dome painted with the mural *Romance of the Skies*. The beautiful courtroom gives a truly magisterial impression. Oak paneled walls, carved wooden ceiling, and rows of portraiture convey the necessary aura of wisdom and sober judgment.

Our walk brought us near the state capitol, completed after a mere twenty-five years of effort, and Empire Square Plaza, the mix of museum, office complex, and performing arts center spearheaded by Governor Nelson Rockefeller in the 1960s. Thirty-six tall columns, comprising the longest colonnade in America, front the State Education Building. City Hall (1882) is a wonderful Henry Hobson Richardson creation of granite and brownstone. Its atrium extends the full height of the building, and the bell tower features a forty-nine-bell carillon.

Formidable bank buildings along State Street reminded us that Albany still ranks as the twentieth largest banking center in the country. At State and Broadway sits a building reminiscent of a flatiron, but with a rounded nose.

A right on Broadway brought us to the Delaware and Hudson

Building. Now housing central administration for the State University of New York (SUNY), this onetime railroad headquarters features Gothic design. Flags representing each SUNY campus decorate the long, vaulted corridors.

Atop outer walls of the former post office, now the James T. Foley U.S. Courthouse and the Custom House, are marble friezes. One depicts the processes of mail delivery. Inside, marble, decorative cast aluminum, and elegant writing stands give the impression of quite a sumptuous place in which to mail a letter. The 186-foot-long lobby ceiling boasts nine colorfully painted maps interspersed with relief sculptures of notable Americans featured on postage stamps.

Next came Union Station, bespeaking the grandeur appropriate to a major rail terminal, and a Beaux Arts creation built in 1900 as a trolley headquarters. Another block returned us to our starting point at Quackenbush Square.

We concluded our day by experiencing the Hudson River Way. Going above highway and rail track, this pedestrian bridge restores the historic link between downtown and the Hudson River. Lampposts painted with subjects of local significance make the walk across more interesting. Once by the river, there's access to Riverside Park with its amphitheater, green space, and miles of trail for biking or hiking.

******

Barely twenty miles southwest of Albany stands John Boyd Thacher State Park. In 1914, Emma Thacher donated land to New York State in memory of her husband, a state legislator and former mayor of Albany. Subsequently enlarged, the 1,800-acre park includes the Helderberg Escarpment, one of New York's most dramatic geologic features.

In essence a rock ledge several miles long, the escarpment resulted from the erosion of softer sedimentary rocks adjoining more resistant limestone. Along with the dramatic cliffs, the processes of nature have led to cave formation and underground streams. Fossil lovers will find a wealth of examples to study. Bird watchers can look for 171 avian species catalogued here. Those who come simply for the scenery will be more than amply rewarded, as views from the 1,300-foot-high ridge are extraordinary.

We began with the Cliff Top Trail, a 2.3-mile level path at the edge of the escarpment. Signs continually remind of the importance to respect split-rail fencing along the rim. The trail occasionally passes through picnic areas, giving easy access to restrooms and tables for snacking. Don't be surprised if a family reunion or a wedding fills a pavilion. Thacher Park has been the site for many such family occasions.

Scenic vistas are omnipresent. Gazing upon adjacent cliffs has its fascination. In the distance, look for the Catskill Mountains, the Berkshires, and even the Adirondacks. We could see the government buildings and performance center (The Egg) on the Capitol Mall in Albany. Closer at hand, there's a wonderful patchwork of valley, forest, and farmland. From the Glen Doone Lookout, we watched a farmer mow his field into windrows. More than a few turkey vultures gliding on air currents followed our progress.

Branching off the Cliff Top Trail is the locally famed Indian Ladder Trail. Well worth the detour, this descends from the top of the escarpment, down steel staircases about sixty feet, to a well-worn cleft in the rock face.

Native Americans used this route to reach Henry Hudson's early trading post; later, they depended on it as a gathering place. They indeed fashioned a tree into a ladder to traverse a particularly steep segment. Amazingly, this became part of the Indian Ladder Road used by nineteenth-century settlers moving goods (and later tourists) between Albany and the Schoharie Valley.

Along the 0.4-mile walk, we followed boardwalks over underground outlet streams, watched waterfalls arch over our heads, and studied the layers of sedimentary rock. A few caves present themselves. Particularly impressive are areas in which softer layers of limestone have eroded, leaving overhanging rock above. Signs "reassuringly" pointed out that most rockfalls occur after heavy water flow during the spring thaw!

In all there are over twelve miles of trail in Thacher Park, with connections to longer walking routes. The nearby Emma Treadwell Thacher Nature Center offers additional short loops. It's also well worth taking time to examine the exhibits in the Center.

Information:
Albany Heritage Area Visitor Center, 25 Quackenbush Square, Albany, NY 12207. Phone 518-434-0405 or 800-258-3582.
John Boyd Thacher State Park, 1 Hailes Cave Road, Voorheesville, NY 12186. Phone 518-872-1237.

Indian Ladder Trail at Thacher Park

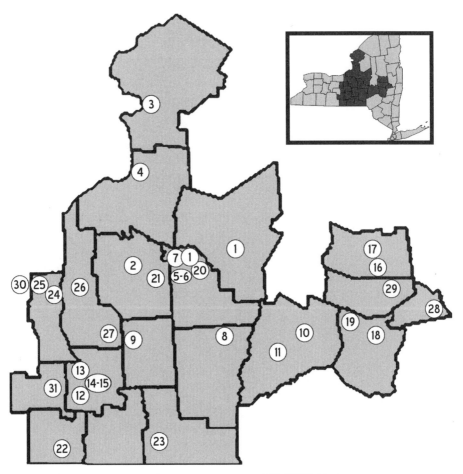

1.	Old Erie Canal State Park	17.	Willie Wildlife Marsh
2.	Camillus	18.	Howe Caverns
3.	Sackets Harbor	19.	Sharon Springs
4.	Selkirk Shores	20.	Oneida
5.	Cazenovia	21.	Pratt's Falls
6.	Stone Quarry	22.	Elmira
7.	Chittenango Falls	23.	Endicott
8.	Rogers Environmental Center	24.	Seneca Falls
9.	Homer	25.	Waterloo
10.	Cooperstown	26.	Auburn
11.	Gilbert Lake	27.	Fillmore Glen
12.	Robert Treman State Park	28.	Schenectady Stockade
13.	Taughannock Falls	29.	Schoharie Crossing
14.	Cornell University	30.	Geneva
15.	Cornell Plantations	31.	Watkins Glen
16.	Johnstown		

CENTRAL – LEATHERSTOCKING

I'm defining central New York quite loosely as an area west of Interstate 88, south of the Adirondacks, and through most of the Finger Lakes. It includes what is commonly referred to as Leatherstocking Country, the Mohawk River valley, and much of the Southern Tier.

Construction of the Erie Canal opened much of this region to development. Some villages expected the canal but were bypassed by the project; a few, like Cazenovia, nonetheless flourished. Waterpower served to make industrial sites. Relocation of much manufacturing elsewhere during the mid-twentieth century led to economic decline in many communities. Walking tours reveal much of this history.

Glaciation and river erosion produced geologic wonders in the Finger Lakes and nearby glens. Day hikes give a sense of these impressive features.

Ideas as well as cargo traveled the Erie Canal. Walks point out the beginnings of women's movements in America and some utopian experiments.

Old Erie Canal State Park • Camillus

Daring though the concept of a canal from Lake Erie to the Hudson River must have seemed in 1816, Dewitt Clinton managed to convince New York's legislature to support the idea. When completed, the Erie Canal not only represented an engineering marvel, but a major spur to economic growth. Settlement blossomed all along the waterway. Buffalo grew into a major city. New York City became the busiest port in America.

A financial success right from the start, canal construction had been completely paid off within a decade. By 1835, work began to enlarge "Clinton's Ditch" from forty feet wide and four feet deep to a channel seventy wide and seven deep. Although the process didn't reach completion until 1862, freight and passenger traffic increased sufficiently to allow elimination of all tolls by 1882.

Railroads threatened to cut into canal revenue. Indeed, trains began to carry much of the cargo between New York and the upper Midwest. Still, the canal stayed busy enough that by 1903, the state committed to yet another enlargement of the system.

This time, a decision was made to utilize existing waterways, thus eliminating the need to build expensive aqueducts over rivers and streams. The Seneca River was incorporated into the route. And although the newer Barge Canal follows closely the course of the original Erie Canal in the western half of the state, east of Syracuse innovative movable dams allowed the route to take advantage of the Mohawk River.

What wasn't foreseen was the explosive growth of the automobile and the highway system. The twentieth century saw a continual diminution of the need of a canal for trade. Opening of the St. Lawrence Seaway gave new access to midwestern ports from the Atlantic Ocean, further obviating the need for the Barge Canal. Commercial traffic dwindled, ceasing completely in 1994.

Old Erie Canal State Park comprises a thirty-six-mile segment of canal that, though bypassed by today's Barge Canal system, remains naturally filled with water. It offers possibilities for canoeing, biking, and hiking, while giving a sense of canal ambience during the nineteenth century.

Beginning off Butternut Drive in Dewitt, just east of Syracuse, the route quickly passes a series of interpretive signs. Within a mile of walking, one sees maps of the canal's enlargement in 1862, learns a little about local plant and animal life, and begins to understand how the canal not only transported goods, but also new settlers and new ideas. Not by coincidence did western New York become such a hotbed of religious revival and reform during the mid-1800s.

Following the towpath on which mules pulled boats about fifteen miles a day, we came to Butternut Creek Aqueduct. The impressive stonework introduces one to the solid construction typical of canal efforts. Few sights testify better to the audacity of canal builders than the image of carrying the canal trough over rivers and streams along the way.

There are many access points to the trail, some of them in the midst of villages spurred by canal traffic and surviving after such commerce ended. Chittenango had a grain elevator by 1851 and had active canning operations through the 1940s. The local garden club has planted trees appropriate to the canal era.

The Chittenango Landing Museum offers insight into the canal heyday. The main building pays homage to canneries operating here from early canal days through the 1940s. Remains of a dry-dock facility give a sense for nineteenth-century boat repair. Volunteers are building a ninety-six-foot canal boat with methods appropriate to an earlier time.

From Chittenango, it's a gentle and peaceful seven-mile hike to Canastota. To my amazement, we actually passed a couple of people fly-fishing at one spot. There's another smaller canal museum here, plus, of all things, the International Boxing Hall of Fame. The Canastota post office features a canal-themed New Deal mural.

The route intersects with the Barge Canal at Lock 21, allowing an opportunity to watch boats being locked through if the timing is right.

Old Erie Canal State Park terminates in Rome, near Erie Canal Village, a replica nineteenth-century town. Another worthy objective in Rome is Fort Stanwix, the reconstruction of an important stronghold during the American Revolution.

******

Camillus is another useful point from which to ponder the canal. It's the exact midpoint of the revamped route operational from 1836 through 1917—175.47 miles to Albany, 175.91 to Buffalo. Local history buffs in the Town of Camillus, just outside Syracuse, have been instrumental in preserving canal structures, including an aqueduct.

Seven miles of abandoned canal, dry since 1922, have been cleared and filled. Towpaths have been similarly reclaimed, giving a four-mile path for hiking or biking. There's road access at each end of the park, and to the cluster of buildings at the center. A tour boat operates during the summer.

Sims' Store, built in 1856, served canal travelers for years. Long out of use, it burned in 1963. A reconstruction, open on weekends, offers interesting displays. I liked a diorama of longer locks built near the end of the canal's heyday. Using just one extra mule, canal men could pull double loads, thus presaging the tractor-trailers that run on our highways today. Also check out the diagrams of a stump puller, one of the more ingenious inventions of early engineers.

Photos and re-creations depict the offerings of Sims' Store in its busier days. Note the clay pipes, products of one of three such factories once active in Camillus.

Outside we roamed over to a lock-tender shanty, an original lock gate, and a blue and yellow buoy boat from the 1930s. A small tobacco patch stands testimony to an important area crop once upon a time.

The towpath runs about two miles in each direction from Sims' Store. Terrain is flat, and therefore easy walking. About a mile to the east, we came to Nine Mile Creek Aqueduct. Volunteers are at work restoring the 140-foot-long stone structure. Originally built in 1844, it's another fine example of the construction methods brought into play almost two centuries ago.

Information:
Old Erie Canal State Historic Park, R. D. 2, Andrus Road, Kirkville, NY

13082. Phone 315-687-7821.

Erie Canal Park, Town of Camillus, 5750 Devoe Road, Camillus, NY 13031. Phone 315-672-5110.

Chittenango Falls

Sackets Harbor • Selkirk Shores

With the Revolutionary War over and settlement proceeding in northern New York, one Augustus Sacket, a New York City attorney, came north to seek his fortune. In 1801, he found a protected harbor on Lake Ontario. The port, combined with the rich timber resources nearby, promised to make him a wealthy man.

Sacket began to prosper, especially with trade in potash, a key ingredient in gunpowder. What he hadn't envisioned, however, was renewal of British-American hostilities, leading the young colony to pass an Embargo Act in 1808.

The law prohibited commerce with England and its colonies. Sacket and his compatriots sold their goods largely to Canada. When the naval battleship *Oneida* arrived to enforce the embargo in 1809, Sacket picked up and left.

Once the War of 1812 began, the British attacked that ship. Their effort failed, but the American army decided to make Sackets Harbor the northern headquarters for troops. Zebulon Pike became their leader.

Great Britain attacked again in May 1813. Though outmanned, the Americans held their ground in what became known as the Battle of Sackets Harbor.

After the War of 1812, the harbor declined as a shipbuilding center. In 1815, the Army established a presence with Madison Barracks. A naval station opened in the 1830s. Combined civilian commerce and military growth led Sackets Harbor into an era of prosperity. A resort community also began to develop.

The navy, army, and New York Central Railroad all left Sackets Harbor after World War II, leading to a downturn in the economy. The population, over 4,000 in the mid-1800s, dropped to just 1,313 in 1990. Heritage tourism now bids to bring new growth to the area.

Our visit began at Augustus Sacket's home, an 1801 Palladian-style mansion used as both officers' quarters and hospital during the war. Now the house, directly across from a marina and the village bandstand, serves as a Visitor Center. Exhibits oriented us to the area's history.

An excellent booklet available at Sacket Mansion helped guide us on a walking tour.

The variety of architectural styles is remarkable for such a small village. We passed Italianate homes, ornate Queen Anne houses, and compact Greek Revival cottages. A few places were particularly noteworthy, including the three-part, limestone George Tisdale House and the elegant Corinthian-columned George Sacket House. The Elisha Camp House, a beautiful Federal brick home built in 1816, is still occupied by descendants of the original family.

Among notable churches are the United Presbyterian (1900) with round windows, a tall square tower, and Tiffany stained glass, and Christ Episcopal, featuring a trio of Gothic arches. Though small, downtown had its own architectural gems. Brick Italianate storefronts caught our eye; so did the Central House Hotel.

We continued with a walk around the battlefield. Plaques detail the attack of May 29, 1813, giving a sense of British strategy and the American defense. Fort Tompkins has critical significance. Elevated above wooden cribs filled with stone, this was the fortification that protected the harbor. British soldiers were never able to penetrate its walls.

Enemy troops finally retreated to Horse Island, there to board ships and return to Kingston. Their casualties exceeded 30 percent.

At one time the grounds had returned to farmland. However, citizens recognizing the historical significance established a park by 1864. Improvements accompanied observance of the Battle of Sackets Harbor Centennial in 1913, when Franklin D. Roosevelt came to dedicate a monument. The state park system eventually assumed responsibility, ensuring Sackets Harbor State Historic Site will continue to tell an important story of survival for a fledgling America.

We completed our day with a walk through Madison Barracks, one of America's first specifically designed military bases. It's a very appealing campus. Old Stone Row housed soldiers as far back as 1816. One was Ulysses S. Grant, who spent two tours of duty here before his days of heroism during the Civil War. Five handsome brick buildings were home to officers. Fiorello LaGuardia grew up in one; his father led the 11th Infantry band.

Much of the base, now in private hands, has been redeveloped for residential and commercial purposes. One impressive building still awaiting reuse is the limestone hospital, which sits right at the lakefront. Dr. Samuel Guthrie allegedly pioneered the use of chloroform for anesthesia here in 1832.

Perhaps the most unique structure is the water tower. Built in 1892 in Romanesque Revival style, complete with observation deck on top, this edifice would seem at home in King Arthur's time as easily as in the nineteenth and twentieth centuries.

Sackets Harbor has its share of small museums to visit.

The Pickering-Beach Home (1817), donated to the village when the last family member died in 1941, holds an interesting assortment of furnishings and curiosities.

The former Union Hotel is one of the village's most impressive buildings. Built in 1817 at the beginning of Sackets Harbor's prosperity, this stately four-story stone edifice now serves as the Seaway Trail Discovery Center.

Two homes built for the Naval Station in the 1840s are part of Sackets Harbor Battlefield State Historic Site. The Lieutenant's House has been in continuous use since 1847. Inside are displays pertinent to the Battle of Sackets Harbor.

The Commandant's House, accessed only by guided tour, has been restored to its appearance in the mid-1860s.

******

Port Ontario, on the eastern end of Lake Ontario, was once expected to become a major harbor and commercial center. Settled early in the nineteenth century, the Port Ontario Land Company had begun formal development by the 1830s. Within forty years, however, the village of Oswego had clearly surpassed Port Ontario in importance. Considerable land stayed untouched as the population dwindled.

In 1925 New York State acquired some of this land and added Selkirk Shores to the state park system. Civilian Conservation Corps workers built cabins, campsites, and other facilities during the 1930s. Subsequent land purchases brought the park to almost a thousand acres in size.

A network of short trails offers gentle hiking. The routes are broad and well maintained, with almost no hills along the way.

We began on the Red Trail, which initially brought us through a maple-dominated hardwood forest. When we diverted onto the Blue Trail, we began to see evergreens, especially tall pines, and large white birches.

Several trees forge unique personalities! The thick trunk of one pine split into three parallel, straight posts as it reached for the sky. Acorns on the ground alerted us to oaks above us. We passed two more pretty pine groves as we completed our two-mile loop.

Separate from the above network is an easy trail (with a parallel asphalt bike trail) along the bluff above the lake. There aren't many unobstructed views until one passes a nicely shaded picnic area and then reaches the park beach. But there are spots where it's possible to look out over the broad vista of Lake Ontario. Expansion of this lakeside trail would make Selkirk Shores a more attractive destination.

Right here you're in the heart of the "lake effect," so central to northern New York winters. Many of the region's legendary snowstorms come from this area. Lands to the east, including the Tug Hill Plateau, have some of the state's largest snow accumulations. Cross-country skiers would find Selkirk Shores a nice warm-up preparatory to more strenuous outings.

Information:
Sackets Harbor Battlefield State Historic Site, 504 West Main Street, Sackets Harbor, NY 13685. Phone 315-646-3634.
Pickering-Beach Museum, 501 West Main Street, Sackets Harbor, NY 13685. Phone 315-646-1529.
Augustus Sacket Mansion (Sackets Harbor Visitor Center), 301 West Main Street, Sackets Harbor, NY 13685. Phone 315-646-2321.
Selkirk Shores State Park, 7101 State Route 3, Pulaski, NY 13142. Phone 315-298-5737.

Cazenovia • Stone Quarry • Chittenango Falls

Back in the 1790s, John Lincklaen came to set up Cazenovia, just east of present-day Syracuse. The unusual name derives from Theophile de Cazenove, Philadelphia-based American representative for financiers in the Netherlands. It turns out Dutch investors became quite enamored of opportunity in America during the 1780s. The Holland Land Company ultimately purchased well over five million acres in New York and Pennsylvania.

As agent of the Holland Land Company, Lincklaen laid out a street plan for the village, built his own mansion (Lorenzo), and awaited inevitable prosperity. Early New York turnpikes brought settlers. Agriculture flourished. A seminary opened.

What wasn't anticipated, however, was the Erie Canal. When that engineering marvel (and subsequently, the railroad) bypassed Cazenovia, growth halted. The great city Lincklaen envisioned never came into being.

Such events may have discouraged Lincklaen and his early settlers. But the vicissitudes of history sometimes leave silver linings. When America entered its so-called Gilded Age after the Civil War, Cazenovia Lake became a favored summer resort, a sedate alternative to the wilder activities of Newport, Rhode Island.

Summer cottages sprung up (they called them cottages; we'd term them mansions). The seminary became the nucleus for a college. Beautiful residential avenues were spared development pressures. Unspoiled four-mile Cazenovia Lake remained a vacation draw. The automobile era brought travelers pleased to find a village little changed from the nineteenth century.

Cazenovia turns out to be a wonderful place for strolling. A brochure suggested five possible walking tours; we did them all. If you'd like to brush up on the differences between, say, Queen Anne, Federal, and Italianate architecture, this is the place to do so.

Albany Street, the main thoroughfare, is a treasure chest of architectural styles. Gothic Revival Bob-O-Link, currently the town offices, looked especially appealing. My favorite place was Century House. Facing Cannon Park (home to a Farmers' Market in season), this Greek

Revival home features two-story Corinthian columns, slate mansard roof, and two covered porches.

There's a classic nineteenth-century downtown core, with the decided advantage of having almost every storefront thriving. The public rooms of Lincklaen House, a hotel dating to 1835, are worth a visit.

The library, a formidable 1820s Greek Revival, has a new addition tucked unobtrusively behind. It boasts a Museum of Curiosities. Mainly gifts from townspeople over the years, holdings run the gamut from Chippewa beadwork, to an elephant trap from Ceylon, to locks made by the Cazenovia Lock Company before it sold out to Yale Lock in 1878. And how many small-town libraries have their own Egypt room, complete with mummy? The older section has been remodeled into comfortably furnished reading rooms, emulating Victorian parlors with intricate moldings and marble fireplaces.

Chenango, Mill, and Sullivan streets had their own highlights. Then we walked a bit along Chittenango Creek, past Carpenter's Pond to Lakeland Park. Here lawns roll down to the lakeshore. A gazebo provides a nice spot for sitting and appreciating the view.

Lincklaen Street is another handsome residential area, with styles ranging from Greek Revival and Italianate, to gambreled Dutch Revival and bungalow. Adjacent Cazenovia College, founded in 1824, includes very pretty public areas. Williams Hall, built of stone and with a handsome brick facade, anchors the campus.

******

Another satisfying walk can be found at nearby Stone Quarry Hill Art Park, a mile east of Cazenovia. Founded by Robert and Dorothy Riester in 1991, this 104-acre property not only preserves a beautiful environment, but challenges with its outdoor sculptures, many of them created specifically for the site. Some, including recent works fashioned of hay and straw, are specifically designed to gradually recycle back to nature.

We walked most segments of the interconnecting four-mile trail network. The routes ranged from open hilltop, to hardwood forest, to a mown grassy trail around a meadow alongside an excavated former quarry site. Remnants of stone fences add texture, while strategically placed benches beckon for rest and meditation. From the Vista Trail we could see Oneida Lake, thirty-five miles away, while nearby Cazenovia Lake came into view at the crest of Old Quarry Trail.

The short Hilltop Habitat Trail runs near an A-frame studio and shop. An accompanying brochure adds insights into flora and fauna of varying habitats—garden, pond, hedgerow, meadow, and woods.

Man-made creations blended remarkably well into the various landscapes. There's a ceramic that resembles a cut tree trunk, a monstrous creation of willows, and a boxed, open-air enclosure entitled *Meditation Space*. *Rhythm Trail*, built of wood slats and pipe over a narrow trench, urges one to walk down it with a strumming stick. Tall glass plates with etched images form a 9/11 Memorial.

I'll best remember *Contemplating Man* as the emblem of the park. Sculpted of copper on steel armature by Dorothy Riester, still an active artist well into her eighties, the figure gazes from the hilltop out onto the grand rural vista. The view encompasses the gift the Riesters have given all of us who take the time to visit.

******

A few miles from the village of Cazenovia, Chittenango Falls flows through a narrow gorge. The cascade supported a stone quarry, sawmills, and a paper mill during the 1800s.

When a gunpowder manufacturer bought the property in 1887, Helen Lincklaen Fairchild sought to preserve this beautiful spot for public use. She formed the Chittenango Falls Park Association before purchasing the land for use as a public park. In 1922, New York added Chittenango to the state park system.

Signs explain the formation of the gorge and its falls during the last ice age, a mere twelve thousand years ago. The water cuts through fossil-laden ledges of limestone and dolomite. There are some rare plants here, and the Chittenango ovate amber snail, found nowhere else in the world. But it's the sheer force of water that attracts visitors.

I find this one of the most fascinating waterfalls in the state. It can't claim the sheer raw power of Niagara, nor the romanticism that made Kaaterskill so popular among Hudson River school painters, nor the mythology that surrounds Buttermilk Falls near Long Lake. But each level of rock gives Chittenango Falls a different look.

We gazed into the chasm, feeling the full height of the falls' descent. A trail took us from the picnic area down stone steps and wood staircases to a lookout point, where trees perfectly framed the scene.

There's a wonderful mix of water effects. A broad flow at the top is fed by a shorter falls and a narrow "stairstep" tributary at the far end, widening to a lacy network of water with continual variations in texture. After a ferocious flow down most of the 167-foot height, the roiling current forms more of a bridal-veil effect down a series of rock steps.

We continued down a rocky (and somewhat slippery) trail to another viewpoint, and then followed switchbacks to a footbridge just downstream from the falls. From the bridge, there's a commanding view of the entire falls. It's entrancing. We could have stayed for hours watching the variations in texture as the water traversed the rocky ledges.

Climbing up the east side, we had another spectacular vantage point and new close-up perspectives. My wife Marty noted one hardy cedar growing straight out of the rock, its roots cantilevered at an angle from the ground.

There are other places to walk in the state park. Options include forested areas and a few spots of meadow with tall grass. The Chips Trail derives its name from the Skaneateles Charcoal Chips chapter of the National Campers and Hikers Association; they created the route in 1982.

Information:
Cazenovia Chamber of Commerce, 59 Albany Street, Cazenovia, NY 13035. Phone 315-655-9243.
Stone Quarry Hill Art Park, 3883 Stone Quarry Road, Cazenovia, NY 13035. Phone 315-655-3196.
Chittenango Falls State Park, 2300 Rathbun Road, Cazenovia, NY 13035. Phone 315-655-9620.

Rogers Environmental Center • Homer

Rogers Environmental Education Center in northern Chenango County offers a nicely interpreted network of trails, plus a host of interesting exhibits. Previously this had been the site of Sherburne Game Farm, operated by Harry and Gertrude Rogers. Begun by the Rogers' in 1909, this was once the longest continually operating facility of its kind in the United States. Transition to an educational nature preserve run by New York's Department of Environmental Conservation serves as a fitting memorial.

Several of the trails begin at the Visitor Center, and then crisscross the six hundred acres of preserved land. There are also two remote trailheads. We briefly looked at an outdoor composting demonstration. Nearby there's a unique living willow structure, woven in the shape of a geodesic dome. It would be interesting to return regularly and see how this evolves over the years.

First on the agenda was Channels Trail. It's a flat 0.7-mile stroll with a few boardwalks. Education focused on wetlands, an oft-neglected aspect of our terrain. Over half of America's wetlands have disappeared over time, raising important questions for environmental advocates.

Our printed guide helped us see the adjacent marsh not as an inconvenience to be filled, but as a sponge that helps absorb excess rainfall and snowmelt, while also serving as a breeding ground for a vast assortment of birds and fish. Though we didn't spot many species from the observation decks along the trail, we certainly heard sounds that confirmed their presence. Wetlands also play a key cleansing role, helping to remove nitrogen and phosphorus that accumulate from agricultural and human use.

By definition, marsh includes only soft-stemmed plants, while swamps are filled with shrubs and trees. Here we saw plenty of both. The green layer of duckweed on the water's surface, not slimy as one might expect, provides an important food source for ducks, geese, and muskrats. Insects are part of that food chain. One species we did see in abundance was dragonflies.

It's instructive to realize these waters flow eventually into Chesapeake Bay. Thus, what happens to the environment here can have a

148

significant impact on the important fisheries of that distant region.

Next we did the 0.3-mile Spruce Ridge Trail. Emphasis here turns to wildlife management. Norway spruce trees, planted during the 1930s by Civilian Conservation Corps workers, give shelter, prevent erosion, and add a pleasing fragrance to the air. There's also pine, cedar, and ash in this forest. Natural and man-made nesting areas are pointed out, as are issues of invasive plant species that threaten to crowd out naturally occurring ones.

South Trail (0.4 mile) goes along the Chenango River. It has ecological succession as its theme. The brochure calls attention to the changes that overtake an abandoned field, or that gradually fill in a marsh. As soil characteristics are altered, different plants will thrive, with ultimate evolution toward a climax forest. Every dead log will play a role! The river's flow also continues to be a force for perpetual change.

Across the road lie the Farm Tower Trail and Pine Ridge Trail.

The Pine Ridge Trail includes a few different ecosystems. There's a white pine forest, and also sections dominated by hardwoods, especially aspen. These aspen are early arrivals in the forest. Over time, they'll be overtaken by taller species before falling, decaying, and becoming part of the soil now beneath them.

Hedgerows and ground holes serve as shelter for various animals and birds, as do many of the young saplings. So does the occasional fallen tree, which, though dead itself, brings new life to fungi, mosses, and a host of flora and fauna. Even the huge boulder erratic will eventually be worn down into soil, thereby making its own contribution to the environment.

From the Pine Ridge Trail, we veered onto the Farm Tower Trail. Though only a half mile in length, this uphill climb took more energy than we had expended on the other routes. Our exertion was suitably rewarded. From the top we enjoyed a panoramic view over the Chenango Valley and its rolling farmland.

Exhibits inside the Visitor Center also deserve attention. Taxidermy is highlighted by a great horned owl, and a red-tailed hawk positioned with wings spread. An Eastern forest scene includes fisher, wild turkey, and porcupine. At the bee exhibit in one corner, we could slide doors open and look down into the continuous vibration of activity inside the hive. And think about this when you complain how long it takes to make a meal—it takes a bee over forty thousand trips to a flower to make one pound of honey.

A quote from naturalist John Muir is posted: "When we try to pick anything by itself, we find it hitched to everything else in the universe." Time at the Rogers Center helps underscore that cautionary message.

******

Every small village has an interesting native son, a few notable snippets of history, and some architectural gems. It's just that Homer, in Cortland County, has packaged such assets into a very nicely conceived walking tour. There's beautiful rural scenery in all directions surrounding Homer—that's just a bonus.

Now a quiet place of ten thousand people, Homer companies once manufactured carriages, printing ink, fishing line, and wrenches. The Underground Railroad stopped here. So did four stagecoaches a day.

One of Abraham Lincoln's private secretaries hailed from Homer. So did Amelia Bloomer, a notable advocate for women's rights, but unfortunately best remembered for a type of clothing that bears her name.

Our walk began on Clinton Street at an unusual dark green building with red trim. It turned out to be a railroad watchtower, dating to 1854. A few steps away we came upon an octagon house, representative of a craze that swept upstate New York during the nineteenth century. The oldest home on the tour (1799) was just a few doors down.

Most of the remainder of the tour focused on Main Street. There are handsome public buildings, including Town Hall with its impressive dome and pediment. Marble stairs and oak woodwork mark the Phillips Free Library. Though not listed in our brochure, the post office has a WPA mural inside.

The compact downtown includes the formidable Union Building and the Barber Block, once containing a hardware store and an opera house.

There is no shortage of beautiful residential architecture. An especially pretty brick home, remodeled in the 1880s with dormers and a mansard roof, belonged to the family of Andrew Dixon White. He grew up to become the first president of Cornell University.

A simpler Federal home across the street was owned by David Hannum. He engineered one of history's greater hoaxes, the Cardiff Giant. Ballyhooing his "find" as an ancient human, Hannum confirmed P. T. Barnum's assertion that a sucker is born every minute.

We saw fine examples of other classic architectural styles—Greek Revival (one as old as 1836), Queen Anne (Elm Street has a host of them), and Federal (including the stately, thirty-two-room brick home built for prominent businessman Jedediah Barber in 1826).

Such is the wealth of fine homes in Homer that two of our favorites weren't listed on the walking tour. The Elizabeth Brewster House is an ornate Greek Revival. A gorgeous three-story Victorian near the corner of Elm and Main impressed us with its columned porches and windows.

Maple trees and a tile-roofed bandstand help distinguish the Village Green. The adjacent Homer Baptist Church, Romanesque in style and featuring a tall bell tower, was constructed from local brick. Then there's a more modest Federal building that was once a "temperance tavern"—whatever that means!

Information:
Rogers Environmental Education Center, 2721 State Highway 80, Sherburne, NY 13460. Phone 607-674-4017.
Cortland County Convention and Visitors Bureau, 34 Tompkins Street, Cortland, NY 13045. Phone 607-753-8463.

Cooperstown • Gilbert Lake

Contrary to what many people think, Cooperstown was not named for early American author James Fenimore Cooper, though his book *The Pioneer* centered around a fictionalized version of the village. Rather it was Cooper's father William whom the appellation honors.

A land speculator in New Jersey, Cooper bought up some 250,000 acres of the Otsego Patent in 1786. Instead of renting land, he sold off plots and held the mortgages. This chance for ownership lured settlers from New England and elsewhere.

By the 1800s Cooper presided over the most prosperous community west of Albany. Agriculture, especially a thriving hops industry, tied many people to the land. The Erie Canal and the railroads bypassed Cooperstown, however, and the village remained bucolic.

Other names have also become interwoven with local history—Augustus Busch, founder of Budweiser; the Clark family, scions of attorney Edward Clark, who partnered with sewing machine manufacturer Isaac Singer; and Abner Doubleday, promulgated by some as the inventor of baseball.

Informative guided tours are offered during summer and fall. A visitor can also pick up a nicely annotated map and explore on one's own.

On Pioneer Street, just off Main, a stone building called The Smithy (1786) holds title as the oldest structure in town. Originally a blacksmith shop, it still holds remnants of forges and bellows. A gallery now occupies the space.

The original courthouse stood at Main and Pioneer. Grounds included the wood-framed jail (even bars were wooden, facilitating frequent escapes), stocks, whipping post, and hanging yard. Farther along Pioneer stands an unobtrusive real estate office built in 1830. Abner Doubleday lived here while attending military school. Go one more block and you'll see the lake.

Otsego Lake, enshrined by James Fenimore Cooper as "Glimmerglass," attracts natives and visitors alike to its shores. Ten steamboats once plied the waters, but now there are only pleasure boats. Lakefront Park, with its bandstand and terraced lawns, makes a good place to contemplate the scene. Look for Kingfisher Tower, a piece of ornamentation built to resemble a medieval castle. As you ponder, consider how this lake serves as headwaters of the Susquehanna River, which continues to Chesapeake Bay, some four hundred miles away.

At the corner of Lake and Fair streets stands Greystone, a beautiful Federal home dating to 1831. One block down on Lake Street is Edgewater, a trim 1813 brick Federal built for Isaac, William Cooper's fourth child. Isaac was one Cooperstown resident not enamored of baseball. He saw the game as a nuisance and worked to ban it from the streets.

From Council Rock Park, at the end of River Street, look for the namesake rock peeking above the water. The Iroquois once used this as a meeting place. Go up River to Main, where stands a 1790 frame structure that's the oldest residence in town. Across the street find a handsome stone home with rows of herringbone design. William Cooper built this for his daughter, Ann.

Continue on River Street past examples of Gothic Revival, and then look for the Cooper plot in Christ Churchyard. The entire family's remains rest here, plus those of Joseph Stewart, "Born a slave ... loved and faithful free servant of Judge Cooper."

The Baseball Hall of Fame sits on the block William Cooper selected for himself. Local lore reports his wife didn't want to come here, and that she had to be bodily put onto his wagon. Hopefully the large brick mansion her husband commissioned helped assuage those feelings. A statue of James Fenimore Cooper denotes that site.

The Clark family built the Hall of Fame, originally as a gymnasium. Edward Clark, the patent attorney who became Isaac Singer's partner, built a Greek Revival structure (Main and Fair streets) with ten Ionic columns for a YMCA; this now holds a library and village offices. Clark purchased the Otsego Bank across the street as an office for his family's enterprises.

Cooperstown is a place for wandering—along its pretty streets, by the lake, and to other attractions besides the Baseball Hall of Fame. The Otesaga, a venerable resort hotel on Lake Street, deserves a visit. Fenimore House, home to the New York State Historical Association, holds wonderful collections of folk art and Native American artifacts.

Save some energy for The Farmers' Museum, a re-creation of a nineteenth-century farming community. Stroll toward the Printing Office and see how a flatbed press turned out 240 four-page copies an hour. Stop in the Pharmacy and observe processes for making pills and gel caps. Find the skeleton stored in a closet of Dr. Jackson's Office.

At the Lippitt Farmstead, there's a red clapboard home, the canvas-roofed turkey house, and a pigpen featuring red Durocs, a breed established in 1823. Look also at the hop house, where exhibits explain the processes of drying and storing this critical brewing ingredient. During the 1800s, New York led the nation in hop production.

Other exhibits at The Farmers' Museum include a broom-making shop, and the American Paper-Staining Manufactory, which still produces replicas of historic wallpaper. Under a blue and white tent, you'll find the Cardiff Giant. A ten-foot carved gypsum figure, this "ancient man" attracted hundreds of paying visitors daily before being exposed as a hoax.

End with an uphill walk to the Seneca Log House, built around 1780 for a Seneca family and used until 1930. Relocated here in the 1990s, the solid hewn-log structure with shake roof interprets Seneca life of the mid-nineteenth century.

******

Gilbert Lake State Park in Otsego County stands as a testament to the work of the Civilian Conservation Corps, one of the most successful New Deal work programs. What sets this place apart is the decision to memorialize those efforts of the CCC, not just with a monument, but with an interesting museum.

Named for a Revolutionary War veteran from Connecticut who settled in the area, Gilbert Lake saw the presence of mills and considerable logging over the years. In 1926, New York purchased the land for a new state park. Improvements began, but accelerated when the CCC located a camp here from 1933 to 1941.

Trails in the park traverse stands of red pine planted by CCC workers. We took an easy walk along the Deer Run Trail, beginning in pines, and then entering a mixed forest, some of it lined by lush rows of fern growth. The CCC Trail also starts amidst pines. This route passed an area of blowdown from a tornado that swept through in 1998. There's another route, a 2.5-mile loop to several ponds. When rain began to fall, we appreciated having the giant hemlocks as a shield.

A self-guided nature trail, 1.3 miles in length, circles the perimeter of Gilbert Lake. We found a few markers were missing, a shame since the accompanying brochure is one of the better written, more informative ones that we've seen.

Along the latter walk, we got to see a few of the buildings erected by the CCC. Made of fossil-laden fieldstone, they remain sturdy six decades after their construction. Briggs Pavilion, also of stone, dates even earlier, having been put up by the state in 1926. It's situated on a beautiful spot above the lake, just beside the dam.

Our trail guide pointed out economic uses of selected trees. Maple, of course, provides sap for syrup, along with fine hardwood for furniture. Red oak has significant economic value for its high quality wood. White ash finds a role in the manufacture of baseball bats, some of which are enshrined in the Baseball Hall of Fame at nearby Cooperstown.

Tips on tree identification are also highlighted. Numbers of needles in a cluster distinguish pine species. Two white lines underneath flat needles characterize hemlock, once prized as a source of tannin for the region's tanneries.

An area opened by a blowdown let us learn a bit about forest succession; implications for wildlife are also denoted.

By all means spend some time in the CCC Museum while you're at Gilbert Lake. Photos, scrapbooks, and newspaper clippings tell the story of the camps, designed to provide employment and training during the Great Depression. Run by the army, they paid young men $30 a month for their strenuous effort; $25 of that got sent home to help their families. Memorabilia ranges from enrollee handbooks and instructional manuals, to uniforms and ice-cutting tools.

Information:
Cooperstown Chamber of Commerce, 31 Chestnut Street, Cooperstown, NY 13326. Phone 607-547-9983
Gilbert Lake State Park, 18 CCC Road, Laurens, NY 13796. Phone 607-432-2114.

Robert Treman State Park • Taughannock Falls

Whereas the Adirondack Mountains dominate the topography of northeastern New York, glacially carved lakes and gorges hold sway in western parts of the state. Untold thousands of years ago, huge glaciers carved the basins for the deep, narrow bodies of water we know as the Finger Lakes. Torrents of water melting from retreating ice fields rushed over steep valleys, creating a series of gorges, or glens.

Once exploited for industrial potential, the surging waters also attracted nineteenth- and early-twentieth-century travelers who stayed in fancy hotels with impressive vistas. The mills are now quiet. The resorts are gone. Preservation by New York State, however, has protected much of the scenic beauty for generations to come.

Robert Treman State Park, near the southern end of Cayuga Lake, may be the least known of these spots. Treman, an Ithaca banker and devoted philanthropist, purchased almost four hundred acres around Enfield Glen. In 1920 he deeded the property to New York State. Holdings have since expanded to over a thousand acres.

During the 1930s, there was a Civilian Conservation Corps camp here. Many of the improvements, including fine stonework along the trail, can be attributed to their efforts.

There is no better way to appreciate the beauty of Enfield Glen than by hiking the Rim Trail.

We began near the campground at the lower end of the glen. After ascending a few shallow stairs into the woods and completing a fairly steep initial jaunt, the way levels out, following a well-cleared route. Our path hugged the side of a hill, and the protective chain link fence to our left was very much appreciated.

Teased almost from the start by glimpses of rapids far below, we eventually came to our first open view of tumbling rapids and a falls. The water flows over a series of broad, shallow ledges. A short spur took us to water's edge; a long, steep set of stairs followed almost immediately. Soon we came to another cascade, one that reminded my wife of her first-communion veil. Now at every turn we came to a new variant of the cascading waters, listening always to the mesmerizing sound of the running stream.

Just beyond a grassy area bright with pink and violet phlox and vinca, we encountered a falls that stretched the full width of the stream. Impressive stonework, dating to CCC days, brought us to a scenic spot with broad rocks perfect for a picnic.

The flow now alternated between gentle falls and more turbulent flow. Natural features like the high cliff to our right competed for attention with man-made ones, including staircases and walkways along the glen.

Near the two-mile point, a bridge crossed over the water. Shortly thereafter, we came around a bend to our best view of Lucifer Falls. Two initial segments roll over a series of rocks. Then, diverted by a resistant rock wall, the water makes a curve in its rush to the bottom. Framed by high cliffs (as much a wonder as the falls itself) on both sides, the 115-foot drop must have thrilled travelers staying at the Enfield Glen Hotel a century ago.

We continued on, passing a few more falls as we proceeded. The upper glen has the feel of a gorge with its dramatic rock ledges and winding channel. Other hikers told us the walls are mostly shale—"scrape a little and you should find a trilobite."

A three-story mill dating to 1847 dominates the upper limit of the glen. Built by Robert Treman's grandfather, it replaced an earlier gristmill built in 1817. The mill was the centerpiece of a hamlet called Enfield Falls that once thrived here. Only the mill, which operated until 1917, and a miller's cottage survive. The community's post office had already been closed in 1902.

Enfield Falls enjoyed brief fame as a resort destination, too. Movies were filmed in the gorges and near the waterfalls. The Enfield Falls Hotel, known not only for its surrounding scenery but for its Saturday night dances in the second-story ballroom, had its heyday in the second half of the nineteenth century, but didn't make it into the twentieth. It was abandoned when Robert Treman began buying his land.

Several people had already gathered inside the nearby stone picnic shelter, anticipating the inclement weather about to come.

But even a steady rain during our walk back to the campground couldn't dampen our enjoyment as we retraced our steps past a dozen waterfalls along the two-and-a-quarter-mile trail.

Plan about two hours each way for the hike, or perhaps spot cars at each end (the upper park is accessible by automobile). There's not a good map immediately available, but the way is well marked. Bring a picnic to enjoy on the broad rocks, and perhaps wear a bathing suit underneath hiking clothes.

******

A shorter trail for a rewarding view leads to Taughannock Falls, among the tallest cascades in New York. Standing at the head of a glacially carved gorge, the falls, at 215 feet, is higher than even Niagara. Park literature proclaims this "the highest vertical single drop waterfall in the Northeastern United States." The Gorge Trail runs a short three-fourths mile from the parking area to the base of the falls.

A churning rapids right at the beginning would strike one as impressive were there no expectation of what was to come later. We frequently veered off the trail to the water's edge. Taughannock Creek itself was quite shallow, ideal for our dogs. A steep shale cliff with lots of talus at its base marked the terrain across from us. The trail side of the river has a less precipitous slope, gentle enough to allow forestation with some maple and beech, plus a few tall evergreens.

Mesmerized by the persistent rush of water over the sandstone bedrock, we almost forgot about the giant cataract ahead. We came around a gentle bend, and there it was, plunging head-on from its course over two hundred feet above. There's no way the unwary traveler could have expected such a sight.

A bit reminiscent of Montmorency Falls near Quebec City, it's the hanging falls of all hanging falls. A bridge allowed excellent views before providing a crossing for closer scrutiny. A microclimate with mosses thrived. We could feel the spray several hundred feet away.

Settlement in the area began in the 1790s. Not surprisingly, the waterpower fed a variety of mills. Others earned a living cutting sandstone. Steamboat travel on Cayuga Lake in the nineteenth century brought travelers to the site. Two hotels, the Taughannock House and the Cataract House, once faced each other across the gorge.

Hotel business faded by the early 1900s. In 1924 development began for a state park. Civilian Conservation Corps workers built trails and facilities during the New Deal era. A campground and bridge were added later.

Nearby Taughannock Falls Inn was originally the home of wealthy Philadelphia businessman John Jones. One can imagine the pleasure he and his guests found in having the falls almost in his back yard. Much of Jones' farm has become part of the state park.

Information:

Robert H. Treman State Park, RD 10, Ithaca, NY 14850. Phone 607-273-3440.

Taughannock Falls State Park, Box 1055 (Route 89), Trumansburg, NY 14886. Phone 607-387-6739.

Empire Carousel at The Farmers' Museum in Cooperstown

Cornell University • Cornell Plantations

Ithaca strikes many as the quintessential college town. The sprawling Cornell University campus dominates one end of the city. High above on a hill to the south sits Ithaca College. In all, close to thirty thousand students come into Ithaca during the school year, almost matching the permanent population.

Ithaca also makes a terrific walking destination. In planning a trip, consider going after the college graduations, when rooms and restaurant reservations become more easily available. But Cayuga Lake, nearby vineyards, and plenty of scenery attract travelers throughout the summer, too.

Our stay began with time at Cornell. Self-guided walking tours are available, but we chose to line up with the prospective students and their parents awaiting one of the tours beginning at regular intervals from Day Hall.

Ezra Cornell founded the college in 1868 and set the ambitious goal of providing any course of study for any person. Partly private and partly New York's land grant university, Cornell comes close to doing just that with its seven undergraduate colleges and six graduate schools.

The one-and-a-half-hour guided walk gave us a flavor for the architecture, history, and educational philosophy of the school. Often hailed as America's most beautiful campus, Cornell's buildings range from the traditional Gothic of the Baker Complex, to mansard-roofed stone structures on the Arts Quad, to columned Greek Revival Goldwin-Smith Hall, to a collection of more modern styles.

Our guide, Ilyse, an exuberant engineering student who clearly loved being here, pointed out steep-roofed Sage Chapel, whose stained-glass panels depict figures of philosophy and knowledge rather than religion. Many marriages take place here, though Ilyse conceded, "It's creepy to me to have the bride get ready in a crypt."

Willard Straight Hall, a stone building with tall chimneys, served as one of the first student unions in the United States. It owes its name and existence to the donation of an undistinguished 1901 architecture grad who specifically bequeathed funds for a non-academic building. Its Memorial Room features fine oak wainscoting, a high wood ceiling, and carvings of some of Straight's professors.

McGraw Tower provides one of Cornell's most recognizable land-marks. Three chime concerts ring out from here each day. Competition to be a chimesmaster is intense, we learned, perhaps partly because the task allows the school's only exemption from the physical education requirement. Daily climbs of the 151 stairs certainly provide some conditioning, though.

From an overlook with views of West Campus (and Lake Cayuga), we saw the Gothic buildings of Baker Complex. Mansard roofs distinguish Morrill Hall and McGraw Hall (both built from stone quarried on the campus) on the Arts Quad. Inside Greek Revival Goldwin-Smith Hall, freshmen complete required writing seminars.

More modern construction includes the sleek, brick-and-glass Space Sciences Building, and futuristic Rhodes Hall, with its tall glass towers at each end and Cornell's supercomputer inside. Consider also the Campus Store, sited largely underground so as not to impede views of more venerable buildings.

Our guide then took us past the hotel school. The 150-room Statler Hotel serves as an exceptional learning laboratory for the students. Its marble-floored lobby with wood paneling and columns makes a strong first impression. Faculty here also offer Introduction to Wine and Spirits, one of the most popular courses at the college.

As we walked the campus of hills, gorges, and new buildings aesthetically nestled amidst the old, the guide also pointed out a few personal favorites. Inside Comstock Hall, for instance, is the entomology department's bug museum. At the veterinarian school, she recommended the dairy bar—"Greatest ice cream I've ever had." The Herbert F. Johnson Museum of Art, designed by I. M. Pei, offers a vista from the fifth floor "even better than the art work."

By tour's end, I found myself wishing I could go back to being an undergraduate again myself.

******

Don't let a Cornell sampling end with just the campus tour.

We bought a walking guide and found our way to adjacent Cornell

Plantations. Part arboretum, part botanical garden, and part nature reserve, these three thousand acres would be among my regular jogging sites if I lived in Ithaca. A detailed guide to trails is available locally. You'll find more botanical and geological information than you'll ever be able to absorb.

My wife loved the Botanical Garden and especially the well-labeled Rock Garden, with its yellow snowdrops and delicate pink cinquefoil. Deep purple Siberian iris and blue spiderwort complemented the broad white and rich pink blooms in the American Peony Society Garden. I'd love to have the nicely terraced Rhododendron Collection atop Comstock Knoll, enriched by penstemon and hostas, or the sixteen thematic beds crisscrossed by slate walks and grassy paths in Robison York State Herb Garden.

Walking the one-mile Beebe Lake Loop, we saw scenic stone bridges (that made us think of picturesque European ruins), remnants of a hydraulics lab, and handsome stone walls. There's a nice mix of old hardwood trees. We watched five baby goslings cavorting with their parents beneath a sycamore.

The Cascadilla Gorge Path had more than its share of dramatic views. Adjacent to the college campus, it's both a shortcut to downtown and a nature oasis along Cascadilla Creek. Its impressive trail work owes much to the efforts of Civilian Conservation Corps workers.

All this, and we didn't even step onto the Fall Creek Path, the Arboretum Loop, or the Mundy Wildflower Garden Loop. When we return to Ithaca, we'll allot at least a full day for Cornell Plantations. Marty will study the flowers and plants, and I'll walk and take photos along the lake and creek-side trails.

******

Birdwatchers flock to Sapsucker Woods, a 200-acre sanctuary outside of town managed by Cornell's ornithology department. Named for the yellow-bellied sapsucker found nesting there in 1909, the reserve includes a visitor center and four miles of trails. Inside we perused information on the Cornell Laboratory of Ornithology. Afterwards, we looked through an observation window out to a pond and songbird garden. Most intriguing of the displays was a nineteenth-century glass parlor case with ninety-eight species of hummingbirds.

We walked meticulously kept trails, going over several nice board-walks and appreciating the regularly spaced benches. Even though we failed to sight a single exotic bird, there was no shortage of geese, ducks, and red-winged blackbirds. Plus we enjoyed the pleasure of a forest walk that included hardwood areas, scrub brush sections, and a spruce plantation.

Information:
Cornell University, Day Hall, Ithaca, NY 14853. Phone 607-254-INFO.
Cornell Plantations, Ithaca, NY 14850. Phone 607-255-3020.
Cornell Laboratory of Ornithology, 159 Sapsucker Woods Road, Ithaca NY 14850. Phone 607-254-BIRD.

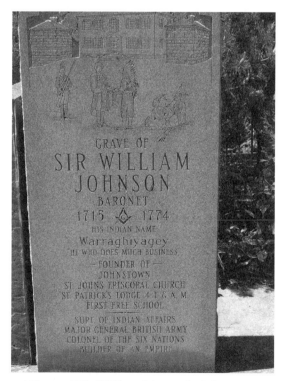

Grave of Sir William Johnson in Johnstown

Johnstown ● Willie Wildlife Marsh

Today Johnstown looks like many other cities in the Mohawk Valley, rebuilding an economy after closure of factories—in this case, glove factories—that once brought prosperity. During the late eighteenth century, however, Johnstown was a British stronghold in North America.

Sir William Johnson (1715–1774), commander of British forces at the Battle of Lake George during the French and Indian War, had become Superintendent of Indian Affairs for the northern half of British North America by 1760. He proceeded to build a mansion as the headquarters of his large estate. Then Johnson laid out a proposed village, built houses for teachers and artisans, and began seeking settlers from Europe.

Johnson developed a reputation for fair dealings with Native Americans. Marriage to a Mohawk woman, Molly Brant, further cemented the respect in which he was held. Merchants, political leaders, and military officers visited Johnson Hall frequently. Johnstown ranked as quite an important place.

Until the American Revolution. Johnson died just before the Declaration of Independence was signed, but family members remained loyal to the British. When hostilities ended, Johnson's holdings had been seized by the colonial government. New centers of prominence left Johnstown behind.

Maps for a walking tour are readily available throughout Johnstown. We even found them used as placemats in a local restaurant!

We began in Sir William Johnson Park, in the center of downtown. Four detailed historic plaques give details about Johnson's life. He's buried at the adjacent Episcopal Church, a handsome stone edifice with heavy oak doors and arched stained-glass windows. This building replaced the original chapel commissioned by Johnson himself.

Simply walking a three-block radius shows the impact of the village's founder. There's St. Patrick's Lodge, established by Johnson in 1766. The handsome brick county courthouse he commissioned first saw service in 1772; it's New York's only courthouse continuously used since colonial times.

Drumm House, though, qualifies as the oldest building in John-

164

stown. This simple clapboard home with wood shake roof is the sole remaining example of six such houses that Johnson constructed in 1763 for teachers and artisans he sought for the fledgling community.

A plaque commemorates the first free public school in New York, another accomplishment attributed to the town's foresighted founder.

Strolling a bit farther we came upon Fort Johnstown, ordered by Johnson just before his death in 1774. Two brick wings flank a central stone unit. Barred windows on the latter testify to its use as a prison early in the Revolutionary War. George Washington came for an inspection in 1783.

Other famous personages spent time in Johnstown. Across from Johnson Park, a historical marker denotes the birthplace of Elizabeth Cady Stanton. Her father's law office stood around the corner. At Mrs. Henry's Boarding House, a trim white home just a block away, Stanton and Susan B. Anthony wrote a volume of their *History of Women's Suffrage*.

Union Hall, a red clapboard inn, dates to 1798. Nick Stoner, one of the earliest legendary Adirondack guides and raconteurs, operated this as a tavern. Farther south is the very impressive Knox Mansion with its Corinthian columned porches. After the premature death of her husband, Rose Knox built Knox Gelatine into a twentieth-century household essential.

The tour also brought us to the battlefield where the final skirmish of the American Revolution took place—six days after the British had surrendered to Washington in Yorktown, Virginia! I suspect some participants in that encounter are buried in the nearby Colonial Cemetery. We noted gravestones dating to 1782, most tragically a single marker set out for three infant children. On a more positive note, at the Cemetery we bumped into an enthusiastic local elementary school class also doing a historical walking tour. It's great to see teachers introducing young people to the immediacy of history in their home town.

Not formally on our tour, but of interest, was a War of 1812 historical marker east on Main Street. A wealth of Victorian, Greek Revival, and Federal architecture graces South William and South Melcher streets. We also ran across a few abandoned glove factories. The leather industry began here as early as 1803. Even as recently as the 1940s,

Johnstown ranked among the world leaders in glove production. Most of that survives only in memory now.

The memory of William Johnson, however, is anything but dead. A visit to Johnson Hall State Historic Site should be the capstone of your visit to Johnstown.

Georgian in style, the home is built of wood painted and scraped to simulate marble. Two adjacent stone buildings facilitated Johnson's business and political responsibilities, plus provided housing for domestic staff and selected guests. A tunnel beneath one gave servants access to the house's basement kitchen.

Period furnishings testify that Johnson sought fine goods even though he lived in a frontier setting. Much came from Europe, though there are a number of Native American items as well. Large windows let in more light than I'm accustomed to seeing in colonial dwellings.

Upstairs, the spacious hall doubled as a dance floor when parties filled the house. There are four guest rooms, each with fireplace and small tea table. Two in front boast canopied beds, fancy wallpaper, and Queen Anne and Chippendale pieces. The back rooms are whitewashed and less sumptuously furnished.

A "British" America would probably revere Johnson as one of its heroes. Policies influenced by Johnson might have made subsequent relations with Native Americans far more constructive. Instead his name has been almost forgotten. Johnson Hall helps memorialize a man whose four decades in the New World included military and economic success, and a determination to live in harmony with those around him.

$$******$$

Willie Wildlife Marsh in Fulton County appears to be well known locally, but doesn't seem to find its way into the usual guide books. The trailhead, just south of the Blue Line that demarcates the Adirondack Park, can be reached by turning off Route 10 onto Route 29A. Go six miles, and then turn right at Willie Road. There's a parking area 1.8 miles down Willie Road. Our walk began across the road.

The trail begins in a pleasant mixed forest heavy on maple, beech, and birch trees. Conifers appear to include hemlock and tamarack. Following yellow markers, we crossed a tiny stream on a plank bridge. After about ten minutes, marsh becomes visible through trees on the left. High-pitched birdcalls and the deep, throaty sounds of frogs greeted our arrival.

There's a junction with the red trail, but we continued on yellow, crossing the first of three boardwalks. A much longer, curving boardwalk crosses a large body of water just a bit farther on. The water was high, actually a few inches over our bridge near its center, so we took extra caution. Yellow water lilies and gleaming dragonflies added color to the setting. The bass symphony of frogs picked up accompaniment from the staccato percussion of woodpeckers.

Once across, we found ourselves on the needle-carpeted paths of the red loop. A third boardwalk traversed marsh. Later came a wood plank viewing platform, but also some flooded areas that required inventive detours. Suddenly we emerged in a clearing with open water. Our Labrador retriever deemed this the best part of the walk.

Continuing around the water and then crossing a bridge, we reached that junction of red and yellow trails at the beginning of the first boardwalk. From there we retraced the route back to our car. All told, we had spent a leisurely hour.

Consider wearing long-sleeved shirts and long pants regardless of the weather. Mosquitoes certainly thrive here. Perhaps bring a nature guide, too. We had been told an interpretive brochure would be available, but this turned out not to be the case. Alternatively, signage along the trail might be a welcome addition in the future.

As you leave, give credit to Cub Scout Pack 4 of nearby Gloversville. They've done a lot of the work to create this trail, as part of the Department of Environmental Conservation's "Adopt-A-Wetland" program.

Information:
Johnson Hall State Historic Site, Hall Avenue, Johnstown, NY 12095. Phone 518-762-8712.
Willie Wildlife Area – Fulton County Regional Chamber of Commerce and Industry, 2 North Main Street, Gloversville, NY 12078. Phone 1-800-676-3858 or 518-725-0641.

Howe Caverns • Sharon Springs

Lester Howe farmed in the Schoharie Valley, southwest of Albany. One hot May afternoon he noticed his animals gathering near a clump of bushes rather than at the pond. He went to investigate.

To his surprise, he found a cool breeze. Exploring further, he found a hole leading into the ground. Intrepid, he slithered down and found himself in a cave. Returning with lanterns, Lester walked the winding passages for almost a mile. Howe's Caverns had been discovered.

An entrepreneurial bent apparently came easily to Lester. Within two years he opened the spot as a tourist attraction. For fifty cents, not an inconsequential sum in those pre-Civil War days, visitors got hip boots, oilskin coats, and oil torches, and then followed Lester for eight hours of spelunking. Mrs. Howe even contributed lunch.

The enterprise lasted until 1870, when Lester went bankrupt. A cement company purchased the land and began quarrying, destroying the first one thousand feet of the cave (and the original entrance) in the process.

In the late 1920s, a newly formed corporation took over and constructed walkways, placed electric lights, and blasted out an elevator shaft. Howe Caverns reopened to the public in 1929.

We paid our admission fees at the mock-Tudor Visitor Center before descending 156 feet (about fifteen stories) in elevators to our starting point.

A guide oriented our group of eighteen. After some basic history, geology, and safety lessons, we started the one-mile route. The brick surface, though never slippery, required paying attention. Frequent stops assured maximum benefit from the experience.

Twisting passages to the right brought us within view of the River Styx, which carved the cavern through limestone bedrock eons ago. The source of this underground stream continues to elude detection, but we do know the water stays at forty-two degrees year-round. Only a few mosses (near areas of artificial illumination) and occasional bats inhabit the caves

We saw such interesting features as "balancing rock," a twenty-two-ton specimen that fell perhaps ten thousand years ago, forming a bridge. Weak carbonic acid dissolves the underpinning limestone; re-sultant calcite drips from the ceiling. Travertine patterns are mesmer-izing.

Now remember some basic geology. Stalagmites rise from the ground; stalactites adhere to the ceilings. Flowstone can be found any-where in between. Formations develop slowly. It can take a century to produce a cubic inch.

The largest stalagmite, Chinese Pagoda, sits within the largest vault in the cavern complex, Titan's Temple. The Pagoda stands a full eleven feet high, impressive even in comparison to the fifty-five-foot height of Titan's Temple. With a flashlight, our guide demonstrated the trans-lucency of calcite, and then pointed out an intricate array of flowstone known as Cathedral Pipe Organ.

There are also grottoes, products of erosion in the caves. Lester Howe explored them all, finding the largest went forty feet into the wall. Some suggest fantastic forms, most notably the Witches of the Grot-toes.

Over the course of half an hour—and half a mile—we had de-scended to our lowest point. We came upon Howie, the cave's "pet turtle." Two stalagmites in the turtle's formation provide guidance as to water levels. On rare occasions, flooding can close the cave, as it did for a full week in 1937.

Now we enjoyed a gentle boat ride along the Lake of Venus, formed by a natural dam. We watched the walls, ducking when necessary, and noted stalactites folded like curtains. The guide briefly turned out all lights, leaving the intimidating presence of total darkness. I briefly pon-dered Lester Howe's wisdom in setting out for the unknown in 1842.

Time on the boat let us appreciate details. Colors are diverse. Dis-solved minerals convey unique hues—red for iron, yellow for sulfur, green for copper, and so forth. The widest range of color can be ap-preciated in the so-called Bronze Room. Here also was the ledge where Lester Howe served his wife's lunches.

It's worth noting Lester built a new raft for each group of visitors. In his mind, this best gave the experience of the first exploration. One wonders how such attention to detail would fly in the impatient twenty-first century!

Walking back, we came to the Bridal Altar. In 1854, Howe's daughter Elgiva became betrothed to Hiram Dewey at the natural entrance to Howe Caverns. Some years later this altar was set up, complete with heart-shaped stone on the floor. Over four hundred weddings have subsequently taken place there.

The tour ended with a slow walk through Winding Way. This convoluted series of narrow passages includes thirty S-turns within its three-hundred-foot course. Passages are only one to four feet wide, so we had to be alert to avoid mishaps. We were rewarded with close-up looks at incredible patterns of flowstone, with fascinating photographic angles everywhere. This part of our trip likely best approximated the sense of discovery greeting the cave's earliest visitors.

The one-mile walk plus boat ride takes about an hour and a half. The way is not strenuous, but one must be in decent physical condition—and not be claustrophobic. Wear a jacket or sweater; interior temperatures are fifty-two degrees all year.

******

Sharon Springs, built near a rock ledge south of the Mohawk River, once had a reputation around the world for its medicinal springs. The Pavilion Hotel attracted travelers as early as 1836. Within fifty years some sixty hotels and a scattering of boarding houses could accommodate as many as ten thousand visitors at a time. From 1870 to 1930, trains came here directly from New York City.

Fashions and fads change. During the late nineteenth century, spots like Saratoga and Newport began to draw the visitors who once would have frequented Sharon Springs. Health resorts based around springs began to decline further "when doctors didn't send people for the waters anymore."

Sharon Springs enjoyed an interesting renaissance after World War II. Jewish prisoners who survived the Holocaust received reparations from the German government. Spa stays, long a staple of European life, were often included among the benefits. When Sharon Springs was designated as an eligible destination for this purpose, Jewish visitors, not only from the United States but from around the world, began flocking here. The remote village took on an international air. Historian Dorcas Comrie told us that in the 1950s "the streets were packed with people—you couldn't walk on them."

Many of the hotels are long gone. Yet enough remain to give the village a distinctive flavor. And the springs are still here, several housed in pavilions that convey a lasting grandeur.

Renovation efforts have enhanced a few properties, as local boosters hope for another prosperous era in the town's history.

A walking tour of Main Street (Route 10) won't take you an hour, unless you end up exploring every nook and cranny like we did. Twenty well-designed plaques offer vintage photos and engaging text, helping bring Sharon Springs' history to life.

We started by the Adler Hotel, still in operation during the summer. Former New York Mayor Ed Koch once spent a summer waiting on tables here. Progressing up the street, we passed the American Hotel, built around 1850 and now nicely rehabbed. Roseboro Hotel, formed in the 1920s by joining three adjacent buildings, has also been updated. The broad covered veranda that fronts the long white building beckons for an afternoon in a rocking chair.

Each spring pavilion deserves a look. The Magnesia Temple, yellow with a domed top, is especially elaborate. You'll quickly detect its strong sulphurous odor. Next door at White Sulphur Spring, there's a ladle with which to sample the waters.

The white stucco facade of Imperial Baths (1927) has begun to crumble a bit, but this remains a place one can get the spa treatment. Then there's Chalybeate Spring, covered by a simple white temple. Iron-laden waters, "reputedly enough to turn one's teeth brown," were not only used for baths, but were bottled and sold as treatment for anemia.

Main Street became steep as we approached what was the separate municipality of Rockville until its amalgamation with Sharon Springs in 1871. The old Lehman Hardware Store, where owner Eugene Lehman once made fine violins, still stands. We enjoyed the views as we retraced our steps back to the point of origin.

Since the plaques are permanently mounted along the street, one can enjoy this walking tour anytime. A locally available architectural guide allows extension of your walk to neighboring streets with impressive residences and churches.

One reason to make the journey in summer, however, is the chance to visit the Sharon Historical Museum. Inside we found all sorts of vintage photography and memorabilia from the heydays of Sharon Springs. A register from the Pavilion Hotel showed Oscar Wilde's signature from 1882. Then there's the wicker "mud pack chair." One would sit in anticipation of being covered with Czech-imported mud mixed with local sulfur water.

There's also a one-room schoolhouse used until the 1930s. The outhouse had separate areas for boys and girls, with slanted seats to accommodate younger children.

Information:
Howe Caverns, 255 Discovery Drive, Howe Cave, NY 12092. Phone 518-296-8990.
Sharon Historical Society, Box 363, Sharon Springs, NY 13459. Phone 518-284-2327.

Pratt's Falls

Oneida • Pratt's Falls

Okay, put down your fork or spoon. Does it happen to be an Oneida utensil? Best known for its production of tableware, the company began as a utopian community that manufactured animal traps. At the Oneida Community Mansion House, just east of Syracuse, we learned more.

One John Humphrey Noyes (1811–1886), Vermont native and Dartmouth graduate, had a conversion experience in 1831. He began preaching, and then tried to create a religious community in Putney, Vermont, in the 1830s. Believing that Christ's second coming occurred in 70 A.D with the fall of Jerusalem, Noyes espoused Perfectionism, the concept that men and women could achieve lives of grace on earth.

As with other inspired leaders in the nineteenth century, he put forward some ideas that were quite unconventional. One was that of complex marriage. All men are considered married to all women, and vice versa. Children were raised in common rather than in nuclear families. By 1848, he no longer felt welcome in Putney. Along with forty-five supporters, he moved to present-day Oneida.

Here his disciples lived in a single large home, expanded as necessary when more recruits joined. Emphasis on continuing education and self-sufficiency united Noyes' followers. The leader also understood the need for a firm economic base. Fruit and vegetable growing provided some income, as did the canning and sale of preserves.

Invention of an improved animal trap by Sewell Newhouse in 1855, though, became the core of Oneida's business. Manufacture of eating utensils began later, at an offshoot community in Wallingford, Connecticut.

As utopian experiments go, Oneida proved successful—both economically and philosophically. Local outrage over complex marriage caused trouble, however. In 1880, fearing arrest, Noyes fled to Canada. Soon afterwards, those remaining at Mansion House decided to disband the community and make the transition to a stock corporation.

Oneida Limited prospered under the leadership of Noyes' son Pierrepont (1870–1959). Indeed the company continues to prosper.

Mansion House, no longer functioning as home for a communal group, now offers more conventional housing. The forty apartments are occupied by families, college students, and a handful of descendants of

Noyes' original followers. A few rooms are reserved for traveling bed-and-breakfast guests.

Mansion House has the feel of an elegant old apartment building with its tall ceilings, interior archways, and varnished woodwork. A tour includes the Court, originally a true courtyard before being enclosed to provide more living space; the Library; and the Historic Manufacturing Room, where items of Oneida design are exhibited.

The Family Hall was the heart of the building. It featured a stage, balconies, wooden benches, and an ornate painted ceiling. The plank floor sloped upwards from the stage, assuring adequate views from all seats. Every evening Noyes would address the residents here. Sometimes the talks centered on business, other times on social or ideological issues. Here also might occur sessions of "mutual criticism," a safeguard against excessive individualism or boasting.

We peeked into a typical sleeping area. All members in the communal house were entitled to private rooms. A bed, bureau, corner shelf, table, and chair filled the space; each room had at least one window. At nine feet by twelve feet, the area compared reasonably well with my college housing.

After a tour of the interior, we wandered the expansive grounds. Only in this way could we fully appreciate the enormity of this sprawling brick edifice. Stone corner quoins, cornices, dentil work, and square towers adorn the structure. Slate mansard roofs are a unifying feature.

Expansive lawns include a formal garden with hedge borders, a variety of perennial and annual flowers, and a small pool. The rustic summer house features twig work and a tile pagoda-style roof.

A brochure describes several nearby walks. Some, including Burling Street and the O&W Railroad bed, are quite short. Another leads to The Larches, passing a golf course on its way to a wooded area.

One path circumscribes Sunset Lake, created in 1901 for fire protection. We traversed both shaded and open areas on our way to the outlet dam, where we found a spur to the large spillway. Kids swam nearby, and we happened upon a few fishermen. A flock of geese had taken residence in the middle of the lake, and our dog flushed some grouse. Lily pads added colorful blooms to the scene.

Next we followed directions to East Park. A left turn led to a well-maintained, grassy path along the tree line. Then we continued along Oneida Creek. Eventually the trail backed up to a series of very beautiful residences with deep backyards.

Two additional routes, called the "little square" and "big square," cover three and five miles, respectively. Going along city streets, these give a good sense of present-day Oneida. Each has a few hills, though neither is difficult.

******

Only by chance did we stop one day at Pratt's Falls, just south of Syracuse and part of the Onondaga County park system. We dropped our one-dollar suggested donation into the box, and found a shady spot to park the car.

Manoah Pratt and Abraham Smith established mills here as early as 1796, with Pratt continuing operation of a gristmill until he died in 1841. A millstone and vertical saw once used here are on display, and the stone-walled flume also survives.

A century later, Onondaga acquired the 306-acre parcel. Civilian Conservation Corps workers planted trees, built shelters, and otherwise helped to develop the site as a county park. One unusual feature is a field archery course with fifty-six targets.

An overlook gives a sense of the depth and power of the 137-foot drop that Limestone Creek makes on its course through the deep gorge. But the view from below is much more rewarding.

The Blue Trail (0.6 miles) begins with a steep descent. We climbed down stone stairs to a broad, well-maintained trail through an airy forest. Maple and beech trees predominated. I passed what looked to be an old cistern; subsequently, I saw a huge uprooted tree that exemplifies just how tenaciously a root system spreads. Birdcalls provided the background music.

Soon we diverted onto the steep spur to the lower falls. A few more sets of stairs assisted the climb down. Quickly we found the cascade, nicely framed by rock ledges and greenery in the foreground.

It's a surprisingly high and pretty falls. Water drops precipitously at first, before spreading out along a series of rock layers as it plummets to the bottom of the gorge. Reminiscent of Chittenango Falls, though not quite as wide, it's a very nice visual treat, worth driving out of one's way to see.

After our climb back up, we picnicked in a nicely shaded grove of conifers and hardwoods, the sound of the water constantly alongside us. Rested and satiated, we walked the park's other two trails.

The Yellow Trail winds 2.6 miles, much of it along the rim of the gorge, while the Red Trail's 1.2-mile length traverses second-growth forest. Our dog, consigned to waiting while we hiked down to the falls, found these routes very much to his liking. Both probably make excellent cross-country ski trails in the winter.

Information:

Oneida Community Mansion House, 170 Kenwood Avenue, Oneida, NY 13421. Phone 315-363-0745.

Pratt's Falls Park, 7671 Pratt's Falls Road, Manlius, NY 13104. Phone 315-682-5934.

Mark Twain Study on campus of Elmira College

Elmira • Endicott

Elmira, founded in the 1780s by a group of Revolutionary War veterans, was allegedly named after the raucous daughter of one. This place offers a venerable city center, broad-lawned residential areas, and a college campus for strolling. For those not in the mood to exercise, tours on a replica 1910 trolley offer an alternative to walking.

We began by an impressive grouping of government buildings near Lake and Market streets. The restored brick courthouse survives from Civil War days. A sandstone city hall features ornate columns and a tall bell tower. Across the street is the red brick Greek Revival Arnot Art Museum, an 1833 mansion that's one of a number of local attractions meriting a visit.

A turn onto Church Street brought us near a cluster of notable ecclesiastical structures. One boasts an unusual all-brick steeple. Park Congregational Church, stone with brick trim, has a dome based on St. Peter's in Rome. Out front stands a statue of Thomas Beecher, brother of Harriet Beecher Stowe and an ardent abolitionist. Several local churches played active roles in the Underground Railroad, leading escaped slaves to freedom.

Veering left off Main Street led to College Street. The story here revolves around Jervis Langdon, a staunch supporter of education and women's rights. He and several colleagues established Elmira Female College in 1855 as the first institution of higher learning exclusively for women. Elmira College is now co-ed, but females still well outnumber males.

Wandering around campus revealed Coles Hall, the original college building, with its cupola on top. White columns front the appealing President's Home. The college is also a good place to learn about one of Elmira's most noted citizens.

A writer named Samuel Clemens met Jervis Langdon's son Charles on a Mediterranean cruise in 1867; he became infatuated with a picture of his new acquaintance's sister. Within a year, Clemens visited Elmira. In 1870, Clemens, better known as Mark Twain, married Olivia Langdon. The bride's father had his doubts, describing Clemens as "trying, tedious, and socially inept," but the union succeeded.

In 1874, relatives built Clemens an octagonal study with two chimneys, modeling the design on a riverboat's pilothouse. The study, in which the author worked on many of his most notable books, was moved to the Elmira College campus in 1952. "Student ambassadors" give tours of the interior, pointing out the stone fireplace, bulls-eye windowpanes, and windows on seven sides (conducive to diffusing smoke from the many Cuban cigars Twain smoked each day).

Just up the street, in Hamilton Hall, there's a collection of Twain photos and memorabilia to examine.

Clemens spent most of his summers in Elmira, and he gave instructions to be buried here when he died. A long walk up Davis Street leads to Woodlawn Cemetery, a 180-acre site that holds over eighty thousand graves in addition to the plots of the Langdon and Clemens families. Other local notables buried here include football star Ernie Davis, film producer Hal Roach, and former slave John Jones, who helped hundreds of escapees along the Underground Railroad.

One section with rows of uniform headstones serves as a National Cemetery. Soldiers of the Confederacy are well represented here, too. Elmira had a prison during the Civil War that rivaled Andersonville in notoriety (many dubbed it "Hellmira"). A majority of the three thousand prisoners who died there, many of smallpox, malaria, and malnutrition, are buried at Woodlawn.

The prison sat south of Water Street. Remnants from its wooden stockade likely found use in some of the nearby houses built after the war. The prison commandant's home, over two hundred years old, now serves as a doctor's office.

Along Water Street we entered the Near Westside District, a twenty-two block section that lays claim to being the largest residential area on the National Register. There's a cavalcade of Victorian homes and architectural features that can occupy hours of exploration. (Another impressive district lies along Maple Avenue, south of the Chemung River.)

In 1972 Hurricane Agnes caused disastrous flooding from the Chemung River, bringing water well over a cement flood wall. The heart of downtown was destroyed. Walking along Riverfront Park today, with its brick plazas and pretty fountains, it's difficult to contemplate how awesome—and awful—the destruction must have been.

At the corner of Lake Street and East Water Street, the 1833 Chemung Bank Building now holds the Chemung Valley Historical Museum. Another must-see stop along our route, the exhibits inside detail local history. There's also more Twain memorabilia, including his typewriter and marriage certificate.

Our walk's origin was just a couple of blocks up Lake Street. Those desirous of more exercise can cross the river and take in Brand Park (originally farmed as tobacco fields), the Maple Avenue District (including The Christmas House, an ornate Queen Anne painted in sixteen colors), and Dunn Field (the minor league baseball stadium where Don Zimmer was married at home plate in 1952).

******

Short walks in Endicott introduced us to a pair of local heroes, businessmen who made both national and regional contributions during their lifetimes.

George Johnson (1857–1948) built a small shoe company into Endicott-Johnson, which employed as many as twenty thousand workers making fifty-two-million pairs of shoes during its peak years. Johnson grew up poor in Massachusetts and worked in a shoe factory by age thirteen. He remembered his harsh treatment and became determined to be an enlightened employer.

His company boasted of the "Square Deal," treating workers well and including health benefits, recreational opportunities, and company housing at low cost, while expecting loyalty and productivity in return. Immigrants flocked to Endicott, joining the many area residents at the firm. Johnson was heralded as "a philanthropist of the first degree."

Thomas Watson (1874–1956) sold pianos and sewing machines from horse-drawn wagons. He then marketed cash registers before coming to Endicott as leader of the Computing-Tabulating-Recording Company. He developed products to serve the business community, moving from time clocks to scales to early versions of the computer. Research and education became priorities as the firm grew into International Business Machines, or IBM.

Though he offered superb working conditions and challenging

tasks, Watson expected high standards and sought "an image of efficiency and respectability." Employees, even those on assembly lines, were to wear white shirts and ties. Strict dress codes were accompanied by similar guidelines on personal behavior. His motto for the company was "THINK."

We began at Endicott's Visitor Center, a columned mansion built for Johnson's executive secretary Julia Bowes. Inside, video clips and photo collages show vignettes from the lives of Johnson's employees. In the Thomas Watson Room, we inspected examples of early machines, including the International Autograph Recorder and an Electromatic Typewriter.

A block away stands a horse barn, the only surviving structure from Johnson's estate. Then we came to a war memorial commissioned by Johnson to honor company workers who died in World War I. Handsome black plaques have been added to memorialize local victims of subsequent conflicts.

Two creations show the fondness Endicott-Johnson workers had for their boss. One is a marble statue of George Johnson, the other an impressive arch over the main street. (They built another in nearby Johnson City.) On top are the words "Home of the Square Deal." Ironically, there is a set of more familiar golden arches next door. Time marches on, I guess!

Company homes, simple but sturdy structures, were built; they were subsequently sold at cost to employees. We passed rows of them on Main Street.

Another walking tour focused on IBM. There's a special dignity to this campus, probably just what Watson wanted. The original brick Georgian-style IBM laboratory, built in 1933, would blend well with Colonial Williamsburg. The motto "THINK" is engraved into either end of the frieze work.

Other buildings are art deco in style. Relief sculptures of an abacus, scales, and hourglass are part of the design in the main complex. Ornate details surround a clock in the training building, where the likes of Ross Perot began careers. Copper eagles guard a flagpole built in tribute to IBM casualties during World War II.

Also on the tour are the Lyric Theater, financed by Johnson on the promise its owner would always charge ten cents for children, and the First Methodist Church, for which Johnson donated the land and the pipe organ, while Watson provided the furnishings. A WPA (Works Progress Administration) mural inside the post office purports to show the "ideal factory."

If you seek a driving tour to complete the day, try riding all six carousels that George Johnson donated to the region. Johnson decreed that these would be free of charge, and so they remained for over six decades.

Information:
Chemung County Chamber of Commerce, 400 E. Church Street, Elmira, NY 14901. Phone 607-734-5137.
Endicott Visitor Center, 300 Lincoln Avenue, Endicott, NY 13760. Phone 607-757-5355.

Seneca Knitting Mills along canal in Seneca Falls

181

Seneca Falls ● Waterloo

On the surface Seneca Falls could be just another ordinary upstate New York city. Waterpower fueled early economic growth. A canal provided necessary transportation. Products from pumps to fire engines made the town reasonably well known. A prosperous citizenship began building substantial homes and commercial structures.

What put Seneca Falls firmly on the map, however, was its early role in the movement for women's rights.

Local interest in the abolition of slavery and the fight for temperance grew rapidly. Quakers were early supporters of both. In addition, the Wesleyan Methodist Church, committed to abolition, broke off from the Methodist Episcopal Church. Its new chapel in Seneca Falls offered a welcoming place for speakers on often controversial issues.

Into all this arrived Elizabeth Cady Stanton. Born in Johnstown, New York, she moved to Seneca Falls after marrying attorney Henry Brewster Stanton. An ardent abolitionist, she also felt acutely the lack of opportunity for women in a newly industrialized society. As she and her friends discussed issues of slavery, they extrapolated their thoughts to the status of women. At this point in American history, women not only couldn't vote—they couldn't attend college, make contracts, or even own property.

In 1848 Stanton and her associates made the daring decision to host a convention on women's rights. That session attracted three hundred people, most—but not all—female. Organizers presented a Declaration of Sentiments closely modeled after the Declaration of Independence. Its theme, however, broadened the key concept to one claiming "that all men and women are created equal."

The National Park Service has recognized the importance of the event with establishment of Women's Rights National Historical Park. After browsing exhibits in the Visitor Center, one should follow the walk outlined in the "Women's Rights Trail" brochure.

Our trip began at the remains of the church where the convention was held. Long ago sold by the Wesleyan Methodists, the building saw use as an opera house, auto dealership, and even a laundromat before the Park Service purchased the site in 1985. The surviving brick shell has been stabilized and surrounded by an open-air stone pavilion. On the west wall, water flows gently over stone tablets engraved with passages from the Declaration of Sentiments.

From adjacent Elizabeth Cady Stanton Park, one can look across the canal to Seneca Knitting Mill, a handsome reminder of peak industrial days in the village. The falls themselves, so critical to local growth, were obliterated by flooding concurrent with expansion of New York's Barge Canal in 1918.

Over the course of walking about two miles, we passed an assortment of homes once owned by some of the one hundred individuals who signed the original Declaration of Sentiments. Along with Stanton's close allies were thirty-two male businessmen and attorneys who undoubtedly faced local censure for their decisions.

Elizabeth Cady Stanton's own home, a modest white clapboard house with green shutters, has been incorporated into the National Historic Site. Tours are given regularly by park rangers.

A marker commemorates another notable reformer, Amelia Bloomer, who also lived in Seneca Falls. Better remembered for designing the once-shocking woman's outfit that still bears her name, Bloomer published *The Lily*, a newspaper devoted to reform causes.

On Bayard Street stands an impressive bronze statue commemorating three early heroes of the women's rights movement. Sculptures depict Amelia Bloomer introducing Elizabeth Cady Stanton to Susan B. Anthony during a chance meeting on a Seneca Falls street in 1851.

Seneca Falls boasts other sites worth visiting. There's the Seneca Museum of Waterways and Industry, Seneca Falls Heritage Area, and an especially fine historical society in a Queen Anne mansion. Additionally, one should stop into the National Women's Hall of Fame.

We expanded our walk via two suggested tours provided by the Seneca Falls Heritage Area. One highlights architecture. There's an array of classic downtown buildings. Furthermore, Seneca Falls boasts a remarkable number of fine nineteenth-century homes. The range of design styles includes Federal, Italianate, Greek Revival, Second Empire, and Queen Anne. Cayuga Street alone merits a stroll; it's a true showplace of wonderful residential architecture.

Another walk focuses on Reform. Though this walk included several stops we'd already made, it offered further insight into issues of the day. Social upheaval produced by industrialization is highlighted. Stops illustrate a growing impetus to address inequality, largely related to slavery or women's rights, and to ameliorate such selected "sins" as alcohol and prostitution.

And here's a final miscellaneous fact to take away. A plaque on the bridge over the canal asserts that Seneca Falls was the inspiration for Bedford Falls, the fictional village in Frank Capra's immortal movie *It's A Wonderful Life.* Alas, I did not see an image of Jimmy Stewart.

******

Just ten miles west of Seneca Falls sits Waterloo. Settled in 1792 near a Cayuga native community, the village had factories producing woolens, wagons, coffins, and pianos during the nineteenth century. More modern manufacturing included the classic "Woody" car bodies so popular in the 1950s. Notables from the town included Dick Clark and the original Elsie the Cow. Waterloo can now claim a Super Bowl champion, too—Tom Coughlin, coach of football's New York Giants.

A walking-tour brochure produced by retired journalist Doris Wolf provided our route of discovery.

We began at Lafayette Park in the center of the village. Presciently set aside as open space right from Waterloo's founding, its name celebrates Marquis de Lafayette's visit in 1825. A monument denotes the spot of a Cayuga village destroyed by colonial troops during the American Revolution, punishment for Cayuga support of the British.

Two homes on our route belonged to men instrumental in perhaps Waterloo's most notable claim to recognition. General John Murray and pharmacist Henry Welles conceived the idea of paying tribute to Civil War veterans. Consequent to their urging, a day was set aside in 1866 for decorating soldiers' graves. Thus was Memorial Day (originally called Decoration Day) created.

Though now observed nationally on the last Monday in May, local residents continue to celebrate the event on its original date, May 30th. There's a Memorial Day Museum on Main Street that's well worth visiting. Staff there can also tell you how to find a large tree outside of town in which are embedded scythes put there by farm boys before going off to the Civil War.

Other stops highlight Waterloo's participation in reform issues. The McClintock House is part of the National Park Service's Women's Rights National Historic Park. Lucretia Mott and Elizabeth Cady Stanton were among the notables joining Mary Ann McClintock in planning the landmark women's rights convention in 1848 at nearby Seneca Falls. Fatzinger Hall, on the second floor of the nearby Waterloo Library, hosted the likes of Susan B. Anthony, Frederick Douglass, and William Lloyd Garrison as speakers.

As we strolled Virginia Street, our guidebook told us about the home where pop music impresario Dick Clark spent his summers. On Main Street we found a house belonging to the man who developed the modern concept of embalming, and another whose occupant patented a couch put to use by George Pullman in his sleeping cars. Each in his own way had an impact on how we live today.

Late in our tour, we saw the site of the original settlement, just over today's Cayuga-Seneca Canal. Samuel Bear had seen the potential for power along the Seneca River. Ironically, Cayuga natives played a significant role in helping him build his first mill. Canals proved important in development here, as elsewhere in western New York. We passed the filled-in bed of the original canal connecting Seneca and Cayuga Lakes. Later, linkage was created to the larger Erie Canal system.

Information:
Women's Rights National Historical Park, 136 Fall Street, Seneca Falls, NY 13148. Phone 315-568-2991.
Seneca County Chamber of Commerce, P.O. Box 70, Seneca Falls, NY 13148. Phone 1-800-732-1848.

Auburn • Fillmore Glen

The largest city in Cayuga County is Auburn. Settled by Revolutionary War veteran John Hardenbergh in 1793, the community had seventeen active mills by 1810. The decision to build a major state penitentiary in 1816 fueled further growth. A prominent religious institution, Auburn Theological Seminary, began offering classes in 1821. The school thrived through 1939, at which time it was relocated next to Union Seminary in New York City.

Over the next century, Auburn's industries included rope-making, buttons, shoes, and a manufacturer of farm equipment that ultimately formed part of International Harvester. That button factory made a prototype plastic penny for use during World War II copper shortages, but steel was chosen instead to make the coins for 1943.

A locally available walking tour of the South Street Historic District has been developed by the Community Preservation Committee. The one-mile route gives a good sense of the wealth and industry that helped build Auburn.

Begin by the Phoenix Building (2 South Street). Its impressive clock tower serves as a downtown anchor. The nearby art deco theater awaits redevelopment. Next comes Memorial City Hall, designed by a notable Boston firm. Design features that stand out include Ionic columns and a gold cupola. The building was given to the city by the family of David Osborne, former mayor and owner of an agricultural equipment manufacturer that became part of International Harvester.

The tour continued with a turn onto Grover Street, a small residential avenue on which even houses not listed in the guide looked impressive. It's a good place to brush up on such architectural features as pilasters, fine dentil work, and mansard roofs. Notice the stick-style home at number 19 and the ornate, dark-green roof brackets on number 37. Several houses along the street date back as far as 1825.

Grander homes along South Street boast turrets, Palladian windows, and wraparound porches. Styles range from Tudor, Federal, and Colonial Revival, to "stick," Greek Revival, and Italianate.

We especially liked the decorative details of two Queen Anne creations, at 48 South (home to the owner of Auburn Button Works) and

85 South. Notable Boston architects Coolidge, Shepley, Bulfinch, and Abbott designed the sixty-five-room Tudor mansion at 108 South for Theodore Case. His early inventions, on display in his restored laboratory downtown behind the Cayuga Museum, laid the basis for "talking" movies.

Even a Vanderbilt would feel comfortable at Queen's Court (number 63), a mansion with ten fireplaces, eight master bedrooms, and a third-floor billiard chamber. The nearby brick Craftsman-style house (number 67), modest by comparison, was once owned by Reverend Allen Dulles. A professor at the Auburn Seminary, he raised sons who became secretary of state and director of the Central Intelligence Agency.

A young attorney named William Seward came to visit an Auburn woman in 1823. He stayed to practice law with her father, Judge Elijah Miller. Seward and Frances Miller eventually married and moved into the house (33 South) Judge Miller had built in 1816. Brigham Young was among the carpenters who worked on the home.

Ambitious and well-read, Seward rose to become governor of New York, and later a United States senator. He was also targeted by the conspiracy leading to the assassination of President Lincoln, but he survived his wounds. While secretary of state in 1867, he engineered the purchase of Alaska (remember Seward's Folly from your high school history?). The house, lived in by subsequent generations of the Seward family, offers an interesting tour.

The Westminster Presbyterian Church on William Street, final stop on the formal tour, stands out with its gray stone construction, red sandstone trim, and central bell tower. Inside are three Tiffany windows.

At Fitch Avenue, it's well worth taking a detour to Fort Hill Cemetery. Situated on the site of ancient burial mounds, the scenic compound serves as a superb example of the nicely landscaped rural cemeteries that replaced less sanitary graveyards during the nineteenth century.

The Cayuga Museum provides a walking guide to the cemetery. Thus, we learned that the impressive stone entry gates were designed by locally noted architect Julius Schweinfurth (whose grave lies here). Atop the hill is a stone obelisk dedicated to Chief Logan. The memorial honors the Cayuga natives who lived here three centuries ago, but also reminds of the earlier Owasco peoples.

Wandering the park-like grounds, we found resting places of such prominent Auburn citizens as William Seward, Theodore Case, Allen Macy Dulles, and David Osborne, all discussed above. Revolutionary War veteran John Hardenbergh, founder of the city, lies here. So does a veteran of the Battle of Little Big Horn.

Another notable resident is Harriet Tubman, the former slave who became so important in the Underground Railroad during the Civil War era. There's also Martha Coffin Wright, sister of women's rights activist Lucretia Mott.

More anonymous but quite poignant is Jane Rogers, who died in 1893 after directing the Cayuga Asylum for Destitute Children for over three decades. She chose to be interred in the orphanage plot with fifty-nine of the children she cared for.

******

For a different type of experience, we headed for Moravia in southern Cayuga County. Fillmore Glen is another of the impressive glacially carved gorges in the Finger Lakes area. It is, however, the only one named after a president. In fact, near the trailhead there's a re-creation of the log cabin in which Millard Fillmore was born just a couple of miles from here.

Once started on the Gorge Trail, the best of several hiking options, it's easy to forget about presidential politics. We crossed a stone bridge and found ourselves at the base of Lower Falls. Nicknamed "Cowsheds" for the way cattle would hide here on hot days, this alcove in the cliff wall provides a good vantage point for watching the forceful stream plummet over a resistant rock ledge. I suspect that this is as far as the majority of visitors come. They're missing a lot if they don't continue.

Back across the bridge, we climbed up 133 stone steps to begin our hike. The trail continues for a couple of miles, crossing nine more bridges along the way, and occasionally passing through a mixed conifer-hardwood forest. Steep gorge walls and the rushing waters of less-than-aptly named Dry Creek dominate the scenery.

We took time to appreciate some of the man-made features, too.

Many of the footpaths and stone steps were constructed in the 1930s by Civilian Conservation Corps workers.

About halfway along the route, we climbed a bit, then walked carefully next to walls of crumbling shale. The fifth and sixth bridges nicely framed a very pretty rapids. The channel subsequently narrowed. A broad, feathery flow of water cascaded down a side wall, offering some nice photo opportunities. (The entire hike beckons to the creative camera user.)

Stone steps led upward again. Just as we approached a bend by the eighth bridge, a large falls came into view, to be followed by another only a few yards farther ahead. Signs pointed to an alternative return path along the rim, but we chose to retrace the more dramatic route at water level.

Along the way back, my wife identified a variety of plant life—trillium, Solomon's seal, foamflower, and on one wall, red columbine. As for me, I just stayed entranced by the movement of the water. Nature doesn't put on many better shows.

Information:
Cayuga County Office of Tourism, 131 Genesee Street, Auburn, NY 13021. Phone 315-255-1658.
Fillmore Glen State Park, 1686 NY Route 38, Moravia, NY 13118. Phone 315-497-0130.

Surviving arches that once supported canal aqueduct over Schoharie Creek

Schenectady Stockade • Schoharie Crossing

When someone first told me about the Schenectady Stockade, I assumed the reference was to a fort. Indeed it was, at least once upon a time. The defensive walls have been down for years. But the Stockade survives—in fact thrives—as New York's oldest historic district.

A Dutchman named Arendt Van Curler purchased land from the Mohawk Indians in 1661, and then settled here along with fourteen other families. Roughly carved trees provided a protective barrier around the four-block plot—the original Stockade. Inside the walls was also a Mohawk longhouse, important both for friendship and trade.

The English, arriving in New York, respected the property rights of Van Curler and his compatriots. However, Frenchmen from Quebec, accompanied by their own native allies, did not. In 1690, these invaders burned forty homes, massacred much of the population of three hundred, and dragged survivors north as prisoners.

Encouraged by a Mohawk known only as "Lawrence," who personally worked to bring ninety prisoners back to Schenectady, the remaining Dutch families rebuilt their houses. A second stockade served to protect the now expanded area. In 1776, the third and last stockade would be built.

Goods moving east or west along the Mohawk River had to be portaged around Cohoes Falls, and Dutch settlers thrived on the economic trade for many years. In 1819 a disastrous fire destroyed over a hundred homes and commercial buildings within the Stockade. Completion of the Erie Canal soon obviated the need for the Schenectady port.

By the time the Edison Machine Works (later to become General Electric) and other industries transformed the local economy, businessmen no longer needed water access. Further growth came elsewhere in the city. Consequently, the Stockade District has managed to remain remarkably intact over time.

Self-guided walking tours are readily available from local museums, including the Schenectady Historical Society at 32 Washington Street (518-374-0263). For over an hour we strolled and enjoyed an immersion into history and architecture.

As a starting point, we chose the Stockade Inn, right in the center of the historic district. Built in 1816 as a bank, the dressed-stone building saw service as a girls' school and men's club before its more recent transformation to a bed-and-breakfast and restaurant. The elegant lobby includes hardwood floors, interior arches, and Corinthian pilasters. Rooms have a Victorian feel. For guests so inclined, there's even a billiard room. The well-appointed dining room, complete with brass chandeliers, makes a good place for a pre- or post-walk lunch.

We walked down Union Street past a regal stone Dutch Reformed Church built in 1862. This was the seventh such structure. The first, complete with whipping post, had stood a block away. The Yates House, dating to 1725, features small handmade bricks assembled in a "butterfly" pattern.

Just across sits the white, columned original courthouse (1833). Glassed-in basement windows prevented peeking into the jail cells. At the corner of Ferry Street stands a brick building with a bay window. From 1796 to 1804 this served as the first home of Union College. Later it became Schenectady's City Hall.

Two adjacent brownstones epitomize luxury with their turrets, parapets, and arched third-floor balcony. These Romanesque brick and sandstone mansions were home to members of the Ellis family, founders of the American Locomotive Company and donors to Ellis Hospital.

Retracing our steps to Ferry Street, we came to St. George's, a compact stone building claiming distinction as the oldest Episcopal Church in the Mohawk Valley. For a time, the Presbyterians shared the premises. One denomination used the front door; the other entered on the side! This turns out to be a good place to peruse weathered grave markers, with their symbolic engravings of urns and weeping willows.

At Ferry and Front, a statue of Lawrence the Indian holds forth on a brick island. This was the site of Queen's New Fort, easternmost wall of the original Stockade. Continuing on, we arrived at a pumping station by the river. A marker on the building's corner notes heights of water during past floods—the highest came in 1914.

A brick promenade leads to a riverside walking path and adjacent parkland. North America's longest covered bridge once spanned the water here. At another spot, early travelers could pull themselves across the Mohawk via a rope ferry.

Joseph Yates, Schenectady's first mayor and fourth governor of New York, occupied a large brick home (1760) on Front Street. He used the attached wing as his law office. Marquis de Lafayette visited Yates here during his tour of the United States in 1825.

The Hendrick Brouwer House, just up Church Street, claims title to being the oldest house. Inside the original 1665 foundation there's a tunnel that goes to the river. Apparently several Stockade homes have such tunnels, the significance of which has been lost with time.

On Washington Street there's a house that headquartered America's first subway, a carriage route under the river that operated from 1832 to 1838, by which time frequent flooding had proved it impractical. A 1680 powder magazine once filled the site now occupied by modest brick houses built to house General Electric employees.

More than anything, we enjoyed the eclecticism of the architecture. We'd be walking past handsome brick row houses reminiscent of Georgetown or downtown Philadelphia, and then suddenly we'd happen onto a gambrel roof or a Tudor home. A Gothic Revival cottage enlivened Front Street. Small gardens between homes caught our eye. So did a beehive oven behind the Teller House.

Few residential neighborhoods boast as many plaques and historical markers. We found homes where George Washington slept (really!), the modest first Schenectady residence of General Electric genius Charles Steinmetz, and the site from which the world's first television broadcast emanated.

We also stopped into the Schenectady Historical Society. Housed in a handsome, pale-yellow Georgian home built for Dora Jackson in 1895, the museum concentrates on eighteenth- and nineteenth-century community history. Among offerings are oil paintings of the covered bridge over the Mohawk, a boardroom table at which such notables as J. P. Morgan and Thomas Edison made decisions, and a dollhouse created for Governor Yates' granddaughter. The Shaker Room commemorates that group's first settlement in America at nearby Watervliet.

******

Farther west, along the Mohawk River near Amsterdam, Schoharie

Crossing State Historic Site provides a unique opportunity to view all phases of Erie Barge Canal development.

An easy half-mile walk along the Mohawk River Trailway brought us to abandoned Lock 20, one of eighty-four on the original 1822 Erie Canal. By crossing a wooden bridge we gained access to the "modernized" and larger Lock 29 ("Empire Lock"), built when the Erie was revised in 1840. Two 110-by-18-foot bays replaced the single 90-by-15-foot capacity of Lock 20.

It's impressive to see the workmanship that left these stone structures durable enough to survive a half century of vigorous use, followed by almost a century of neglect.

Two more miles along the towpath brings one to Lock 28, a double-bay affair called Yankee Hill Lock. Just across stood Putman's Store. This Greek Revival stone building, mustard-colored with mauve trim, typified the many such places found along the canal's route. Lodging was offered, and crewmen could stock up on food, liquor, and harness materials.

Still structurally strong, the store contains historical exhibits and information on provisions purveyed at the time. There's also an important concession to modern day travelers—clean rest rooms!

Most remarkable about the site, however, is the Schoharie Aqueduct. Originally, the Erie Canal simply went across Schoharie Creek; ropes towed boats through the north-flowing stream. On occasion, turbulent waters led to loss of both property and life. When the canal was enlarged, the decision was made to carry the channel in an aqueduct over these waters.

Fourteen arches supported a 624-foot viaduct at completion in 1841. Thus, the stone-bedded canal trough and the adjacent towpath continued directly over Schoharie Creek. Clambering up to the top of the aqueduct, I got a close-up look at the seven remaining arches and pillars. Much of one towpath is still in place, and we clearly saw where the canal trough would have been carried across the arches.

The Schoharie Aqueduct further testifies to the boldness and confidence that accompanied construction of early canals. It's appropriate having these arches survive as engineering artifacts.

Information:
Schenectady County Historical Society, 32 Washington Avenue, Schenectady, NY 12305. Phone 518-374-0263.
Schenectady Heritage Area Visitor Center, Nott Terrace Heights, Schenectady, NY 12308. Phone 518-382-7890.
Schoharie Crossing State Historic Site, 129 Schoharie Street, P.O. Box 140, Fort Hunter, NY 12069. Phone 518-829-7516.

Costumed guide at Schenectady Stockade

Geneva ● Watkins Glen

Our wanderings brought us to New York's Finger Lakes region. At the northern tip of Seneca Lake, Geneva boasts a college campus, a remarkable collection of American architecture, noteworthy tourist attractions, and the lake itself.

To gain a sense of the city, try beginning with a walking tour put together by the Geneva Historical Society.

When, in the 1790s, Pulteney Associates of England purchased the million-acre land patent that included present-day Geneva, they hired Charles Williamson to be their agent. Williamson in turn laid out the main grid and marketed the land.

Agriculture, and especially nurseries, fueled early growth. The area became a leader in farm innovation; there's still an agricultural research center in Geneva today. Early industries produced glass products, engines, and cereals. Commitment to education, present almost from the city's founding, continues to be central to the economy.

Using our brochure as a guide, we strolled South Main Street, which follows the lakeshore. Early land purchasers were guaranteed rights to both sides of the road, thereby assuring lake access for the homes built on the west side of the street. As time passed, many owners sold the lakeside lots, allowing construction of more houses. Along part of South Main, however, the original views are retained. Benches encourage walkers to sit and enjoy the panorama.

The village began around Pulteney Park, at the north end of the street. There we began our walk.

By 1800, there was already a hotel, a post office, and the Geneva Academy surrounding the green. The Geneva Hotel (1796) survives as an apartment house. At one time it also saw use as a sanitarium. Row houses around the park, reminiscent of those in Georgetown, date to the 1820s.

South Main Street is a good place to cement knowledge of architectural features. Examples of Federal, Greek Revival, and Gothic Revival styles are plentiful. Two homes described as Jeffersonian turned out to be college fraternity houses. The President's Home, a columned Greek Revival mansion, truly makes a statement.

Continuing south, we approached the campus of Hobart and William Smith Colleges. Two of the earliest buildings, Geneva Hall and Trinity Hall, date to 1822 (the year of Hobart's founding) and 1837. We examined the corner quoins; early graduates' names are carved into the stones.

Next door sits St. John's Chapel, designed by the same architect who designed Trinity Church in New York City. Just behind we found the Hobart Quadrangle, surrounded by its own wealth of venerable architecture. Go a few steps farther for a glimpse of Smith Hall, built for newly established William Smith College for Women in 1907.

Farther south, a wooded area encloses Houghton House. Ensconced in its secluded setting, this is home to the college's art school. Nearby stone walls surround a sunken garden.

Working our way back north, we came upon a frame house built in 1787; an Italianate home with a square tower; some Second Empire buildings with mansard roofs; and a collection of steep-roofed Gothic Revival cottages (one was constructed of adobe and wood planks). Outside 493 South Main, a state historical marker denotes the site of Geneva Medical College. In 1849, this institution accepted Elizabeth Blackwell, the first woman to study medicine in the United States.

Not quite ready to stop, we went a couple of blocks into the downtown area. Two buildings made strong impressions. A sandstone Romanesque structure, now the Geneva Athletic Club, originally served as the YMCA. I especially liked the Smith Opera House. Built for the city by William Smith in 1894, it has been substantially renovated into a performing arts center. Relief sculptures of William Shakespeare and nineteenth-century actor Edwin Booth stare down upon entering patrons.

Those desiring more walking could turn onto Washington Street, another nucleus of impressive residences. A stone edifice fronted by four Roman pillars originally served as the Pulteney Land Office. Just off Washington, on Delancey Drive, sits the Van Gleason Foote house. This large white Greek Revival has hosted a girls' school and a sanitarium during its long life.

Another option, Castle Street, was a lane of country estates in the days when nurseries dominated local business. Three Italianate homes were the residences of Theodore, Thomas, and William Smith. At number 760, there's a two-story octagonal house that became notable locally when it was built with *two* bathtubs.

It's worth asking directions to Jay Street to see Ashcroft, an imposing Gothic Revival cottage designed by Frederick Law Olmstead's associate Calvert Vaux.

There are also beautiful waterside paths in the village park and Seneca Lake State Park at the northern tip of the lake.

While in Geneva, take time to visit Rose Hill, an elegant restoration of a Greek Revival mansion dating to 1836. A short distance away, there's the Mike Weaver Drain Tile Museum, likely the only entity in the world exclusively devoted to this architectural engineering phenomenon. Both are operated by the Geneva Historical Society.

******

Much of Watkins Glen's fame comes from the association with auto racing. For years an American race on the Grand Prix circuit took place near here. But Watkins Glen itself has been a tourist attraction since journalist Morvalden Ells opened the marvel to the public in 1863. Long in private hands, and once flanked by resort hotels, the land became part of the New York State park system in 1906.

The glen dates back to the ice age. Glaciers initially carved the deep trough, and the flowing waters of Glen Creek have continued the process of erosion.

When you park and face the gorge, you'll already find yourself in the midst of tall cliffs. The trail will stretch a mile and a half; a sign warns there will be 832 steps along the way. Shuttles take visitors to the upper entrance for a one-way hike. If, as I did, you plan to walk both directions from the main entrance, allow a good two or three hours for the trip.

Look for the entry tunnel and climb through to begin your journey. The forces of nature become apparent immediately. The power of water—churning, rushing, plunging over vertical falls—has sculpted a remarkable series of rock formations.

Cavern Cascade proves an early highlight. The route winds along twisting channels to a point where you can stand behind the waterfalls and marvel at the inexorable force. The eeriness of being just behind the flow can make you think this is an amusement park ride, but no theme park can satisfactorily reproduce this sense of awe.

Soon you'll come to a suspension bridge eighty-five feet above water level. The Glen Mountain House once stood at one end. It staggers belief, but floodwaters in 1935 came within five feet of the span.

Next comes the Narrows, a shaded area with considerable plant growth. After climbing another set of stairs, you'll note how the chasm widens. The air feels a bit lighter. Sedimentary rock layers, hardened over hundreds of millions of years, make their presence known.

The next notable point is Central Cascade. Crossing a bridge allows a view from the top as well as alongside. Though narrow and less imposing than Cavern Cascade, at sixty feet this is the highest falls in Watkins Glen. Soon a very pretty falls spreads out from the wall to the left, forming a nice contrast with adjacent moss-covered cliffs. This is Rainbow Falls. Once again, erosion of shale in the cliff wall allows the trail to wind behind the flow of water. I walked on an overcast day, so I didn't get to experience the array of colors that gives the spot its name.

In contrast, Pluto Falls, coming from an overhanging lip, is just a wisp of a cataract.

A clearly marked junction designates Mile Point Bridge. You might be tempted to turn around here, but don't. A stroll along the next—and quieter—segment of the gorge could be like walking along any broad babbling brook, but time here will clear the sensory palate for the splendors you'll see again on the return to your origin. The trail will end at the steep staircase known as Jacob's Ladder, which gives access to the upper entry point for the gorge.

Though I could have made my way back along the South Rim Trail, I chose instead to retrace the Gorge Trail.

I lingered a bit near the Spiral Tunnel. Then I made my way into a notch behind a waterfall. It's quite a feeling when you suddenly realize that the full force of Glen Creek now races above, indeed almost atop, you.

At both Rainbow Falls and Cavern Cascade, I stopped and spent some extra time. From behind the latter, I enjoyed what were almost stop-action perspectives of the flow of water.

It's impossible to come away from Watkins Glen without an appreciation of the power of water to transform a landscape. Indeed, this is one of Mother Nature's great amphitheaters—it's her show. Pay attention, though, to some of the man-made additions. Stone bridges and walkways have been well crafted both for sturdiness and their ability to blend in with the environment. Such accomplishments should not be overlooked.

Don't rush when walking the Glen. There are photo opportunities at every turn. I've hiked Watkins Glen twice, both times in mid-afternoon. Next time I'll come in early morning or closer to dusk, when I'm sure the light will give an entirely different feel to this magnificent place.

Information:
Geneva Historical Society, 543 S. Main Street, Geneva, NY 14456. Phone 789-5151.
Watkins Glen State Park, Route 14, Box 304, Watkins Glen, NY 14891. Phone 607-535-4511.

Stone bridge at Fillmore Glen

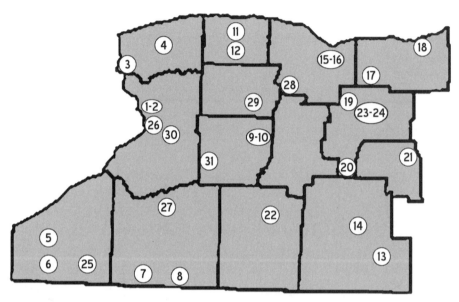

1.	Buffalo	23.	Sonnenberg Gardens
2.	Allentown	24.	Canandaigua
3.	Niagara Falls	25.	Jamestown
4.	Lockport	26.	Charles Burchfield Nature & Art Center
5.	Chautauqua Institution	27.	Griffis Sculpture Park
6.	Panama Rocks	28.	Genesee Country Village
7.	Allegany State Park	29.	Genesee Forest and Park
8.	Rock City	30.	East Aurora
9.	Letchworth State Park	31.	Beaver Meadow
10.	Mount Morris Dam		
11.	Cobblestone Country		
12.	Albion		
13.	Corning		
14.	Bath		
15.	Rochester		
16.	Mount Hope Cemetery		
17.	Palmyra		
18.	Chimney Bluffs		
19.	Ganondagan		
20.	Cumming Nature Center		
21.	Keuka Outlet		
22.	Palmers Pond		

WESTERN – NIAGARA

Western New York comprises the Niagara Frontier, much of Lake Ontario's shore, the Allegheny region, and the state's second- and third-largest cities. Though Niagara Falls may be the area's most famous natural feature, there's also the "Grand Canyon of the East" in Letchworth State Park, and unusual rock formations in the southwest corner of the state.

Buffalo boasts a wealth of American architecture surpassed perhaps only by Chicago. Rochester built its industrial growth on the rushing waters of the Genesee River, still a dominant point in the city's center. Walking tours provide insights into the history of these metropolitan areas.

Corning became world famous for its manufacturing of glass products. The Victorian village of Chautauqua became noted as the first summer educational institution in the country, leading to a Chautauqua movement across America. Small villages produced such important entrepreneurs as George Pullman and Henry Wells.

In the aftermath of Erie Canal construction, artisans built unique cobblestone houses; nowhere in the world is there as great a concentration as in western New York. Creativity still thrives, as shown by the outdoor sculpture complex one family built in Cattaraugus County.

Buffalo • Allentown

A century ago, Buffalo ranked as one of America's ten largest cities. Success began with the building of the Erie Canal. Completion of that revolutionary transportation channel made Buffalo the hub between the Midwest and major port cities in the East. The coming of the railroad simply cemented its commercial importance. Availability of hydroelectric power from nearby Niagara Falls fueled more growth.

By 1901 it seemed only natural for Buffalo to have a World's Fair. Unfortunately, that event, the Pan American Exposition, gets remembered more for the assassination of President William McKinley than for Buffalo's status as host city.

Still, it was Buffalo that became America's first city with electric streetlights. It was Buffalo that witnessed invention of the grain elevator. It was Buffalo that made Cheerios. The luxury automobile Pierce-Arrow had its home in Buffalo. Ellsworth Statler began his famous chain of hotels here.

Such commercial success brought in its wake a remarkable variety of architectural creativity. Virtually every notable architect of the era designed a building in Buffalo. Frank Lloyd Wright drafted plans to be implemented in Buffalo. So did his mentor Louis Sullivan. Henry Hobson Richardson made a mark here. Frederick Law Olmstead did, too.

Economic times have changed here as elsewhere in the Northeast. Major employer Bethlehem Steel has been gone for two decades, and Pierce-Arrow even longer. Still, two state colleges and a few smaller private ones flourish, as does a medical school and famed Roswell Park Cancer Institute. High tech grows. Buffalo native Ani Difranco contributes by recycling an abandoned church into her "Righteous Babe" studio.

The serious walker has the opportunity to savor a virtual museum of structures, many now recycled for new uses. In fact, a long stroll around Buffalo gives an American architectural survey second perhaps only to that of Chicago.

Begin downtown. If you're fortunate enough to find a "Walk Buffalo" booklet, this details an excellent two-mile tour. Other readily available brochures map out similar routes.

Niagara Square, the center of government for Buffalo and Erie County, makes a good starting point. A monument to William McKinley stands in this park, while across the street stands the thirty-two-story art deco City Hall. Next time I'll tour on a weekday, so I can look out from the twenty-eighth-floor observation windows.

Then turn your attention to the red brick Statler Building. This, the second hotel built by Ellsworth Statler, now functions as an office building.

Winding my way counterclockwise to Franklin and Swan streets, I passed St. Joseph's Cathedral and the Guaranty Building. Frank Lloyd Wright mentor, Louis Sullivan, designed the latter structure, one of America's first to utilize all-steel framing. It's notable for its elaborate terra-cotta facing. (There is a handful of Wright creations in Buffalo, but none close enough to be on the walking tour.)

The nearby Dun Building, housing the credit firm that became Dun and Bradstreet, is another early skyscraper (ten stories!). Cast-iron facades farther along Pearl Street harken back to what was once a leading industry in Buffalo. St. Paul's Episcopal Cathedral owes its design to Richard Upjohn, also responsible for New York's Trinity Church.

The Old Post Office on Swan Street is magnificent. Transformed into Erie Community College, the granite structure's massive size and its towers give it a commanding presence. Across the street stands Buffalo's baseball stadium. Designed by the same firm that developed Baltimore's Camden Yards and Cleveland's Jacobs Field, the 1988 facility blends well with the city landscape.

Most of my way now followed along Main Street.

There are few interior spaces more grand than that of the Ellicott Square Building, named in honor of Joseph Ellicott, who in 1797 drew up plans for the settlement that would become Buffalo. Chicago architect Daniel Burnham designed the complex, the largest business center in the world at its completion in 1896. There's a wonderful skylit atrium, each individual pane of glass etched with a starburst pattern. Wrought-iron staircases lead from the mosaic tile floor (twenty-three million individual pieces!) to the balcony level. Even the bronze panels on the elevator doors are decorative, with scenes ranging from a log cabin, to a grain elevator, to a (surprise!) buffalo.

Lafayette Square, another of the nice parks scattered throughout Buffalo, had been called Courthouse Square before being changed to honor Marquis de Lafayette. Immediately adjacent are the Liberty Building (notable for two replicas of the statue in New York Harbor), and Lafayette Hotel (designed by Louise Bethune, the country's first licensed female architect).

In contrast to the Statler, a hotel turned into office space, the Hyatt makes use of the 1923 Genesee Building for the city's largest hotel. A block down Huron stands the Niagara Mohawk Building, a favorite landmark that owes its design to the Electric Tower at the 1901 Pan-American Exposition. The traditional New Year's Eve ball falls here.

The prominent gold dome turns out to be only one of the ornate, decorative features of the Beaux-Arts style M&T Center, but its presence proved formidable enough that Buffalo Savings Bank once changed its name to the Goldome Bank. Market Arcade, a nineteenth-century edifice that foreshadowed later malls, has interior skylights, and terra-cotta buffalo heads over its entry doors.

I'm partial to oddities like the Cyclorama Building. Hard as it may be to believe, before the days of television and motion pictures, huge circular painted scenes attracted droves of spectators. Specially designed structures were needed. Not many remain, but this multisided brick building, now an architectural firm, is a good example. Nearby St. Louis Roman Catholic Church, built of Medina sandstone by German immigrants, includes an unusual open spire in its Gothic construction.

Among other areas that reward the walker are Elmwood Village and Allentown. Delaware Avenue boasts an array of mansions and elegant old apartment houses once occupied by Buffalo's most successful citizens. Henry Hobson Richardson and New York's McKim, Mead, and White are among architects represented.

The Knox Mansion reminded me of the Vanderbilt Mansion in Hyde Park. The gray limestone Clement Mansion, designed to simulate an English manor house, now headquarters the Red Cross. The Mansion on Delaware has been renovated into a sumptuous boutique hotel. Row houses on the 400 block are more modest.

One place on Delaware, the Wilcox Mansion, has national historic importance. After William McKinley's assassination in 1901, Vice

President Theodore Roosevelt rushed to Buffalo from an Adirondack hunting trip. Learning en route that the President had died, Roosevelt went to the home of a friend, Ansley Wilcox. Wearing clothes borrowed from his host, the new President took the oath of office here.

Allentown includes a terrific variety of nineteenth- and twentieth-century residential architecture. Nancy Vargo of the Buffalo-Niagara Convention and Visitors Bureau helped me see a representative sampling.

We began at Arlington Place. Frederick Law Olmstead lived here while working on Buffalo's park system. He convinced other architects to build homes here, thereby ensuring an impressive group of residences around a central green. Plaques indicate most houses date from the 1870s to the 1890s. Especially notable are Gothic Revival creations, well demonstrating the decorative carpentry of that style, and a lone example of Dutch Colonial.

Turning left onto Wadsworth and then onto Allen, we passed Nietzche's, notable as the place where the Goo Goo Dolls got their start. Allendale Theater, its movie days behind it, has become a home for young people's theater.

On Mariner Street, I found a range of styles. There are mirror-image brick homes dating to the 1860s, a wonderful multicolor clapboard worker's cottage, and others quite reminiscent of New Orleans shotgun design. On Cottage Street, one formidable brick house features contrasting stone corner quoins and a turret.

Days Park takes its name from Thomas Day, who ran the city's first brick kiln. The two homes he built for his sons in the 1820s still stand. An ornately repainted Victorian with a parapet merits attention.

We ended at Symphony Circle, where the First Presbyterian Church features Tiffany stained-glass windows. Across the street stands Kleinhan's Music Hall, designed by Eliel Saarinen and his son Eero (designer of the Gateway Arch in St. Louis).

Information:
Buffalo-Niagara Convention and Visitors Bureau, 617 Main Street, Suite 200, Buffalo, NY 14203. Phone 716-852-0511.

Niagara Falls • Lockport

Few natural features in the world combine myth, legend, and geological uniqueness to the degree that Niagara Falls does. Honeymoons by the score have been celebrated by these roaring waters. Tightrope walkers challenged the chasm for years. So did daredevils, who attempted to conquer the cascades in barrels, or even less.

Engineers worked to bridge its span, and then to harness its waters for power. Entrepreneurs built sideshows and garish souvenir stands to attract tourists. Other enterprising types built boats to bring visitors close to the spray. New York began its state park system there with the Niagara Reservation.

No end of famous personages has been associated with the falls. King Gillette, inventor of the disposable razor blade, built a complex here devoted to his interest in world peace. Ed Delahanty, an early baseball star now enshrined in the Baseball Hall of Fame, plunged to his death from a railroad trestle over the falls. John Roebling built a suspension bridge across the raging waters before he became world famous for his Brooklyn Bridge. Frederick Law Olmsted, most noted for New York City's Central Park, advocated for the Niagara Reservation, so as to preserve a natural view of the falls. Thomas Edison and Nicolas Tesla came with designs to harness the waters for electric power.

Indeed everyone deserves to see this remarkable sight, in all seasons if possible. And no one can deny the attraction of riding close up on Maid of the Mist. An elevator goes down to Cave of the Winds, a niche created by erosion behind the falls. But perhaps a walk around Goat Island best builds appreciation of the falls' majesty.

First I stopped in the Visitor Center. Displays discuss the geologic and human history of the Niagara River. Niagara Falls had become the "honeymoon capital of the world" by 1802. Frederick Law Olmstead made his first visit in 1869. The Niagara Reservation, New York's first state park, was established in 1885.

There are impressive photos, one of the Biddle Stairs, an eighty-foot spiral staircase built in 1829 to allow walking access to the base of the American Falls. It was demolished in 1927. Another dramatic shot shows the collapse of Schoellkopf Power Station in 1956.

I began my walk at an observation deck just outside the Visitor Center. This gave me a close-up look at the tumultuous American Falls. Just before the precipice, swollen rapids warn of the riverbed change. Water striking the rocks far below creates a mist, and a persistent fog gave the sight a moody feeling. Moving a few steps to Prospect Point let me stand right at the crest of the falls, the roiling river tumbling down just in front of me.

I walked upstream along the rapids and turned onto the Pedestrian Bridge. Constructed with three stone arches, the bridge brought me to Goat Island. The name celebrates a lone goat from the herd of early settler John Stedman that survived a particularly bad winter. Olmstead praised the island's beauty, deeming it a good spot for "quiet contemplation of nature." His description belies the omnipresent sound, for if anything is constant around the falls, it's the continual roaring of the waters.

A tiny bridge gives access to Luna Island, named for the "moonbows" (nighttime counterpart of rainbows) commonly seen here during the nineteenth century, before artificial light deadened the effect. There I stood at the precipice of Bridal Veil Falls, the smallest of the three cascades by which the Niagara River falls from Lake Erie to Lake Ontario. A glance back gave a stunning view of the American Falls.

Retracing to Goat Island, I followed the road to Terrapin Point, just a few yards from the Canadian, or Horseshoe, Falls. Though a wood walkway that gave access to this spot as early as 1820 is long gone, the remarkable panorama remains largely the same. Almost a half-mile wide, this falls drops 167 feet back to the Niagara River. Rarely during a lifetime will anyone feel such a source of raw power as when standing on this site.

Anyone complaining that the Niagara Falls area has become too commercialized and "touristy" need only come here for a reinforcement of the magic and majesty of this natural wonder. I've had the opportunity to view the falls in all seasons, and it never loses its allure.

Continuing the 1.5-mile circuit around the perimeter of Goat Island, I next came to the Three Sisters Islands. Named for the daughters of an American general, these are reached via another pedestrian bridge. Here are the Horseshoe Rapids, where the river picks up power en route to its dramatic drop across the falls.

Farther along, interpretive signs told of early portages and military activity. British settlers had built roads for driving cattle by the late 1700s. Forts were established early to guard this critical border.

I continued past the American Rapids, and back to the pedestrian bridge. Crossing, I returned to Prospect Point overlooking the American Falls. Words don't adequately express the emotions stirred by the site.

Less traveled and more rustic trails lead to the Niagara Gorge and Whirlpool, both worthy destinations. The loop around Goat Island, however, serves as an excellent introduction to Niagara Falls, an introduction you'll be happy to have again and again on return visits.

******

Farther east in Niagara County, the city of Lockport merits a stop. When the Erie Canal was built across New York, a massive rock ledge called the Niagara Escarpment posed a major barrier. Ingenuity, plus backbreaking effort with drills, black powder, and sledgehammers were required to overcome the hurdle.

Five consecutive locks were required to raise boats over the escarpment. Substantial remnants of this stonework still stand today, though boat traffic now traverses two larger locks close by.

Interpretive panels along Riley's Way, named for former City Historian William Riley, give background on this and other aspects of local history. One can also stroll the refurbished towpath. Should the spirit move you, the path goes about seventy miles eastward, past Rochester and all the way to Palmyra.

The highlight of the walk is, of course, the series of locks. Each of the original five locks raised a boat ten feet. A series of falls flows over the remains. In comparison, enlarged Locks 34 and 35, opened in 1918, each lift (or lower) twenty-five feet in under ten minutes. During the summer, one should have only a brief wait to see boats being locked through.

Lockport bridges are worth noting. One is nicknamed the "upside down bridge," its steel truss facing downwards instead of up. Fiercely competitive railroads were not above building in such a manner, so as to prevent large boats from being able to ply the waterway.

Advent of automobile traffic led to installation of lift bridges; there are two in Lockport. You shouldn't have to wait long to see them in operation, either.

Then there's the Big Bridge. At 299 feet, it's purported to have been the country's widest such span at the time of its construction.

Notice how commercial buildings could unload right onto canal boats. And find two stone arches. These mark the hydraulic cave race-way, an ingenious creation blasted out in the 1850s to divert water and provide power to local industry. Birdsill Holly, an inventor whose other patents include the fire hydrant, is credited with the idea.

Going east of Lockport along the towpath, there's a series of hand-some stone houses. Consider them products of rock blasted from the escarpment and the efforts of stonemasons originally brought to work on the canal. A stone church was built by one resident in nostalgic memory of his home parish in England.

Lockport's Memorial Tree Garden and Widewaters Marina marked our turnaround point. Those with enough energy could continue east for hours.

Information:
Niagara Reservation State Park, Box 1132, Niagara Falls, NY 14303. Phone 716-278-1796.
Niagara County Historical Society, 215 Niagara Street, Lockport, NY 14094. Phone 716-434-7433.

Chautauqua Institution • Panama Rocks

Chautauqua County sits in the far southwest corner of New York State. The farmland is beautiful, lake access is abundant, and a traveler should never run out of things to do.

Perhaps the area is best known for the Chautauqua Institution, established in 1874 as a training ground for Sunday school teachers. Its rapid success led to other Chautauqua-like programs elsewhere, such as the Catholic Summer School of America at Cliff Haven near Plattsburgh. Though most have faded into history, the original setup continues to attract thousands of visitors for a week or a season.

Chautauqua can only be fully appreciated during the summer season. The original religious mission has been broadened with a schedule of lectures, concerts, and plays, all of which meld with an array of outdoor recreational opportunities for a rich experience. Speakers and performers in a given summer may include the likes of the Beach Boys and Mary Chapin Carpenter, to former Supreme Court Justice Sandra Day O'Connor and National Football League Commissioner Roger Goodell, to author E. L. Doctorow and cartoonist Garry Trudeau.

Though the spirit is ecumenical and talks are likely to run the full political spectrum, there is still a Department of Religion, and morning services remain a part of the daily routine. The Chautauqua Literary and Scientific Circle, the oldest book club in America, sponsors readings and book signings. Cultural offerings also include a symphony orchestra, ballet and opera companies, and an active theater.

We visited in June, too early for such activity. But with the aid of a map and detailed guidebook, we enjoyed a walking tour that kept us occupied for several hours.

The village of Chautauqua boasts classic Victoriana; virtually every architectural feature of that era can be found. One specimen, the Gingerbread Cottage, looks just that with its decorative Gothic Revival wood trim. A sign on Foulkeholm next door reports "enjoyed by same family since built in 1889."

Lewis Miller Cottage, named for one of Chautauqua's founders, resembles a Swiss chalet. Ulysses S. Grant was a houseguest just after its completion in 1875. Arthur Bestor resided in a 1905 turreted Queen

Anne home during his tenure as president of Chautauqua. There's an Octagon Building, representative of a fad in the late 1800s. Cottages in board-and-batten and other vernacular styles can also be found.

Some designs, such as that for Chapel of the Good Shepherd, were stimulated by the Arts and Crafts movement. Smith Memorial Library is a grand Georgian Revival building. More modest are dozens of compact practice studios reserved for music students and symphony performers. Each boasts the name of a composer. One commemorates George Gershwin, who composed a concerto at Chautauqua.

Not surprisingly for a place devoted to lecture and performance, auditoriums are impressive. The covered, open-air Amphitheater, built in 1893, can seat five thousand. Equally impressive for religious services and rock concerts, it includes a 5,600 pipe organ, reputedly the largest outdoor one in the world. We've seen Washington Post reporter David Broder speak and singer Anne Murray perform there. Visitors in earlier times had the chance to hear the likes of Booker T. Washington and Franklin D. Roosevelt.

Other venues were also appealing. Smith-Wilkes Hall accommodates over four hundred. With its old-fashioned folding wooden seats, it's a space best described as an open-air school assembly room. The columned Hall of Philosophy, with a capacity of seven hundred, resembles Greece's Parthenon.

Our stroll included the well-maintained waterfront, plus such pleasant open spaces as Bestor Plaza, with its central fountain and sculptures. The Ravine offers trails through a preserved wooded area, while Miller Park's shaded expanse became a favored respite spot when we spent a week here ten years ago. Over two dozen small gardens add further variety to the landscape.

Many of the homes offer rooms to visitors during the summer. There are also several small hotels, boarding houses, and a smattering of condominiums. Since 1881, the mansard-roofed Athenaeum Hotel has ranked as the most elegant place to stay. Aided by Thomas Edison's presence at Chautauqua, this became among the first such buildings to enjoy electric lighting.

Of course, one shouldn't forget Chautauqua Lake, with its beaches and marinas. Bells still chime in the Miller Bell Tower, a sixty-nine-foot-tall Italianate structure, completed in 1911, that stands on the lake-front. Boys' and girls' day camps date back to the 1890s. A long walk on the Promenade offers lake views on one side, glimpses of grand mansions on the other.

Enjoyable to walk, and challenging to experience in more depth, Chautauqua offers a unique bridge between the nineteenth and twenty-first centuries.

******

In contrast to the man-made attractions of Chautauqua, nearby Panama Rocks highlights the vagaries of nature. Geologists talk about sea islands formed during the Devonian period. Tremendous pressure atop sedimentary layers created huge monoliths of quartz conglomerate, also called "pudding stone." Uplifting of the earth's crust, followed by the impact of glaciation, produced wide fissures. At the end of the ice age, the formations were finally exposed.

To us, lacking in scientific expertise, the place simply represented an amazing geological anomaly. From a very ordinary landscape, we descended seventy feet on steep steps. Suddenly we found ourselves amidst massive rock formations with deep clefts and crevices, caves, and alcoves. At one turn, we would enter a mystical rock-bordered glade. Then we'd find the semblance of an elephant or a turtle in a rock.

A one-mile hiking trail brought us past huge rock monoliths, a hollowed arch nicknamed Indian Fireplace, and a long cleft rock called Mayflower. There's a beautiful green area behind Eagle Claw and a narrow channel to negotiate at Fat Man's Misery.

Luxuriant moss carpets thrive at Panama Rocks, as does an array of ferns. Surrounding forest includes cedar, hemlock, maple, and ash trees. Plenty of carved graffiti decorates the smooth bark of beech trees.

Even the human history qualifies as unusual. The name immortalizes one "Panama Joe," who thought the rocks resembled some he saw during an excursion to Panama. Thus, both a geological curiosity and the nearby village gained their names. Gold from a long-ago robbery is still rumored to be buried nearby. In the mid-1800s, these rocks served as a hideout for a band of counterfeiters.

The site has long been privately owned. In fact, Panama Rocks became open to tourists before New York even had its first state park. During the late nineteenth century, a hotel thrived here. The adjacent picnic grounds date to the 1970s.

As we walked back up the trail, we found snow covering the bottom of one deep crevice (and this was August!). Trees seemed to struggle for their very existence. Roots twisted around rocks to gain precarious footholds, at one spot in such a way as to bring to mind a Chippendale ball-and-claw chair leg. It's a battle of nature that sometimes resembles abstract art.

Information:
Chautauqua Institution, 1 Ames Avenue, PO Box 28, Chautauqua, New York 14722. Phone 1-800-836-ARTS.
Panama Rocks, 11 Rock Hill Road, Panama, NY 14767. Phone 716-782-2845.

Sculpture *The Gaffer* in Corning

Allegany State Park ● Rock City

Allegany State Park, in the southwestern section of the state, is one of the largest components of New York State's excellent park system. A seven-thousand-acre purchase in 1921 led to establishment of the park. Subsequent additions have enlarged the protected recreational area to over sixty-five thousand acres.

Much of the construction of facilities, along with forest and stream bank improvements, dates to Civilian Conservation Corps camps established here during the 1930s and early 1940s. A plaque near the headquarters building pays tribute to their efforts. Considerable old-growth forest survives here. The area is notable as being one of the few sections of New York State not covered by glaciers during the ice age.

Red House Lake is especially scenic. Rolling meadowland joins forested slope in providing scenic views. Animal life proved abundant. We saw plenty of deer, more than our share of woodchucks, plus raccoons and foxes. Beaver are apparently plentiful, thanks to a pair brought here from the Adirondacks in 1937. Displays in the park's small natural history museum focus on wildlife. There's a beautiful diorama with wild turkey, black bear, and ruffed grouse. Also check out the case of raptors, and the skeleton of a snapping turtle.

Right behind the handsome stone and half-timbered administration building in the park's Red House Area are two short walks. The one-mile Red Jacket Trail is a pretty route through old forest on a slope above Red House Lake. We found lettered posts along the way, but no one in the office was able to find us any kind of interpretive brochure.

It's too bad, as we passed intriguing stone formations and a couple of small stone walls that needed identification. We did learn later that some of this remains from ski jumps once on the property. A couple of switchbacks brought us higher on the hill. Hollowed-out tree trunks made us wonder if this had been bear habitat. We saw some burls, and listened to the sounds of water rushing through Red Lake outlet.

For something more vigorous we hiked a three-mile loop up Black Snake Mountain (Park Trail Number 3). The trailhead is near Science Lake, once the site of Allegany School of Natural History. Trail markers were discs with a walking symbol; some had been in place long enough to be partially scabbed over by tree bark.

Early on we noted lots of ferns and plenty of birch trees. Tall shag-bark hickories were the titans of the forest. My wife noted Solomon's seal and mayapple along the ground, while our dogs enjoyed the frequent stream access. A few tree blowdowns necessitated wide detours.

Climbing, steady but never difficult, eventually brought us to an airy maple forest. To our surprise we came upon a stone marker designating one side as New York, the other as Pennsylvania.

Trail conditions were better on the way down. We noted evidence of horse travel. The dogs found a broad pool perfect for cooling off at the end of the afternoon. This route can be managed comfortably in two hours.

Another route, the Flagg Trail, began near the Cain Hollow campground entrance. A historical marker told us that Elizi Flagg first began buying land here in 1832. He built two sawmills. His nephew Robert Cain joined him in the 1840s, helping to establish a steam sawmill and a shingle mill. They remained active well into the 1870s. Many early buildings, including some of these, were submerged when a dam created Quaker Lake in the 1960s.

We'd expected just a gentle meadow walk, but the Flagg Trail turned out to be an energy-consuming woodland hike. Hickory nuts were plentiful on the ground, not surprising as hickory, along with maple, dominated the forest.

Studying tree forms and a variety of fungi occupied our attention. A few fallen trees lay impossibly wedged and balanced amidst their still stalwart neighbors. I spotted a porcupine early in the trip. Fortunately, he (she? I didn't get close enough to check) saw us early enough to avoid confrontation. So we watched it lumber up the nearest tree.

After climbing to the crest of the hill, the trail dropped down near Quaker Lake's beach. Following the road back completed a loop easily done in an hour and a half.

Just before getting back to the trailhead, we watched two ospreys soar from their high nest, and then land after a spectacular display of gliding. The book may officially call it the Flagg Trail, but for us it will always be remembered as the "Porcupine-to-Osprey Walk."

Allegany boasts over fifty miles of maintained routes for hiking and walking. Brochures detail eighteen marked trails, including one that goes to a series of caves. Another features a fire tower. Several end at scenic overlooks.

******

Rock City Park is one of those topographic anomalies that one would never expect to find. Just east of Olean, this place claims to be the largest outcropping of pudding stone, a quartz conglomerate, in the world. Geological studies indicate the rock is over 300 million years old.

Local trolley companies saw the tourism potential early and began running cars to the site by 1890. The Bon Air Hotel and a pavilion once thrived alongside. The likes of boxing champion John L. Sullivan came to visit. John Philip Sousa's band played here.

Still privately operated, it makes for a pleasant hour or two of hiking and studying these truly amazing formations.

Entered via a gift shop and small museum, Rock City first requires descent down a flight of metal stairs. That brought us to a long passage called Fat Man's Squeeze, less challenging than the name suggests, but rather a demarcation point on the trail.

A detailed brochure guided us past triangular Tepee Rock, Dining Hall Pass, and to Three Sisters, a trio of huge rock monoliths. Sentinel Rock reigns as the tallest freestanding formation.

A few shapes—Moray Eel, Fallen Map of New York State, and Old Man of the Rocks—require a bit of imagination to envision. However, there's no mistaking Balancing Rock. It's worth circling around and viewing this thousand-ton boulder from all sides.

Seneca Indians once inhabited this territory. Indian Camp, under a massive leaning rock, was purportedly one of many shelters they used. Signal Rock is reached via a steep and narrow stone staircase carved out by the Senecas; it's not for the faint of heart. Once on top, however, there's an unobstructed view for thirty miles or more. One has no difficulty believing that the natives found this useful as a signaling point.

There are more recent traces of human presence. Graffiti dating back as far as 1880 is carved into rock. Huge wheels testify to another use of the land. Oil deposits were discovered here during the nineteenth century. These wheels were part of drilling apparatus used as recently as the 1960s.

It's instructive to remember that when John D. Rockefeller was just beginning to build Standard Oil, his raw material came from New York and Pennsylvania. The huge oil fields of Texas and the Middle East came later.

The green ground cover of ferns, moss, and laurel adds a bright contrast to the rock formations. Trees appear to have a battle for survival. Pines and hemlocks look small, but we learned they're close to a hundred years old.

Information:
Allegany State Park, Route 1, Salamanca, NY 14779. Phone 716-354-9121.
Rock City Park, 505A Rock City Road, Route 16 South, Olean, NY 14760. Phone 866-404-ROCK or 716-372-7790.

Triple mansard roof in downtown Rochester

Letchworth State Park • Mount Morris Dam

By age twenty-two, William Letchworth had already established his success as a manufacturer of saddlery and hardware in Buffalo. Looking for a country place that might provide relaxation and respite from his hectic city life, he set off by train across the state in 1858.

Near the village of Portageville, he crossed the Genesee River on a wooden trestle that soared two hundred feet above the water. Both shores showed the ravages of logging, but Letchworth saw a special beauty in the place.

He left the train and explored a bit. Within a year he began purchasing land. One acquisition led to another. By the time of his death, Letchworth had accumulated over a thousand acres surrounding the Genesee River, including two major waterfalls.

Upon retirement in 1873, Letchworth became active in social reform issues, especially those concerning children and the poor. For two decades, he served on the New York State Board of Charities. He also devoted more time to his estate along the Genesee River.

Unmarried, and with no close relatives, he ultimately deeded the entire property to the State of New York in 1907 for establishment of a park. Nicknamed the "Grand Canyon of the East," Letchworth State Park now comprises over fourteen thousand acres along a wild stretch of the Genesee River.

A road traverses the length of the park. Lookouts give a nice introduction to the scenery.

One turnout overlooks Mount Morris Dam, built by the Army Corps of Engineers for flood control in 1951. When water builds up sufficiently to require containment, the result can be a lake as long as seventeen miles. In 1972, during Tropical Storm Agnes, that's exactly what happened.

More impressive than the dam are the shale and sandstone walls of the gorge. Sheer rock in some places, and more gently sloped and forested elsewhere, the banks of the Genesee are both daunting and beautiful.

Tea Table Overlook boasts a spectacular view of the river coursing 240 feet below. Great Bend offers a vista 550 feet above the water, where the broad river takes a gentle curve. Farther along, at Archery Field, turkey vultures glided between the 480-foot cliffs, coming close enough for detailed views of their bald red heads. In the southern end of the park, waterfalls become the attraction.

Driving provides quite an exposure to Letchworth, but it takes some hiking to fully grasp the enormity of the canyon. Amazingly, as Park Manager Rich Parker told us, well under one percent of visitors take time to sample the trails. We found plenty of options.

The six-mile Gorge Trail, originally a Seneca Indian footpath, offers incredible views at every turn. Hikers must pay attention. At overlooks designated for drivers, we found protective walls and fences; elsewhere, a six-foot deviation can lead straight into the abyss!

We began our trek at Tea Table Overlook. Proceeding quite lei-surely, we came to the views we had previously enjoyed at Great Bend and Archery Point. Our walk intersected with parking areas for over-looks several times—cars would drive on, while we'd go back into the woods.

From Archery Point, approximately halfway along Gorge Trail, we had generally easy walking (but few fences or guardrails), as we headed for Inspiration Point.

Signs just north of Inspiration Point (a good spot to begin a shorter walk) detailed some of the geological forces involved in creating the landscape. We learned about the sedimentary rocks of the canyon walls, and the eroding effects of glaciers and the river.

Red pines, common in the Carolinas, thrive in Letchworth. They grow mainly on sandy bluffs along the rim of the canyon. Another dis-play told about the Genesee Valley Canal that ran high on the shoulder of the bluff for sixteen years, until superseded by a railroad.

Inspiration Point provides a view of the Middle and Upper Falls of Portage Canyon. The latter is nicely framed by Erie High Bridge, the trestle (still used!) that in 1875 replaced the wooden construction Wil-liam Letchworth crossed on his initial visit.

After savoring the falls views, we began a gentle series of switch-backs down to the gorge rim. Steps went down a spur to a musically cascading tributary stream under a stone arch bridge. We looked often at the cliffs, as wondrous as any falls. The roar of waters from below always accompanied us.

The way progressed briefly along a sidewalk of broad stone before descending to a stone-walled path almost at the level of the Middle Falls. There the river tumbles 107 feet over a rock ledge. This may not be the tallest—nor the broadest—cascade I've ever seen, but the torrent of water on this June day could match its power with any. Spray rebounded higher than the cataract itself.

We walked down to a lookout for a close-up view of this violent confluence of upstream waters. Just as we reached the point where the river drops, we looked back to our left and saw a rainbow—a perfect way to cement the memory in our minds.

The trail winds all the way around the falls, providing a terrific sequence of views. At the crest, we had a good vantage point on the canal notch across from us, plus a landslide on the opposite slope, and ruins of an old bridge. Closer at hand we found a broad lawn and picnic area.

Continuing along a grassy swath, we reached a viewpoint on the Upper Falls. At seventy feet, it was modest in comparison to what we had already seen. Lush greenery thrives on the cliff face bathed by the spray.

Another hike brought us through mixed pine and hardwood forest to Kisil Point. Beginning near Loop 100 of the park's campground, this popular hike goes 1.75 miles each way. The route is gentle and broad, ending with a somewhat steep descent. I wondered if it might once have been a carriage road.

We followed near a cliff's edge much of the time, peeking through clear spots for glimpses of the Genesee River far below. White pine, maple, ash, and oak dominated the adjacent forest, with penstemon among the wildflowers along the way.

At our destination, we were rewarded with impressive vistas high above a gentle curve in the river. It's a nice place for appreciating the depth of the canyon. We weren't the only ones admiring the view. A young deer stood on the opposite slope, at least until he spotted us and ran for cover higher up.

The shorter Lee's Landing Trail brought us down to the river's edge. Here river otters were successfully reintroduced into the region a few years ago. White-water raft rides set out from this area. This also boasts a reputation as a good fishing spot for trout and smallmouth bass. The walk follows a gravel road; be prepared for a slight climb upon return.

Visitors should see William Letchworth's other contributions to the park. He took an active interest in Native American culture. Out of respect for the Seneca Indians, he moved a tribal council house to the park. In 1872, he participated, along with former President Millard Fillmore, in the last Seneca Council ever held.

He also paid tribute to Mary Jemison (1742–1833), "White Woman of the Genesee." Born aboard ship as her parents traveled from Ireland for a new start in America, she grew up at Marsh Creek, Pennsylvania. When she was only thirteen, a Seneca raiding party kidnapped her and took her away.

With time, she became fully assimilated into the tribe, eventually marrying a Seneca leader. Though her life was not without tragedy—one of her sons murdered another—she earned the respect of both native peoples and white settlers. Letchworth had her cabin reassembled on a knoll above his own home, and subsequently brought her body there for reburial in 1874. A statue was dedicated in 1910.

Letchworth's collection of Native American artifacts became the core for a museum in the park's south end. Inside, we found exhibits on Mary Jemison (whose memoirs still remain in print), and displays on the skill of flintknapping, by which natives hammered, flaked, and abraded rock into tools. A fossil room featured the head of a mastodon, a forty-three-inch skull with a ninety-six-inch tusk.

Touring Mount Morris Dam revealed this to be much more than a simple wall for blocking water. (And it's a big wall, by the way—1,028 feet long, 245 feet above the water, and containing 740,000 cubic yards of concrete. My pickup truck, in contrast, holds two cubic yards.) Dina Dreisbach led us through the interior, explaining monitoring functions and engineering principles along the way. By day's end, we knew about the nine hydraulically operated slide gates, the grouting gallery where dam and river-bed come together, and the role of a stilling basin to slow downstream flow.

Once William Letchworth's country home, the columned Glen Iris Inn now hosts guests in fifteen exquisitely renovated rooms, plus offers fine dining. Victorian and Arts and Crafts furniture fills the space. Staff made especially certain that we saw the elegant third-floor library, with its deep-blue, star-studded ceiling and commanding view over Middle Falls.

Information:
Letchworth State Park, 1 Letchworth State Park, Castile, NY 14427. Phone 716-493-3600.
Mount Morris Dam, phone 716-658-4790.

Pullman Universalist Church in Albion

Cobblestone Country • Albion

Upstate New York became a spawning ground for all sorts of new ideas during the early nineteenth century. Religious revivals were plentiful enough to give Western New York the nickname "burned-over district." Canals turned out to be a good idea. One experiment in Utopianism, Oneida, managed to thrive. Concepts like phrenology fared less well.

The state also saw a few architectural crazes. Octagonal houses began to appear, extolled for their spiritual virtues as well as efficient use of space. Another fad was the cobblestone house. Early examples appeared along Lake Ontario, and even today 80 percent of such homes lie within an hour or two of Rochester.

About twelve hundred cobblestone buildings went up in North America, most of them between 1825 and 1860. Local ingenuity, lime for mortar, and an unlimited supply of stones made such construction possible. Many became residences for farmers prospering from wheat and other crops in the days when the Genesee Valley served as the breadbasket of America. Masons, many unknown, made these homes especially pleasing in appearance. The painstaking work eventually made such construction too expensive for a rapidly growing America.

We learned these facts and much more while walking around the Cobblestone Museum in Childs, New York, located about halfway between Rochester and Niagara Falls. The museum opened in 1960 when a onetime Universalist church became available for purchase by a fledgling historical society anxious to bring attention to cobblestone architecture. Now the complex includes two other cobblestone buildings, plus four additional display sites.

C. W. (Bill) Lattin guided us through the buildings. We began outside the church, where we appreciated glacially smoothed rocks graded by height to make uniform rows. What defines a cobblestone? I asked. Bill responded, "A stone you can pick up with one hand." The exterior stones, veneered over a two-foot-thick rubble wall, varied in width, and certainly in color. Square quoins of local dolomite gave stability to the corners. The overall effect was quite handsome.

Inside the church, we examined photos and diagrams as Bill taught us the limekiln process. Mortar was indeed the key to such construction. During the cobblestone era, Portland cement had not yet become available. In one alcove we could inspect an unadorned rubble wall.

There's an opportunity to learn a bit about religion on a visit. Bill explained the early simple decor of the Universalist churches, and how such design matched the beliefs of that order. An 1874 renovation moved the pulpit from the middle of the church to the front. Galleries upstairs accommodated those who couldn't afford pews.

We moved down the road to the 1836 Ward House, an interesting contrast with its smaller stones, sandstone quoins, and green shutters. Briefly owned by Horace Greeley in the 1860s, the last owner, Mrs. Inez Ward, sold it to the Cobblestone Society in 1975, complete with furnishings.

Consequently, Bill could point out details of the Victorian period exemplified in the interior design. Along with a fine selection of furniture, there are such quaint oddities as a pump-operated Regina "Pneumatic Cleaner"; a charcoal-fueled iron; a cumbersome, long hearing tube; and a "Friendship Wreath" made of human hair ("macramé, 1870's-style," Bill quipped).

Next we walked to a one-room schoolhouse, passing two cobblestone homes (still in private hands) along the way. Built in 1849, it served students from first through eighth grades as late as 1952. Distinguishing features include the use of lake-washed stones rather than fieldstones (used at the first two sites), and the fact that a stone veneer has been placed over a standard plank building. The architectural style is Greek Revival.

The Cobblestone Society purchased this holding in 1961 for $125 and decided to keep it as a school. Virtually every student in the county visits here on field trips at one time or another. Ropes control vents in the ceiling. Bill pointed out the incline of the floor, a feature that elevates the desks in the back for better sight lines.

Across Route 104 are four newer additions to the Cobblestone Museum. A blacksmith shop used until 1955 is in the process of reconstruction. "This building is a real gem," Bill told us. He hopes also to restore the southern room into a belt-driven woodworking shop.

The Print Shop, just beyond a green-shingled outhouse with a gracefully curved roof, houses a press and associated equipment donated by a local printer. The electrical system includes restored knob-and-tube wiring of the 1890s.

Contents of John Peters' harness shop in nearby Lyndonville had been given to the museum for safekeeping. Now the leather goods, saddles, liniments, and tools are set up in a nicely finished store with gray plank front and stuccoed sides.

Farmers' Hall was originally the town hall of Kendall, New York. The entry foyer is lined with cases of stuffed birds. Commissioned in 1883, this work was done by David Bruce of Brockport, noted for being one of the earliest taxidermists to put his specimens in natural positions.

A painted backdrop from a Grange Hall reminded me of a similar curtain displayed in Elizabethtown, in Essex County. Nowhere, however, have I seen a smokehouse like the one here. Six feet in diameter, and once used as a chicken coop, the piece was hollowed out of the limb of a sycamore.

******

Not far from the Cobblestone Museum (a two-mile walk should you have the desire) sits Albion, the seat of Orleans County. One short and one long walking opportunity present themselves here.

First, the Erie Canalway Trail goes through Albion, offering a route that extends for miles both west and east. The canal's Floating Plant winters here. When the canal is open, these sixty blue vessels with yellow trim dredge, remove trash, and provide all sorts of maintenance to the four-hundred-mile channel.

Along the well-packed towpath, interpretive signs add a bit of flavor. One told about the kerosene buoy lanterns that marked the original Erie Canal. Each burned thirty-one hours on three quarts of kerosene, creating a "ribbon of red and white dots across the state."

Heading west you'll come to Gaines Basin, the highest point along the canal, and the only place where a highway has been carved underneath the artificial river. Eastward, watch for two lift bridges, which are raised as needed to allow passage of boat traffic. There's a comfortable marina in the small village of Holley.

From downtown Albion, walk up past stalwart nineteenth century architecture to Courthouse Square. You'll pass a few structures built with locally quarried, reddish-brown Medina sandstone. A map in front of the domed courthouse will be your guide to neighboring blocks. (Printed maps seem to be available only irregularly in the area.)

The courthouse itself is truly regal with its silver dome, red brick construction, and four gleaming white ionic columns. Unfortunately, the windowless concrete jail next door marks one intrusion into the otherwise impressive setting.

Many of the nearby buildings are churches. The monumental First Presbyterian Church, built in 1874, uses sandstone even in its tall steeple. Dating to 1844, the brick Christ Episcopal Church is the oldest ecclesiastical building in the county. There's also a Norman Revival structure, the Free Methodist Church (1860), with white plank framing and shingled tower.

Stop especially at the Pullman Memorial Universalist Church. Railroad manufacturer George Pullman began his storied career as a cabinetmaker in Albion. Years after leaving, he built this house of worship for the village. It's interesting with its stained glass, arched entry, turret, and all the unusual angles. Louis Comfort Tiffany himself came up to install the windows.

Wander around and see the nearby Victorian homes and the 1851 Burrows Mansion, long used as the public library. And go inside the post office to view the 1939 mural by Judson Smith depicting village life, complete with pastoral homes, a woman pushing a baby carriage, a factory with smokestack, and a canal boat going under a bridge.

Information:
The Cobblestone Society Museum, Routes 104 and 98, Childs, New York. (Mailing address: P.O. Box 363, Albion New York 14411.) Phone 716-589-9013.
Orleans County Tourism, 14016 Route 31, Albion, NY 14411. Phone 800-724-0314.

Corning • Bath

Corning's historic Market Street offers a walk that will remind many of the vibrant downtowns of earlier generations. Despite the pressures from malls, and a disastrous flooding of the Chemung River in 1972, the city center remains vital and active, drawing locals and tourists.

Corning has become almost synonymous with glassmaking, a business that first came to town in 1868. Products of another old local industry, the manufacture of decorative terra cotta, highlighted our tour. A sampling of modern sculpture adds further artistic touch to the city.

We stopped at the Information Center, where we picked up maps and studied photographic images of the city. Then we began our walk at adjacent Centerway Square. Though generally following a route outlined in a leaflet on Corning's public art, we added other stops of our own.

Centerway Square was rebuilt as a city park in 1989, but it is anchored by a much older structure. The stone clock tower dates to 1883 and remains a dominant local landmark. A newer adaptation hides out of sight; beneath the brick plaza runs a river that aids in flood prevention.

Next we stopped at the First National Bank building, an 1894 sandstone edifice that began its life as a department store. Adding to the Renaissance Revival style is a terra cotta shell-and-wreath motif, manufactured by the Corning Brick and Terra Cotta Works.

Working our way farther down, we saw more elaborate terra cotta, including an owl atop 21-25 East Market Street, a building being renovated into loft apartments. There was originally a public lecture hall on the third floor of the Williams Building (27 E. Market). Corning must have enjoyed an active cultural life, as we later passed two more buildings with similar features.

Kaleidoscopes and decorative glass are offered at The Glass Menagerie, where a transom sign boasted 560 pieces of cut glass. The auto dealership is long gone from under the Becrafts Garage sign at 73 E. Market, where a ramp allowed cars to be raised for prominent display in upper windows.

The Corning Centennial Sculpture marks the end of the street.

Commemorating Corning's incorporation as a city in 1888, the open archway features images of the railroad, a cigar factory, a horse-drawn canal boat, and, naturally, an early glassworks.

We crossed over to the other side of Market Street for more splendid nineteenth-century commercial architecture. The five-story tall, but remarkably thin, Henkel Block features a broad arched window on the third floor with art nouveau lettering done in white terra cotta.

Concert Hall Block (another building with a third-floor auditorium) dates to 1851; it's a survivor of an 1856 fire that destroyed most of downtown. Brown's Cigar Store, a Victorian Gothic structure with a cast-iron facade, has been the site of a cigar and news store continuously since 1889. Sprague Insurance occupies an impressive Romanesque home with terra cotta and sandstone trim. Upstairs is yet another one-time community hall.

Atop the West End gallery (12 West Market), we spotted *A Melting Clock*, a modern sculptural adornment reminiscent of Salvador Dali. Another atypical creation, a sardonic relief sculpture entitled *The Critic*, decorates the side of 89 West Market Street.

T. G. Hawkes Company made fine art glass at 75 West Market from 1898 to 1976. Vitrix Hot Glass Studio creates artistic pieces on the first floor now, a reminder that Corning once boasted over fifty such operations. (A storefront display showed off a remarkable range of glass pieces fashioned by Frederick Carder for Steuben Glass Works.) Elaborate terra-cotta trim around the windows, added in 1924, distinguishes the building.

The massive brick factory building at Walnut and West Market served as home to the Southern Tier Roller Mills from 1879 to 1918. Corning Glass bought the facility in 1926. During the 1972 flood, a radio transmitter on top briefly provided Corning's only link to the outside world.

Via a commemorative brick archway, we diverted onto the park-like campus that Corning Glass occupies along the Chemung River. Erected in 1994, the arch incorporates glass inlays and Steuben mosaics as mementos of the company's long history.

Nearby stands Little Joe, a 185-foot-tall draw tower built in 1912 and used for making tubing until 1973. Corning initially used this major advance in glass manufacturing for making thermometers, then neon tubing, and finally optical fiber. The gleaming white tower has the silhouette of a nineteenth-century glassblower, or gaffer, on its side.

A few steps down sits *Gaffer on Bench*, a delightful bronze sculpture created by Bruno Lucchesi in 1993. It's a fitting monument for the corporation (first organized as Brooklyn Flint Glass Company) that moved to Corning in 1868, and has so long served as a vital force for the city.

There are reasons for diverting off Market Street. On Cedar Street is the Rockwell Museum, a personal favorite, and arguably the best center for Western art east of the Mississippi River. First Street leads to Christ Episcopal Church, notable for its Tiffany windows.

And by all means, return to Centerway Square and cross the pedestrian bridge leading to the Corning Museum of Glass, the area's leading attraction. We peered below at the Chemung River so harmlessly running its course, yet knowing the impact of its flooding in 1972. Historic Market Street's liveliness testifies to the city's resilience.

******

Bath, county seat of Steuben County, dates its history to 1793. The area was part of a one-million-acre land purchase by London's Pulteney Company. Charles Williamson was sent as land agent to supervise settlement. Surveyors blocked off lots and avenues, leaving a large common green. Within a year, thirty families had taken up residence.

British presence at Fort Niagara and across Lake Ontario loomed heavy in local minds. Indians influenced by the British may have posed a more immediate threat. Thus, a blockade and stockade were constructed near the common, now Pulteney Square. When peace became secure, logs and pickets were recycled into new homes and fences.

Pick up a walking guide at Magee House, a stately brick home built by a local congressman in 1831, and now the Steuben County History Center. A few blocks away, you'll find Pulteney Square. Once the location of the town well, and a place for militia training, it's now a peaceful oasis at the south end of the compact village. A gazebo and the 1905 Town Clock add flair to the setting.

The impressive First Presbyterian Church stands south of the park. Built of native limestone, it features a soaring bell tower. Inside are a Rose Window and two chandeliers by Louis Tiffany. Later I saw St. Thomas Episcopal Church, another striking limestone building, in Gothic Revival style.

East of the park, there's a handsome campus of brick public buildings—the Steuben County Courthouse, Clerk's Office, and Surrogate Office, plus the white Greek Revival Balcom home (1819).

Bath has a classic, small, nineteenth-century downtown. Number 7 Liberty is notable for its cast-iron construction. Deep red with black trim, the building was manufactured in New York City, and then brought by train for assembly here. Notice such interesting details as lions' heads and grapevines.

The Purdy Opera House began life as a paint store. Now converted to retail space, the mansard roof and central tower still allow one to imagine its onetime grandeur. If the post office looks a bit familiar, that may be because the designer was Bath native James Wetmore, chief architect for the entire postal service.

Residential properties along Liberty Street show off a sampling of Federal, Greek Revival, and Gothic Revival architecture. Here and there are Italianate, Victorian, and Moorish features. The "Three Sisters," identical Queen Anne homes with octagonal towers, were built to showcase a Bath lumber business.

The fairgrounds are home to the longest continuously running county fair (1819) in the United States. Even earlier, Colonel Williamson held a "world's fair" on the site in 1796 to push land sales.

The Pioneer Burial Ground serves as resting place for many early settlers. The first interment was of seven-year-old Christian Williamson, daughter of the town's founder. She died of "Genesee fever," the common name then for malaria.

Information:
Information Center of Corning, 1 W. Market Street, Corning, NY 14830. Phone 607-962-8997.
Steuben County History Center, Magee House, Cameron Park, Box 349, Bath, NY 14810. Phone 607-776-9930.

Rochester • Mount Hope Cemetery

Rochester makes it easy for the walker. Spiral-bound volumes, readily available at local outlets, outline a half-dozen leisurely tours. The same routes are also detailed online. None are long, and it's easy to string a few together for a satisfying experience with a reasonable amount of exercise.

I'd recommend starting with High Falls. A dramatic waterfall right in the center of a major city makes quite an impression. The Genesee River drops ninety-six feet in a torrent, making it easy to imagine why a community grew around such easy availability of waterpower. Indeed, Rochester became the country's leading flour maker early in its history.

Pont de Rennes pedestrian bridge, fashioned in 1982 from a much older span, offers a terrific view. Amateur geologists will want to study the sedimentary rock layers. I found myself more interested in ruins of former factory sites. It's worth a return in the evening, when the falls is lit.

A turn on Brown's Race Street brings you along the raceway, built to channel water from the river through a variety of mills. The design shows the ingenuity of early entrepreneurs. After passing the former Rochester Water Works, now an exhibit center, you'll come to the remains of the Triphammer Forge Building, where you can see the old waterwheel that was found during excavation in 1977.

One block farther gives access to a plaza. Here you can walk almost to the spot where the river plunges over the falls. Fragments of stone walls surround the viewing area, some of them part of the 1888 Gorsline Building, originally a shoe factory.

Juxtapositions of economic history are readily seen in Rochester. On this same short walk, a stroller will see not only remnants of the flour industry, but many other key players in the city's growth.

The Rochester Button Company was the world's largest producer of buttons at the turn of the twentieth century. Across the street stands Kodak Office Tower, once headquarters of the film and camera company established by George Eastman. Across the gorge, a sign signifies the Genesee Brewery, in its day a major regional beer maker.

Next I doubled back to do the Central City Tour. With the Genesee

River bisecting the city on its northerly course to Lake Ontario, bridges are important landmarks. Historic markers on the Main Street Bridge talk about the Seneca presence before white settlers reached this area.

Especially notable is the Broad Street Bridge. The street itself runs atop a multi-arched aqueduct that carried the Erie Canal over the river. The aqueduct stayed in use from 1842 until the canal was rerouted to the south in 1920. For several decades, the Rochester subway system ran through the abandoned canal bed.

A narrow swath of green called Aqueduct Park follows the west bank of the river. Continuing along Main Street, one comes to the Talman Building, notable as the place where former slave Frederick Douglas printed his abolitionist newspaper.

Now the tour becomes one of architectural grandeur.

The Reynolds Arcade shows off art deco style. It replaced an 1828 building of the same name, which for a time housed Western Union, another of the major corporations begun in Rochester. At Main and Exchange streets is the Wilder Building. Features include brown sandstone on the first floor, brick and terra cotta above, and a series of turrets. One must view it from a distance for full appreciation.

My personal favorite is the Powers Building, now home for M&T Bank. A dominant structure, it's a mix of stone and cast-iron construction. The triple mansard roof is topped by an observation tower. On a return visit, I'll have to go inside and see if the interior is up to the standards of the facade.

The walk continues on State Street past a stolid bank building with Corinthian columns, and then examples of Richardsonian Romanesque, Italianate, and Federal construction. Back at the river, there's the Andrews Street Bridge. Another waterfall, this one eighty-eight feet high, is nearby. It's hidden from view, but I could hear the roar.

Along St. Paul Street, there's the cast-iron H. H. Warner Building that fills an entire block. Patent medicines were made here. The Edwards Building has distinctive white terra-cotta work. I very much liked the 1893 Granite Building, actually made of brick as well as stone, and boasting impressive window styling.

I added a couple of spurs to the above tours. City Hall is only a few blocks out off State Street, at Church and Fitzhugh. It's another dark sandstone Richardsonian Romanesque edifice. But it's the interior that sets it apart, especially the marble-columned, three-story atrium.

Another route takes you east along Main Street to the Eastman Theater and the School of Music, a grand complex given to the community by Kodak founder George Eastman. Peek inside to see the lobby murals, and the medallions molded into the ceiling.

Nearby, on Gibbs Street, is a row of Tudor townhouses, an attractive urban residential area dating to the 1870s. Farther along are a couple of local favorites. Hallman's Chevrolet Building sports art deco at its more flamboyant, with structural steel, lots of black glass, and neon signs and clock. (Some will say this is why art deco passed out of style!) The Little Theater, another art deco creation, has become locally popular for art and foreign films.

******

People die in Rochester, too, of course. Many—over 370,000—are buried in one of the country's most beautiful cemeteries, Mount Hope.

When a cholera epidemic took over 120 lives and led to pollution concerns, city leaders purchased fifty-four acres for a new cemetery in 1837. Controversial at the time, the area was carefully developed as a park. Construction of gazebos and Florentine fountains made this not only a place for honoring the dead, but one for enjoying life with picnics and Sunday promenades.

Mount Hope has grown to encompass 196 acres, with fourteen miles of roadway coursing through. It's the largest Victorian cemetery in the United States. Regular tours are given by an active Friends of Mount Hope organization, which also works to restore buildings and educate the public. Over time, the group has reset almost two thousand headstones that had toppled.

Architectural highlights include the Gothic Revival chapel, which includes a crematorium, and the stone gatehouse, complete with bell tower. Special tours look at these and other architectural features, along with notable monuments.

Susan B. Anthony's grave may be the most visited spot in the park. Frederick Douglas, former slave and ardent abolitionist, is also buried here. A light-gray headstone on a hill memorializes city founder Nathaniel Rochester, a colonel in the Revolutionary War. He freed his slaves before his death. One lies under a stone engraved simply "We Called Her Anna."

"Millionaire's Row" includes many local notables. One man earned his fortune via invention of the hotel mail chute. Another founded Western Union. A few names are nationally known, including newspaperman Frank Gannett, and opticians John Jacob Bausch and Henry Lomb. The largest mausoleum in Mount Hope holds twenty-four.

Tour leader Bill Knapp, a most committed guide, told us about some themed tours. A Heritage Walk highlights resting places of people important in abolitionist and suffrage movements. Another focuses on the Civil War.

With its glacier ridges (called eskers) and kettle holes, Mount Hope is conducive to a geology outing. Trees make the place special, too. Some of the site's original forest was preserved, and additional plantings over the years have further enhanced the setting. A self-guided tree tour brochure is available.

Knapp emphasized that the Victorian cemetery, with its careful landscaping and park-like setting, represents an under-recognized contribution of that era in American history. Such graveyards made public health contributions, but also added places of special beauty to many American cities.

Information:
Greater Rochester Visitors Association, 45 East Avenue, Suite 400, Rochester, NY 14604. Phone 800-677-7282 or 585-279-8300.
Friends of Mount Hope Cemetery, 791 Mount Hope Avenue, Rochester, NY 14620. Phone 585-461-3494.

Palmyra • Chimney Bluffs

Palmyra, about thirty miles east of Rochester, works diligently to preserve its proud heritage. In school, I had learned about Palmyra being the home of Joseph Smith, founder of the Church of Jesus Christ of Latter-Day Saints. But that's just the beginning of this place's history.

Local history precedes Smith a bit. Revolutionary War veteran General John Swift founded the town in 1789. By the time the Erie Canal opened a new era of growth in 1821, Palmyra had already gained notice for its prosperous and well-educated population.

Joseph Smith met the Angel Moroni in 1827 at Hill Cumorah, just south of Palmyra. There he received the golden plates that he published as the *Book of Mormon*. Though hostilities forced Smith and his followers to move west, Mormons still celebrate their beginning annually with a spectacular pageant on this site.

Railroads and then the automobile led to the demise of canal traffic, leaving smaller waterside towns to deal with the vicissitudes of dramatically changing economies. Somehow urban renewal movements left Palmyra remarkably intact. An active preservation group, Historic Palmyra, helped crystallize determination to not just preserve, but also interpret, much of the area's illustrious past.

We began where a towpath stretch reaches Palmyra near Lock 29. Pleasant parkland, with a view of small waterfalls that once powered mills, surrounds the spot. Solid stone arches, once part of an aqueduct that carried the channel of water over Ganargua Creek, still survive. There's one especially unique artifact, the Aldrich Change Bridge, built in 1858, and moved to this site in 2002.

Think of a change bridge as analogous to an interstate cloverleaf. Here mules and drivers could cross the canal without having to be disconnected from their boats. Diagrams depict construction principles, showing the ingenious way compression at certain joints, combined with tension loops and rods, holds the structure together.

The Canalway Trail brought us into the village. Wetlands form a nature preserve along the way, offering a chance to view turtles, frogs, and a variety of birds. Muskrat and beaver live here, too, but we didn't find any. At the corner of Canal and Market streets, we took a right.

Historic Palmyra's first project, the Palmyra Historical Museum on Market Street, proved a good place to get our bearings. Originally a hotel and tavern, the 1826 structure was expanded over the years, adding Victorian touches to earlier Federal styling. Twenty-three rooms offer a broad variety of exhibits.

Just down the street is the William Phelps General Store, built in 1826. When the last generation of the Phelps family closed the store in 1940, contents were left exactly as they were. What remains is a time capsule, a fully stocked shop with jars of indigo for making dye, cigars made locally, and the likes of Oxydol and Dreft on the shelves.

Next door is the Print Shop, where John Jones began manufacturing printing equipment in 1860. Within its brick walls stands a selection of printing presses made locally.

At the corner of Market and Canal streets, a kiosk offered information on notable local residents, from Captain Swift through Joseph Smith. A few names surprised us.

A couple of blocks down Canal, we found ourselves at the home of Leonard and Clarissa Jerome. Not familiar? Well, their daughter Jennie grew up and married one Randolph Churchill. They had a son named Winston, arguably the greatest British leader of the twentieth century.

Turning up Church Street, we passed one of several cobblestone houses in the community. Then we climbed Cemetery Hill. The grave of General Swift lies amidst a grove of shade trees. A new stone denotes the resting place of Joseph Smith's brother, Alvin. Markers point out the sites of the village's first church and school.

Though the Latter Day Saints look at Palmyra with unusual reverence, most other denominations are represented here, too. Four stately churches rule the corners of Main and Canandaigua streets. Amazingly, it's claimed this is America's only major intersection with such a religious stamp.

A stroll up and down Main Street revealed a handsome collection of nineteenth-century commercial buildings. The 1867 Village Hall once boasted an opera house on its second floor. Sturdy iron fencing around Village Park was made by a local foundry over 150 years ago. A large black cannon captured from a Spanish vessel stands in commemoration of another native son, Admiral William Sampson, a key figure in the Spanish-American War. (His home sits at the corner of Vienna and Johnson streets.)

Farther east we approached the residence of Pliny Sexton, a prominent banker. Signage indicated his home also served as an Underground Railroad station. Just across was the location of Wells, Pomeroy, and Livingston, a courier service. Henry Wells gained more fame when he joined with one William Fargo and expanded westward.

Turns onto Canandaigua, Cuyler, and other streets revealed glimpses of Palmyra's wealth of Victorian, Federal, and Italianate architecture.

When Joseph Smith needed to print copies of the newly translated *Book of Mormon* in 1830, he sought out E. B. Grandin, publisher of the weekly *Wayne Sentinel*. His stately brick print shop on Main Street has been restored by the Latter Day Saints as the Book of Mormon Historic Publication Site.

Turn up William Street and finish at the Alling Coverlet Museum. Built around two hundred handweavings donated by Mrs. Merle Alling, this museum in a former newspaper building has earned national notice since its opening in 1976.

Coverlets take center stage, but don't miss the unusual array of framed rug samples fashioned for traveling salesmen a century ago, or the locally made quilts, including one comprised of campaign and encampment ribbons.

******

Chimney Bluffs State Park sits on Lake Ontario about forty miles east of Rochester. There's an attractive sign, clean restrooms, and nice trails. Otherwise this is a relatively undeveloped member of the park system.

Grassy meadowland leads to a group of picnic tables overlooking a sand beach. Looking off to the right, we saw the bluffs that give the place its name. From a distance, the appearance is that of sand dunes, awaiting rearrangement by the prevailing winds. Glacial in origin, some of these clay configurations reach a height of 150 feet above the lake.

We headed eastward on the trail, traversing a maple-dominated forest with an understory of ferns. My wife Marty noticed a few may-apples in bloom with their white flowers. Later, we observed a couple of swallows diving through the air over the lake. I found myself more impressed with some tree blowdowns. Fierce winds must howl here on occasion.

Continuing on, we came to a rocky bluff high above water level. Now we began a gradual ascent across the bluff formations. Some of the trail looms perilously close to the edge. Erosion is an ever-present force here, and it's important not to become part of the erosive process. The concept "slippery when wet" certainly applies.

We strolled in search of changing views before circling behind the bluffs and finding the perfect fallen tree to sit on and use as a lunch spot. These sandstone creations are quite impressive close-up. There's a certain combination of timelessness and fragility mixed together.

One has the feeling that what we saw on our experience will not look the same in ten years.

After retracing our steps back to the beach, and letting our dog have a quick swim as a reward for his patience, we sampled another trail. This one doesn't follow the shore, but instead lets one focus on the wildflowers in the area. Wild columbine was my wife's key find. If it's a windy day, this route offers some protection, as it generally meanders through woods.

This is an obscure part of the New York State Park System. Even some people in the store a few miles away where we bought our sandwiches didn't know exactly where it was. Nevertheless, unusual geology and panoramic views over Lake Ontario make the experience rewarding.

Information:
Historic Palmyra, 132 Market Street, Box 96, Palmyra, NY 14522. Phone 315-597-6981.
Chimney Bluffs State Park, 7700 Garner Road, Wolcott, NY 14590. Phone 315-947-5205.

Ganondagan • Cumming Nature Center

A thousand years ago Iroquois occupied much of upstate New York. Five groups—the Seneca, Cayuga, Onondaga, Oneida, and Mohawk—comprised the Iroquois. The Tuscarora people joined later, completing what became known to the British as the Confederacy of the Six Nations. Known for their longhouses, and for ceremonial customs honoring agricultural cycles, they long lived peacefully even after the arrival of European colonizers.

There was a high degree of social organization within the tribes. Beans, squash, and corn anchored a diet supplemented with wild plants, animals, and fish. Large central granaries were built to store corn over the winter.

The Seneca people constructed four large communities in western New York. One was near Victor, a few miles southeast of present-day Rochester. Now called Ganondagan, this village grew to include over 150 longhouses. In addition, four granaries stood nearby.

French military forces, three thousand strong, swooped down from Canada in 1687 and invaded Seneca lands. Determined to oust a major competitor in the fur trade, these soldiers and their Indian allies burned longhouses and destroyed stores of grain. Surviving Senecas never again developed large communities, deciding instead to scatter into smaller settlements.

Land around Ganondagan changed from forest to field as new settlers arrived and began to farm. Several hills became popular picnic spots by the late 1800s. More than a few visitors began to find native artifacts in the ground, leading to amateur archaeological excavations that also uncovered human remains.

Local historians worked to have the area listed as a National Historic Landmark, finally succeeding by 1964. New York State began purchasing the land for development of a new historic site; dedication was celebrated in 1987. Ganondagan includes a visitor center with introductory exhibits and a short video, but for a true sense of history, it's important to walk the three designated trails.

I began on the Trail of Peace. While enjoying a leisurely pace and some panoramic views, I read a series of illustrated plaques that taught me a bit about the Seneca view of the cosmos, along with some tribal traditions.

Senecas (and the other members of the Iroquois Confederacy) believe that "spirits of the Sky World created the world on the back of a great spirit turtle," to be forever moving in an endless sea. All components of the natural world have spiritual aspects; plants and animals are considered "allies in life." To this day, all formal Seneca meetings begin with a prayer of Thanksgiving acknowledging this connection.

A highlight of this half-mile trail is the full-size replica of a longhouse. Traditionally, four corner posts were sunk, and then the outer frame completed with young elm or hickory trees. Strips of shagbark hickory tied sheets of elm bark to the frame as siding. Pine pitch made the structure watertight.

The Senecas are divided into clans, with several family groups usually occupying each longhouse. A fire ring lay between each pair of family units; a smoke hole directly overhead provided venting. Two tiers of planks lined the walls. People slept on the bottom level and used the upper one for storage.

On the two-mile "The Earth is Our Mother" trail, one learns about traditional uses of plants and trees. My path traversed brush and young forest; a long boardwalk eased my way over a wetland segment.

Twenty-nine plants are labeled. Consequently, I learned the value of sassafras root tea to "thin" the blood, and of cattails as lining for both moccasins and diapers. The bark of wild black cherry could be made into a potion for colds, while a tea brewed from the leaves could serve the same function. I wonder if this explains why so many cough syrups are still cherry-flavored.

Perhaps the most poignant site, however, is Fort Hill, about a mile down the road. Here the Senecas had their largest granary, over 440,000 bushels of corn stored within an oak-palisaded stronghold. When Marquis de Denonville and his three thousand troops vandalized the cache in 1687, the results proved devastating to the Senecas.

The Granary Trail began with a climb up a grassy swath, and then followed a dirt trail to the top of a mesa. Once on the thirty-acre plateau, with its wonderful view over surrounding farmland, it became clear why the Senecas chose this spot for their largest storehouse. No one could have approached the area without being noticed.

Plaques around the perimeter interpret the site and its significance in Seneca history.

Interestingly, France's Indian allies refused to join in destroying the foodstuffs. Such wanton action would have been regarded as sinful. Some of the commentary comes from soldiers' diaries. One quote read, "It is something astonishing, the quantity of corn, both old and new, that we have destroyed." Sadly, such pride in willful destruction can still blind humanity to this day.

Like so many battleground sites, this place holds a quiet serenity today. I found it an appropriate place for reflection on history about which many of us know far too little.

******

The Rochester Museum and Science Center operates Cumming Nature Center, a nine-hundred-acre preserve in the Bristol Hills between Honeoye Falls and Naples, as an environmental education center. A network of short trails allows an outing of almost any length.

A quick stop in the Visitor Center offers photographs and taxidermy work, as well as a chance to pick up a map. Just outside, the short Explorer's Trail will appeal to kids with its life-size wildlife silhouettes.

Three trails, each about three-quarters of a mile in length, gave me a nice sampling.

Broad grass and dirt paths begin the Haudenosaunee Trail, which then enters a birch and conifer forest. Benches are placed at strategic intervals. A bridge goes over a gently percolating stream.

A spur leads to a replica Seneca hunting camp. Thin logs and twigs frame the structure; bark veneers the walls and provides the roof. Inside, twig benches are reminiscent of Adirondack rustic furniture.

The Pioneer Trail goes by wetlands as well as through forest. There's an old homestead, its chinked log construction supporting a stone hearth and wood shake roof. Nearby, a grinding stone, plow, and huge iron cauldron remind of tasks required of early settlers.

There's a sugar house, also made of logs, with a green roof and vented cupolas. Displays explain the process of extracting syrup from the raw sap of maple trees.

I especially liked the Helen Gordon Trail, named for a longtime secretary of the Rochester Museum. There's an Adirondack feel, with its beautiful stands of pine (one sees why these were so prized for ships' masts) and needle-carpeted trail.

A slight breeze and the gurgling of a stream offered a backdrop, while painted signs added color and information about plant, animal, and bird life. A panel that needed an accompanying picture—the one discussing poison ivy—lacked it during my visit.

Two additional loops, the Conservation Trail and the Beaver Trail, bring the walker to a sawmill, a fire tower, and a beaver observation area.

This beautifully maintained complex would be ideal for family outings in summer and fall. During the winter, Cumming offers an opportunity for cross-country skiing.

Information:

Ganondagan State Historic Site, P.O. Box 239, 1488 State Route 444, Victor, NY 14564. Phone 585-924-5848.

Cumming Nature Center, 6472 Gulick Road, Naples, NY 14512. Phone 585-374-6160.

Re-created Seneca longhouse at Ganondagan

Keuka Outlet • Palmers Pond

Keuka Outlet Trail in Yates County links the villages of Dresden and Penn Yan. Following both the route of the unusually named Crooked Lake Canal, and a railroad that ran until 1972, this is a very nice reuse of land. Sam Olivier and her daughter Gloria hiked with us, allowing the luxury of spotting cars at each end.

The outlet connects Keuka and Seneca Lakes; water drops 274 feet along the way. Quiet today, this area saw heavy industrial development as early as the 1780s. Waterpower drove a panoply of mills, some of them built by the Society of Universal Friends, a newly arrived religious group. There were a dozen power dams on the Outlet by 1827.

Development of a canal in 1833, followed by the railroad in 1844, provided improved transportation. Over three dozen mills operated along the short stretch, producing not only flour, lumber, and paper, but also such products as textiles, linseed oil, and liquor. Five concerns lasted into the twentieth century, with one managing to thrive as late as 1968. The railroad ran until 1972.

Detailed trail maps are readily available at local outlets. The recommended route begins at the Dresden end, but we contrarians had decided to start in Penn Yan, near Birkett Mill, once a source of buckwheat flour. Sometimes the trail followed canal towpath, at other times former railbed, and occasionally the canal bed itself.

Not long after starting, we passed a scooped-out area that once held a railroad turntable for turning engines around. Up ahead came High Bridge, a train trestle sitting atop massive stone pillars, dating to 1890. There would be many more industrial artifacts to come.

Our guidebook referred to an almost continuous sequence of old mill and dam sites. Masonry and stonework was more obvious in some places than others. The tall brick smokestack of the former Milo Mill couldn't be missed, however. Alongside stood a seventeen-foot-high, steam-driven flywheel.

A relatively undeveloped segment followed. Ponds stand where locks once existed. Forest has retaken the land. Instead of signs of human industry, we found cut-off trees representing the work of beavers. One solitary whitetail deer stared at us. Along the ground, purple phlox, yellow wild iris, and wild columbine thrived. Those looking for tree varieties will find oak, sumac, cedar, and basswood.

The next highlight came at the Seneca Mill site. This two-story stone mill dates to 1884; it had been preceded by a gristmill as early as 1790. From the second floor, one can see two penstocks dating to that era. Not surprisingly for such an early mill site, there's a significant falls, with water flowing over three tiers of Tulley limestone. Swimmers were making good use of the swimming hole. If we had packed a lunch, the nearby picnic park would have been a good place to stop a while.

We approached another significant complex of buildings. This was formerly the Taylor Chemical Company, once the world's largest supplier of carbon bisulfide. Previously the site had held a gristmill (1827) and then several paper mills; one of the latter exported thin brown paper to Cuba for wrapping cigars. Diagrams explain the layout, including the brick-lined boiler in which sulfur was melted with charcoal to make carbon bisulfide for the rayon industry.

Outlet slopes began to steepen. Our trail guide indicated these gray rock walls were composed of Genesee shale.

One of the more poignant sights was just ahead. We crossed a road that once went to the thriving settlement of Hopeton. A spur to our right, camouflaged by foliage, led to the remains of an iron-truss bridge atop massive stone abutments. This provided a route to prosperous mills when built in 1840. Still sturdy, it's now a bridge to nowhere.

We passed a few more steep cliffs, crossed a couple of wooden bridges, walked beside the old canal for a while, and completed our trek to Dresden at the conveniently located Crossroads Ice Cream Shop. All agreed this provided a suitable reward for successfully finishing the seven-mile hike.

Nowhere is the hiking particularly difficult. Reading the trail guide along the way maximizes the value of this historic walk. All along the Keuka Outlet Trail, there are stone remnants marking ruins and foundations. Bridge abutments can be found; so can sluiceways, dams, and parts of canal locks. The careful observer will make plenty of archaeological discoveries.

With a bit of imagination, small villages can be envisioned along the way, their residents earning livings from the various mills and factories. Think of the Keuka Outlet Trail as a memorial to their industriousness and tenacity.

******

New York benefits from the prescient preservation of huge reserves of state land. The "forever wild" clause in the state constitution that protects millions of acres of Adirondack terrain dates back to the late nineteenth century. Its institution made New York a pioneer in wilderness protection. Application of the same principles to the Catskill Mountain Preserve guarantees further pristine landscapes for future generations.

Less well known is the system of state forests outside the Adirondacks and Catskills. In travels to western New York, we became aware of several such tracts in Allegany County. To sample opportunities, we took Exit 32 off the Southern Tier Expressway (Route 17). Turning left toward West Almond, and then going right onto Miller Road, we reached a trailhead at 1.8 miles. Large parking areas were available on both sides of the road.

This was one of several multi-use trails in Palmers Pond State Forest. Yellow markers pointed the way along a grassy path through forestland. Occasionally we approached nearby cleared pasture, and during the early spring, we had to hop over an occasional rivulet. Aside from a bit of mud, however, the going was relatively easy.

What we enjoyed was a quiet 4.6-mile loop that offered brisk walking and a chance to exercise some powers of observation. Sounds of robins broke the silence. Careful looking revealed plenty of butterflies and frogs.

Luxuriant fern growth and plenty of moss added texture. We spotted white mayapple blooms, the violet color of wild primrose, and stands of wild strawberries.

Though we had the trail to ourselves that day, we noticed evidence of horse travel. Likely this would make for a great cross-country ski experience in the winter.

Across the road was another network of paths. These will await a return visit. We did, however, walk a bit farther along Miller Road, and were rewarded with wonderful views across a beautiful, bucolic landscape.

Detailed maps show further trails in Phillips Creek and Turnpike State Forests, which, with Palmers Pond, comprise the West Almond Trail System. Information on all these trails is available from the New York State Department of Environmental Conservation's foresters, headquartered in nearby Belmont.

Information:
Friends of the Outlet, P.O. Box 321, Penn Yan, NY 14527.
DEC, 5425 County Route 48, Belmont, NY 14813. Phone 716-268-5392.

Bridge to abandoned village of Hopeton along Keuka Outlet Trail

Sonnenberg Gardens • Canandaigua • Jamestown

The country estate Sonnenberg (German meaning "sunny hill") in Canandaigua was purchased by banker Frederick Ferris Thompson (the New York bank he founded went on to become Citibank) and his wife Mary in 1863. After her husband's death in 1899, Mary worked with landscape architects to develop specialty gardens. Upon her own death in 1923, Mary bequeathed the estate to a nephew, who in turn sold it to the federal government for use as a veterans hospital.

In 1973, a local nonprofit group purchased fifty acres, including the mansion and gardens, for potential use as a tourist attraction. Since 2006, the New York State Office of Parks and Recreation has collaborated to operate Sonnenberg Gardens and Mansion State Historic Park. Restoration continues with the assistance of a significant volunteer effort.

Visitors can take a guided tour or wander the fifty acres on their own. A leisurely mile or so of walking brings one past most of the distinctive features. For those so inclined, a tram ride goes by many of the highlights.

It's worth beginning at the greenhouses, which include spaces for palms, cacti, and bromeliads. From there, one walks out onto a landscape not unlike those devised for English country gardens.

Four thousand Jackson & Perkins cultivars fill the Rose Garden, where orchestras once played from the two-story gazebo. The Old-Fashioned Garden, filled with perennials, is set amidst a full quarter mile of boxwood hedging. Elsewhere, the formally geometric Italian Garden with its sunken parterres features colorful annual flowers.

A gentle stream and stone paths introduce the Japanese Garden. The tea house replicates one Mrs. Thompson saw in Kyoto. Other spaces are dedicated to the pansy, her favorite flower, and the Moonlight Garden, dominated by white night-blooming varieties.

For serenity, I'd choose her Rock Garden, with its winding paths, bridges, and stone arch. This natural-looking landscape undoubtedly required the hauling of many loads of limestone. Stairs climb to a rustic stone summerhouse with a nice view. The low fence nearby encloses a pet cemetery. From a bench overlooking two tiny cascades, all seemed right with the world.

The forty-room, three-story Queen Anne mansion replaced a smaller farmhouse in the mid-1880s. Architectural features include turrets, leaded bay windows, oak and mahogany paneling, and interior arches. Medieval influences dominate the Great Hall with its array of taxidermy, while beveled glass doors in the dining room open onto an outdoor breakfast bower.

Complete your day with a stroll around Canandaigua. Established in 1789 as the county seat of Ontario County (comprising thirteen present-day counties), its nineteenth-century heritage is nicely reflected in residential areas and the compact downtown.

Land speculators Oliver Phelps and Nathaniel Gorham bought over two million acres in 1789—at a nickel an acre. Early turnpikes helped lure settlers. Although the Erie Canal bypassed Canandaigua, arrival of the Auburn and Rochester Railroad in 1840 aided an economic boom.

Many commercial establishments served the surrounding agricultural area, but manufacturing played a key role in growth. One company produced enamelware; another made pressed brick. As in so many other young cities, a brewery proved successful, too. Canandaigua Lake brought plenty of tourists, creating an industry that continues strongly to this day.

We stopped at the Ontario Historical Society and picked up leaflets for a self-guided walking tour.

City Hall and the Ontario County Courthouse stand prominently on the edge of downtown. The courthouse looks quite magisterial with its dome and gilded Statue of Justice. It was here that Susan B. Anthony was convicted of unlawfully voting in an election. She refused to pay her one-hundred-dollar fine.

There's the usual smattering of sturdy, nineteenth-century commercial buildings. Niagara Street features a distinctive 1873 fire station, the tower for drying hoses still intact.

Some buildings have been nicely recycled. The 1904 F. F. Thompson Memorial Hospital and the former Canandaigua Academy (built with local pressed brick) have both been transformed into senior citizen housing units; the 1912 post office has become part of the YMCA.

Turning to the residential end of Main Street, we quickly realized how many striking homes didn't even make it onto the tour route. With a range from Greek Revival and Federal, to Italianate and Queen Anne, this would be a good place to cement knowledge of American building styles. There's a cobblestone house, too.

Historical personages have graced Canandaigua. Within a few short blocks are homes that belonged to three men who served in the nation's cabinet, including one who became secretary of war under President John Quincy Adams, and another who served as secretary of war and then secretary of the treasury under President Tyler.

Gideon Granger, the country's longest tenured postmaster general (under Presidents Jefferson and Madison) also called Canandaigua home. His beautiful 1816 Federal-style house stands on spacious grounds. Later a girls' school and a retirement home for congregational ministers, it's now operated as a house museum.

An attorney named Walter Hubbell operated a law school next to his residence. One notable pupil (and later associate) was Stephen Douglas, he of the famed debates with Abraham Lincoln. Nearby lived a young man who lost his life at sea; Herman Melville turned his story into the novel *Billy Budd*. Another notable local was John North Willys, founder of an automobile company that bore his name. Willys Jeeps once were staples for the United States Army.

******

The Jamestown Audubon Society maintains a six-hundred-acre nature preserve in far southwestern New York near the Pennsylvania border. A network of color-coded trails meanders through a mix of wetland, pond, and forest. By combining them, we enjoyed three miles of very pleasant walking.

First, though, we diverted to the Arboretum, between the parking lot and the front of the Nature Center. A mowed path wound its way among sixty trees found in New York State. All are well labeled with both Latin and common names. The most unusual new one for us was the American hornbeam with its corrugated trunk.

We began amidst even rows of red pines. An undergrowth of ferns added contrast to red-brown needles on the ground in this beautiful, airy grove. A right turn took us over a boardwalk, after which we veered left onto the Red Wing Trail. The route alternated between forest and the edge of Spatterdock Pond. Sonorous calls from the water sounded like a symphony of tubas.

Nearing Big Pond, we approached a wooden observation tower that offered a terrific overview of the pristine wetlands. My wife quickly spotted a blue heron in the distance.

Retracing a bit, we turned toward Big Pond. After traversing a boardwalk and strolling through some more woods, we arrived at the northern shoreline of Big Pond. Here we had an unexpected show of wildlife. Huge carp jumped about in the water. On land, we watched two geese lead their four offspring on an exploration of their new home.

From there we followed the Yellow Trail along Big Pond, stopping at a couple of viewing platforms, and then took the twisting Blue Trail (also called the Bunny Trail) back to the Visitor Center.

Benches are strategically placed. The sounds of birdlife followed us everywhere. We also noted deer tracks, evidence of beaver activity, and plenty of frogs. Bring binoculars; maybe you'll do better than we did sighting activity in the duck and bluebird boxes around the preserve. Also consider carrying some bug spray to ward off mosquitoes!

Since you're this close, add the Roger Tory Peterson Institute's headquarters in nearby Jamestown to your itinerary. A native son from a city that also spawned Lucille Ball and Natalie Merchant, Peterson transformed from a kid with a passion into one of the world's best-known naturalists.

Peterson (1908–1996) began studying birds by age ten, sketching pictures and recording observations. As his artistic skills grew, he defied conventional wisdom by designing his field guides not for the scientist, but as aids for the general public interested in identifying birds in the field.

Beginning with *A Field Guide to the Birds: A Bird Book on a New Plan* in 1934, he taught generations how to recognize certain anatomical features rather than simply depending on formal taxonomy. Paul Ehrlich proclaimed, "no one has done more to promote an interest in living creatures than Roger Tory Peterson."

His personal collections were left to this facility, which opened in 1993. The striking design of stone, board-and-batten, and Engelmann spruce pillars, product of an architectural competition, provides a suitable home for early editions of his books, illustrations for texts and Audubon Society periodicals, and especially his detailed paintings.

After learning about Peterson's life and seeing his work, it's time to turn your attention back to the outdoors. From the stunning two-story library, visitors can use binoculars to spy upon birds attracted by the array of birdfeeders just outside the tall windows. Then one can walk the small trail system. An accompanying brochure available in the gift shop gives detailed information on the flora and fauna.

Information:

Sonnenberg Gardens and Mansion State Historic Park, 151 Charlotte Street, Canandaigua, NY 14424. Phone 585-394-4922.

Ontario County Historical Society, 55 N. Main Street, Canandaigua, NY 14424. Phone 585-394-4975.

Jamestown Audubon Society, 1600 Riverside Road, Jamestown, NY 14701. Phone 716-569-2345.

Roger Tory Peterson Institute, 311 Curtis Street, Jamestown, NY 14701. Phone 716-665-2473 or 1-800-758-6841.

Canandaigua home of Gideon Granger, Postmaster General under Presidents Jefferson and Madison

Charles Burchfield Nature & Art Center ● Griffis Sculpture Park

It's not the size of the Charles Burchfield Nature Center that sets it apart. After all, the preserve measures barely thirty acres. It's the idea that I like. Celebrate an artist who's a native son; make use of land in view of his house; and take advantage of the opportunity to showcase scenes he may have painted right by his home.

Add to this some trails marked with reproductions of his paintings. Add a playground, an outdoor amphitheater, and a panoply of whimsical sculptures. Add some historical context. Suddenly (all right, not so suddenly, as I'm certain plenty of planning and time went into the process) you have a unique walking area ready to engage children and adults alike.

Burchfield (1893–1967) hailed from Ohio. He studied art in Cleveland before moving to Buffalo to work as a designer for a wallpaper company. Developing a style influenced by both urban and rural scenes in western New York, he felt confident enough to devote all his time to art after 1929.

By the time of his death, the Burchfield-Penney Art Center at Buffalo State College had been established as the major exhibitor of his work. For over four decades, he lived and worked in West Seneca, only a matter of steps from Buffalo Creek, the stream that bisects the nature center.

My walk began at the Gathering Area, with its perimeter of benches. Displays provide information on Burchfield and his art. He looked for inspiration in both small-town and big-city life; in addition, he looked to create imaginative nature scenes. This center hopes others will sense the emotions Burchfield felt as he painted.

A playground area competes for attention, as do several large-scale metal insects. But I began to follow the trails along Buffalo Creek. Signs along the way offer reproductions of selected works, often adding some of the artist's own words and inspirations.

At one spot, opposite pretty red St. John's Lutheran Church high on the far bank, I learned this land was portrayed in his 1935 painting *Rain and Wind Through the Trees*. Trees would be a frequent theme for Burchfield.

Soon I reached a waterside amphitheater. There's a twenty-five-foot stage, and seating for one hundred. I passed depictions of *Skunk Cabbage*, based upon a fond childhood memory, and *Bee Hepaticas*, paying tribute to an early spring flower.

A boardwalk led to an elevated covered pavilion. Looking across Buffalo Creek, I could see the home where Burchfield lived from 1925 until his death. One conjectures whether someday this could be added to the park's holdings.

I continued along the boardwalk over some wetlands. Pictures of *Fantasy of Heat*, its colors shimmering above the water, and *Untitled/ Gothic Window Trees*, with its sense of spirituality, further immersed me in the artist's view of nature. The rich colors of *Wind-Blown Asters* turned an ordinary scene into "a fantasy."

A spur along the trail brought me to some dam ruins, and later I found myself walking along a former millrace, built to provide water-power. Now further history of the area was introduced.

Members of the Ebenezer Society, an offshoot of the Community of True Inspiration founded in Germany in 1714, came to America in search of religious freedom. They purchased five thousand acres from the Seneca Indians here in 1842. Middle Ebenezer, as the communal settlement became known, included lumber mills and gristmills along the race, plus a tannery, clock shop, and brewery elsewhere in the village.

As per the religion's custom, Middle Ebenezer Cemetery has no gravestones. When the community moved to Iowa in the 1860s, where it became part of the Amana Society, an estimated 180 members re-mained at rest in this burial ground just off the trail.

There's a Meditation Area, with five benches in a semicircle, and a tree dedicated to West Senecans who served at Ground Zero after 9/11. There's also lots of sound—from traffic (the park is right in the village), from children's voices as they frolic in two playgrounds, and from the occasional chiming of bells from the nearby church.

Continuing along boardwalks and trails, I saw how Burchfield tried to capture multiple senses in his paintings. *The Woodpecker* almost makes you hear the rat-a-tat-tat and feel the vibrations as the bird pecks on his tree. He skillfully makes you feel the stream water move and lights twinkle in *Fireflies and Lightning*.

Stop in the Interpretive Center before leaving and see a further sampling of Burchfield's work. *Rainy Day*, a terrific painting of a young boy sitting and reading on a stairway, used his son as model. Each of his children posed for at least one canvas. *The Moth and the Thunderclap*, a watercolor with charcoal, is more abstract. You definitely see the motion and feel the approach of the impending storm.

This center only dates to the year 2000. To a degree it's still a work in progress. Already it offers a satisfying mile or more of walking, with a bit of artistic inspiration and an urge toward reflection.

******

Consider Griffis Sculpture Park for an interesting and unusual outing. Operated by the four-decade-old Ashford Hollow Foundation, the largest number of creations are by three generations of the Griffis family. It was Larry Griffis, Jr., who founded the park in 1966.

There are four hundred acres here, with over 250 outdoor sculptures. A network of trails meshes with fanciful art work for an entertaining experience.

We followed signs closely from the tiny village of Ashford Hollow. Taking a left, we climbed as steep a paved road as you're likely to see, and then made a few more turns to find the Mill Valley Park section of the complex. Admission is on the honor system, with a recommended $5 fee for adults, $3 for students and seniors.

Immediately upon beginning the trail we saw a giant grasshopper made from welded steel rods. Whimsical painted aluminum figures followed soon after. The path crossed a babbling brook on a plank bridge. We then took the Green Trail to Sculpture Pond.

Without question, here was the most remarkable sight of the day. *Ten Aluminum Bathers*, by Larry Griffis, are depicted swimming, diving, floating, and running through the water. (There were also two geese nearby, standing so still that I at first thought they were sculpted as well.) I can't remember the last time I had so much fun studying a single work of art.

A bit uphill, a large field offered such pieces as *Bathysphere and*

Submarine, along with some oversized human figures, one bronze, another aluminum. A glance behind us gave another perspective on the pond and the ten "bathers."

The Blue Trail turned out to be a fairly sustained climb through a wooded area. Just before the top, a sharp left brought us to *Amazones*. Three giant aluminum figures—one seated, another standing, the third supine—greeted us. Their silver glimmer contrasted nicely with the greens and browns of the forest.

The trail peaked on an elevated plateau, with the largest field of sculpture we saw on our visit. Broad vistas of nearby hills and meadows competed for attention with a collection of abstract sculptures. And there's *Castle Tower*, its ladders clearly beckoning for exploration by children (and we young-at-heart adults).

In addition to Mill Valley Park, the sculpture has a Rohr Hill Park section. That will await a return visit. We expect it will be equally satisfying and entertaining.

Information:
Charles E. Burchfield Nature and Art Center, 2001 Union Road, West Seneca, NY 14224. Phone 716-677-4843.
Griffis Sculpture Park, 6902 Mill Valley Road, East Otto, NY 14729. Phone 617-667-2808.

Genesee Country Village • Genesee Forest and Park

Genesee Country Village in Mumford, twenty miles from Rochester, offers a chance to experience life as it was in the nineteenth century. Created by John Wehle, longtime chairman of the Genesee Brewing Company, the fifty-seven buildings moved here for the complex's opening in 1976 make this the third largest collection of historic structures in the country.

The place is laid out as a true small village, giving a visit the feel of an in-depth, self-guided walking tour. Staff in period costume help interpret the exhibits. Artisans demonstrate crafts and trade skills of a bygone time.

We entered via a tollhouse, a reminder of the many plank-road companies that operated in the mid-1800s. A family of three plus a boarder once lived in this modest home. From there we turned onto Maple Street.

In a formidable brick Greek Revival law office, an excellent interpreter discussed the role of a country lawyer. Several houses down stands a shoemaker's shop. Here we learned that until the late eighteenth century, shoes weren't made separately for right and left feet. People would rotate shoes periodically to equalize wear, not unlike the way we rotate tires today.

Hill Street has trade shops. There's a dressmaker, who fashioned clothes with her treadle sewing machine, and a cobblestone blacksmith shop, always popular for its demonstrations. A barrel over the door marks the cooperage. This largely forgotten business made the barrels and buckets critical to commerce before the days of cardboard and glass. In a tackle shop, fly tying gets its recognition.

In the pioneer farmstead, a pleasant fire blazed in the stone hearth, smoke winding its way up the stick-and-mud chimney. This particular structure dates to 1809. The resident interpreter reminded us "this was the wild west then." At the nearby land office, a surveyor explained his work and tools.

The industrial area centers around Orchard Street. There's a pottery shop, wheelwright, an early brewery, and also a gunsmith's shop. Before the days of mass production, a gunsmith relied on a foot-pedal lathe and drill press to make weaponry. Customers would routinely wait six to twelve months for an order to be filled.

Farther along, we found a tinsmith making pierced barn-lamps. To us, these may be quaint antiques, but to early farmers they provided a fire- and wind-proof source of light. Several kids tried to blow out the flame, but none succeeded.

A variety of homes reflect different economic classes. The birthplace of George Eastman, moved here from Waterville, is small but comfortable. I liked the painted window shades. Much more ornate was the Hamilton house, an Italianate villa built around 1870 by a tannery owner. Unique furnishings included a multi-compartment Wooten desk and a parlor chandelier with six kerosene lamps.

Octagonal houses enjoyed a period of popularity in New York State. Touted for efficient use of space and good air circulation, the interiors have lots of angles and unusual room shapes. Though painted in a yellow-green color that only a Victorian could love, the two-story octagon house here had its walls papered to simulate marble. A beautiful cupola sat atop the roof.

An early Shaker Trustees' building was also transported here, allowing a chance to learn more about this group's simple lifestyle. We owe a surprising number of inventions to the Shakers, among them the agitator for washing machines, forced hot-air heat, seed packets, and flat brooms.

Public buildings include an 1822 town hall with its original clock tower, and the Romulus Female Seminary. The Roman Catholic Church, with its tall stained windows and oak pews, joins the Greek Revival-style Methodist Church and Parsonage on Church Street. The simple Quaker Meetinghouse stands elsewhere, on Meetinghouse Road.

Green space dispersed throughout the grounds includes the Great Meadow with its bandstand, the tree-lined Village Square, and a couple of orchards. Several houses boast adjacent gardens. There are also eleven plots planted with heirloom seeds.

If a prolonged stroll in the village induces a desire for brisker exercise, there are almost two hundred acres of undisturbed woodland and wetlands with trails. The longest route, the 1.9-mile Perimeter Trail, passes old pasture and stone walls. Rockhounds will likely enjoy the

1.8-mile Geology Trail.

A pond on the short Web of Life Trail hosts frogs and ducks in the spring, and then dries up in late summer. The Succession Trail gives a sense of how nature reclaims a field once it's been abandoned from human use.

Genesee Country Village also includes an impressive gallery of sporting art (plus some Native American basketry and pottery), a carriage museum, and a clustering of outdoor sculpture. There's more than can be seen in one day, so every visitor is likely to have a different experience. Most will want to return someday.

******

Genesee County Park and Forest in Bethany dates back to 1915, when the first thirty-one thousand trees were planted. The oldest county forest in the state, its woodlands were initially designed as a wood source for the heating and cooking needs of the county poorhouse. By 1935, some 160,000 trees had been set into the ground. In the 1960s, the 440-acre holding, with its three ponds, was turned into a park. Further growth ensued after the county home was closed in 1974.

Addition of the Genesee County Park Interpretive Center in 1998 enhanced the offerings. Stimulating exhibits within the spacious knotty-pine interior include a wetland simulation with a beaver resting in its lodge, information on forest recycling, and a well-interpreted replica bat cave. Among fine taxidermy specimens are a bobcat in pursuit of a snowshoe hare, and a nest with two red-tailed hawks.

We walked a good portion of the seventeen-mile trail network.

Death Row Trail slopes gently uphill past maple, beech, and hickory trees. A left turn brought us onto the Wilderness Trail and then the Forestry Trail. An interpretive sign told us that many of the trails here follow deer runs. At stations on the General Conservation Trail, we learned how white pines in one area were girdled to facilitate growth of Norway spruce (so-called "release cutting"), while red pines were sited on a dry, sandy area ideal for their maturation.

Other routes brought us by brush piles used by rabbits and ruffed grouse for winter cover, and across a walkway to a tiny island in the midst of a small marsh. Toboggan Hill is a mowed path, while Low Road Trail traversed old meadow ringed by thick conifer forest.

One unique feature is the Touch and See Trail. Visually impaired hikers can follow chained posts bordering the path, and read about specific sites on Braille markers.

Volunteers staff the park, and if the ones we met are typical, it's an enthusiastic crew anxious to help visitors find maximal enjoyment. There's also a regular schedule of guided outings and other activities.

Information:

Genesee Country Village and Museum, 1410 Flint Hill Road, Mumford, NY 14511. Phone 716-538-6822.

Genesee County Park, 11095 Bethany Center Road, East Bethany, NY 14054. Phone 585-344-1122.

Aldrich Change Bridge outside Palmyra

East Aurora • Beaver Meadow

East Aurora boasts broad streets lined with trees, a variety of residential architectural styles, and a downtown with a variety of galleries and shops. More than a few homes are classic bungalows. Something called the Roycroft Campus fills a couple of blocks. There's not just a toy store, but a toy factory and a toy museum. The place turns out to be special.

The story begins with a soap salesman named Elbert Hubbard (1856–1915). At age fifteen he was peddling his wares by horse and wagon in Illinois. Within three years he had moved to Buffalo, where he found employment at the Larkin Soap Company. He rose to sales manager, and then became part owner of the concern.

With economic success assured by age thirty-six, he had freedom to follow longtime urges to become a writer. Hubbard sold his share of Larkin and began to travel. While visiting Europe, he happened upon William Morris.

An artist and writer in England, Morris decried the excessive ornamentation of the Victorian era, and criticized the shoddy manufacturing of the industrial age. He called for commitment to hand craftsmanship akin to that of medieval European guilds. Thus began what we now call the Arts and Crafts Movement.

Hubbard had found his mission. He returned to his home in East Aurora and built a print shop, turning out finely crafted materials, plus publishing his own work. In 1899, he composed a missive entitled *A Message for Garcia*, praising accomplishment of tasks regardless of obstacles. Corporate executives, clergymen, politicians, and military leaders bought the monograph. Over eighty million copies were sold. Hubbard became known throughout the world.

Suddenly the enterprise had outgrown the tiny print shop. A bindery was built, followed by a pottery studio, leather and furniture workshops, and a metal shop. People like Stephen Crane and Henry Ford came to see what was going on. Hubbard built a luxurious inn in 1905 to accommodate guests.

He named the complex Roycroft, after two seventeenth-century English bookbinders. Hubbard attracted accomplished craftsmen, while also hiring local people. The mix appeared to work, and Roycroft thrived. Cabinetmakers turned out fine oak furniture. Skilled metal-workers fashioned pieces of silver and copper. Potters sculpted distinctive wares. And there were the books, printed on high-grade paper and bound in stamped leather.

Unfortunately, Hubbard died when a German submarine destroyed the Lusitania in 1915. His son Elbert II (Bert) continued the enterprise, but the Depression ruined the market for expensive goods like those crafted in East Aurora. Roycroft closed in 1938.

Skilled artisans continued to migrate to the area. Earlier efforts to revive the Roycroft Inn met financial barriers, but the Margaret L. Wendt Foundation in Buffalo succeeded, making the inn "not as Hubbard did it, but as Hubbard would do it now." In 1995, the grand lodging place reopened.

A walk around the Roycroft Campus introduces Hubbard and his legacy. The fortress-like stone Chapel, now Aurora's town hall, served as both meeting hall and display area for sales. Next door was the Print Shop, a mix of stone and Tudor construction.

The former Blacksmith and Copper Shop has become a boutique offering both Roycroft originals and fine reproductions. Nearby, in a sprawling green-shingled building, Roycrofters had furniture, leather, and bookbinding shops.

Across Grove Street stands the Roycroft Inn. Hubbard aphorisms are carved into heavy wooden doors. Arts and Crafts pieces furnish common rooms and large suites. During meals, docents give guided tours, pointing out restored murals on salon walls, fine oak wainscoting, and other details.

A couple of blocks away sits the Elbert Hubbard Roycroft Museum, once home to George ScheideMantel, a bellboy at the inn who worked his way up to supervisor of the leather shop. His wife Gladys, upon reaching age 100, donated the house as a museum in exchange for lifetime nursing home care (she died at 106).

The 1910 bungalow itself is a singularly impressive Roycroft artifact. Construction includes narrow-plank oak floors, American chestnut trim, a large stone fireplace, and handsome built-in cabinetry.

Self-guiding walking tours brought me farther into the village.

East Aurora was thriving well before Hubbard arrived. Earlier in the nineteenth century, the place became known for horse farms, the last of which has become a state park.

An earlier celebrity had called East Aurora home. Millard Fillmore practiced law here for a decade before he became president. His 1825 house, restored by the Aurora Historical Society, is the only surviving abode in America built by a president. My route also brought me by Baker Memorial United Methodist Church, a 1927 edifice with seventeen Tiffany windows; Pioneer Cemetery; and the Globe Hotel, built as a stagecoach stop in 1823 and still active.

Toys helped drive the economy in the post-Hubbard years. I crossed an unpaved portion of the original Main Street to Fisher-Price headquarters. The company offers both a comprehensive store and the Toy Town Museum. Inside are products dating back to Fisher-Price's beginnings in 1931.

Bright red-and-white awnings draw attention to Vidler's 5&10, a family-run store that's been a local fixture for over seventy years. Ten cents still buys a bag of freshly popped yellow popcorn.

Trees matter to East Aurorans. On the East End Tour, I saw American linden, sycamore, gingko, and mulberry trees, and a red oak over fifteen feet in circumference—plus well-maintained Victorian homes. The Central Village Loop showed off American beech, flowering dogwood, and catalpa.

A stay at the Roycroft Inn made my visit especially memorable. My comfortable room had Stickley furniture, interior wood shutters, and a brown mica shade lamp. Dinner in the Roycroft Inn's Hubbard Hall came served on Roycroft-design china.

******

A jewel in Wyoming County is Beaver Meadow Audubon Center, a 324-acre preserve owned by the Buffalo Audubon Society. With its visitor center, variety of trails, and enthusiastic staff, this place would be a regular stopping point if we lived close by.

The handsome new visitor center was just being completed when we stopped. It has a discovery room where children can crawl into a

simulated beaver lodge and imagine the life of these fascinating creatures. Display areas have both taxidermy and live amphibians and reptiles. Upstairs programming areas offer a panoramic view of a nearby
pond and wetlands.

Bill Michalak oriented us to the opportunities at Beaver Meadow.
He came for a nature walk as a seventh grader and "I got hooked." Now
he serves as chief naturalist. Taking us to a boardwalk by the pond, he
pointed out the beaver lodge on the far shore. Beavers are nocturnal,
however. The daytime visitor is more likely to see turtles, geese, or an
occasional eagle.

We walked the fern and butterfly gardens with Bill before moving on to the hummingbird garden. He told us about the birds' terri-
toriality—"whatever time they don't spend eating, they spend chasing
other hummingbirds away." It amazes me to realize this species flaps
its wings three thousand times a minute and can fly five hundred miles
nonstop.

Beaver Meadow offers a wealth of programs. Self-guiding trail
brochures enrich several hikes. A Beaver Meadow Mid-Week was going on while we were there. Aimed largely at senior citizens, these
mornings conclude with a group cookout. There are full-moon walks
monthly, and also regularly scheduled nights of viewing the skies from
observatory telescopes.

After spending time with Bill, we drove a short distance to the
Bracken Trail. On this pleasant, forty-five-minute woods walk, we
found a densely canopied maple grove, beech and oak trees farther uphill, and iron remnants of an ancient farm wagon. A cabin and plaque
honor Jane and Glen Bagley, the original owners of Beaver Meadow.

There wasn't time to wander the arboretum, but we did go down to
Jenny Glen. Here the Buffalo Rotary Club has constructed a boardwalk
that encircles and crosses a wetland. Designed also for physically or
visually handicapped visitors, the well-maintained walkway is apparently one of Beaver Meadow's more popular spots. We wished we had
brought a field guide; this would be a good place to hone identification
skills.

Information:

Greater East Aurora Chamber of Commerce, 431 Main Street, East Aurora, NY 14052. Phone 716-652-8444.

The Roycroft Inn, 40 South Grove Street, East Aurora, NY 14052. Phone 716-652-5552.

Beaver Meadow Nature Center, 1610 Welch Road, North Java, NY 14113. Phone 716-457-3228.

Richard Frost grew up in Glens Falls, New York, before leaving for warmer climates. Eventually he made a return to northern New York, where he practices medicine and writes about travel and history.

Since 1988, he has written a weekly regional travel column for the Press-Republican in Plattsburgh, New York. *One Foot Forward: Walks in Upstate New York* is his third book. He lives with his wife, Marty, and his Labrador retriever, Ripken, in the foothills of the northern Adirondacks.